MACROMEDIA®
DREAMWEAVER® MX
2004 AND DATABASES

SEAN R. NICHOLSON

New
Riders
www.newriders.com

800 East 96th Street, 3rd Floor, Indianapolis, IN 46240

An Imprint of Pearson Education

Boston • Indianapolis • London • Munich • New York • San Francisco

Macromedia® Dreamweaver® MX 2004 and Databases

International Standard Book Number: 0-7357-1370-7

Library of Congress Catalog Card Number: 2003104256

Printed in the United States of America

First printing: October, 2003

08 07 06 05 04 03   7 6 5 4 3 2

Interpretation of the printing code: The rightmost double-digit number is the year of the book's printing; the rightmost single-digit number is the number of the book's printing. For example, the printing code 03-1 shows that the first printing of the book occurred in 2003.

Trademarks

Warning and Disclaimer

PUBLISHER
Stephanie Wall

PRODUCTION MANAGER
Gina Kanouse

SENIOR ACQUISITIONS EDITOR
Linda Anne Bump

SENIOR PROJECT EDITOR
Kristy Hart

COPY EDITOR
Kelli Brooks

INDEXER
Cheryl Lenser

COMPOSITION
Amy Hassos

MANUFACTURING COORDINATOR
Dan Uhrig

INTERIOR DESIGNER
Wil Cruz

COVER DESIGNER
Alan Clements

MEDIA DEVELOPER
Jay Payne

MARKETING
Scott Cowlin
Tammy Detrich
Hannah Onstad Latham

PUBLICITY MANAGER
Susan Nixon

Contents at a Glance

*I would like to dedicate this book to my brother, Staff Sergeant Matthew Nicholson.
At the time of this writing, Matt is serving his country as a member of the United
States Air National Guard, thousands of miles away from the family and
friends he loves. Although it is not much, I offer you this dedication as a
token of my appreciation for the sacrifice you make to protect the
freedoms and liberties we hold so precious and sometimes take for granted.*

*Matt, I hope that by the time you read this you are back at home where you belong.
But if, for some reason, your services are still required at the time this book is
published, I hope you will pass along a message to your fellow service members:*

*Thank you and God bless...
We love you and we miss you,
Sean*

Table of Contents

About the Author

Sean R. Nicholson is the Network Administrator and Web Developer for the Career Services Center at the University of Missouri—Kansas City. He and his development team architect, develop, and manage foundation and back-end execution for programs such as the CareerExec Employment Database (www.careerexec.com), UMKC Career Services Web site (www.career.umkc.edu), and UMKC's Virtual Career Fair (www.umkc.edu/virtualfair). Sean also does private contract and consulting work on database and Web development for organizations and individuals.

Sean has a Juris Doctor from UMKC, but opted to follow a career path in technology rather than law. Sean has been working with computers since the day a shiny new Apple II computer showed up at his house when he was twelve (twenty years ago). Sean began building Web pages using Notepad and has been developing sites in Dreamweaver since version 1.0 was released. In addition, he has used DrumBeat, UltraDev, and now Dreamweaver MX 2004 extensively in both Web-based and intranet-based projects.

Sean's technical publications include *Discover Excel 97 (Hungry Minds, Inc., 1997), Teach Yourself Outlook 98 in 24 hours (Sams, 1998), Inside Dreamweaver UltraDev 4 (New Riders, 2001),* and *Dreamweaver MX Magic New Riders, 2002).* He has also written several legal articles ranging in topics from Canadian water rights to the protection of historic artifacts lost at sea.

During his free time, Sean can be found traveling with his family, riding his motorcycle to biker events nationwide, or continuing the development of his site at www.unitedbikers.com, with hope of building one of the largest motorcycle-related sites on the Web.

About the Technical Reviewers

These reviewers contributed their considerable hands-on expertise to the entire development process for *Dreamweaver MX 2004 and Databases*. As the book was being written, these dedicated professionals reviewed all the material for technical content, organization, and flow. Their feedback was critical to ensuring that *Dreamweaver MX 2004 and Databases* fits our readers' need for the highest-quality technical information.

Matt Brown is a consultant based in the Bay Area. He has edited more than 20 Dreamweaver and Photoshop books over the years. He has taught at Foothill College and the Multimedia Studies Program at San Francisco State University. He was on the Dreamweaver team for 5 years in a number of capacities finally as Community Manager. Matt is married to a magnificent woman, Marcella, keeps chickens, loves to cook, and creates all sorts of art.

Mark Fletcher has been in the I.T. industry for 15 years. He began his career as a database administrator, and for the last 5 years he has been a Web developer/trainer for the Virtual Training Company.

Mark is involved in developing training courses on Dreamweaver amongst other Macromedia Internet Products. He is also a member of Team Macromedia for Dreamweaver and a regular contributor to Macromedia's DevNet. Mark is also a training partner for the Dreamweaver extension developer WebAssist.com.

Mark lives on the northwest coast of the United Kingdom with his wife, Vanessa, and with his two children, Joel and Lucy. Mark can be reached on this personal Web site http://www.mark-fletcher.co.uk.

Acknowledgments

First and foremost, I would like to thank the incredible team at New Riders. A huge thank you to Linda Bump for helping shape this project from a simple idea into a great book. I appreciate all your time and effort, Linda; working with you is always a pleasure. Another special thank you goes to Lisa Thibault for making sure the project went smoothly and for keeping me on-task.

Additional thanks goes to my Project Editor, Kristy Hart, and Technical Editors, Matt Brown and Mark Fletcher. Your attention to detail and input are sincerely appreciated.

As is tradition with all of my books that focus on Macromedia products, I offer a sincere thank you to each and every employee at Macromedia for developing some of the best Web development software on the market. I cannot thank you all enough for your dedication to making software that makes my job easier (not to mention a whole lot of fun!).

In addition, I would like to thank TechSmith for allowing me to use their SnagIt Screen Capture program for the images in this book. I highly recommend this handy utility, and you can check it out at http://www.techsmith.com/products/snagit/.

To my wife, Deborah, and children, Emma and Zayne, a single thank you is not enough so thank you, thank you, and thank you. Without your understanding and support, projects like these simply would simply not be possible.

Tell Us What You Think

As the reader of this book, you are the most important critic and commentator. We value your opinion and want to know what we're doing right, what we could do better, what areas you'd like to see us publish in, and any other words of wisdom you're willing to pass our way.

As the Senior Acquisitions Editor for New Riders Publishing, I welcome your comments. You can fax, email, or write me directly to let me know what you did or didn't like about this book—as well as what we can do to make our books stronger. When you write, please be sure to include this book's title, ISBN, and author, as well as your name and phone or fax number. I will carefully review your comments and share them with the author and editors who worked on the book.

Please note that I cannot help you with technical problems related to the topic of this book, and that due to the high volume of email I receive, I might not be able to reply to every message.

Fax: 317-428-3280

Email: linda.bump@newriders.com

Mail: Linda Anne Bump
          Senior Acquisitions Editor
          New Riders Publishing
          800 East 96th Street
          3rd Floor
          Indianapolis, IN 46240 USA

INTRODUCTION

As Network Administrator and Web Developer for the Career Services Center at the University of Missouri—Kansas City, I am often asked to talk with students who are preparing to enter the professional world of Information Technology and who are concerned about their prospects. The questions students most often ask pertain to the job market and what they can do to make themselves marketable to employers. My answer to them is to enhance their skills through hands-on training. Although a degree in the field is usually necessary to be considered for a position, employers are often more interested in what experience the candidate has and what work they have included in their portfolio.

So, what does that have to do with this book, you might ask? Everything.

As a working professional, you are most likely looking for ways to enhance your current skills so you can develop a project that will serve your organization's needs. In addition, because you have picked up this book, it's probably safe to assume that the project will have something to do with a database, a Web server, and a Dreamweaver MX 2004.

Regardless of what you plan to do—build a small organizational directory for your company, an intranet application that enhances communication, or a full-blown eCommerce site that does millions of dollars in sales in the next year—the goal of this book is to help you build the skills you need to complete your project and make yourself more marketable within your own organization or in the job market.

Getting the Most from Dreamweaver MX 2004 and Databases

This is a highly interactive book, meaning that the more you use your computer while reading it, the more you will get out of it. Before you start, however, you can do some things to ensure smooth sailing.

Install the Most Recent Version of Dreamweaver

Although most of the principles covered in the book will work with Dreamweaver MX (or even Dreamweaver UltraDev), there are features that are exclusive to the newest release, Dreamweaver MX 2004. For this reason, it's best to have the most recent version of the software installed. If you haven't purchased the software yet but really want to start on this book, feel free to download a free 30-day trial from Macromedia's Web site at www.macromedia.com.

Read the Manual and Walk Through the Tutorials

The first time I opened Dreamweaver 1.0, I was a little overwhelmed. I had previously been using Notepad for the majority of my HTML coding, and Dreamweaver's layout, menus, and panels were a bit of a divergence from the traditional Windows-based applications. As Dreamweaver has matured and new features have been added, the graphical user interface (GUI) has become more complex. Macromedia, however, continues to produce outstanding manuals and tutorials to help you get acclimated to the Dreamweaver environment. If you are new to Dreamweaver, walk through the tutorials from the beginning. If you are stuck or unfamiliar with a feature, check out the Help section.

Start at the Beginning of the Book

The best way to approach this book is head-on. Part I, "Introduction to Dynamic Applications," introduces you to the key technologies that fuel database-driven Web sites. These first two chapters are more informational than hands-on, but the topics they cover are crucial to understanding how dynamic applications work. I know it's sometimes tough to wade through pages of text when you want to get cracking on the projects, but believe me, building and troubleshooting future applications will be so much easier if you understand how and why (or why not) your application works.

Part II, "Creating Intranet-Strength Applications with MS Access, ASP/CF, and Dreamweaver MX 2004," and Part III, "Building Web-Strength Applications with SQL Server, ASP/CF, and Dreamweaver MX 2004," are the hands-on sections. Part II walks you through the process of using Dreamweaver, Access, and ASP.NET to build an organizational intranet, whereas Part III shows you how to use SQL Server and ColdFusion to build an organizational Web site. Each section begins by showing you how to build the database, set up your Web server, and create connections that allow your pages to interact with the database. Each section has several chapters of hands-on applications to show you exactly how to use Dreamweaver to build your pages.

Because the chapters build upon one another toward the result of a complete intranet or Web site, it's a good idea to walk through them in order.

Experiment with Each Feature

The best way to fully understand how a feature works is to apply it in a manner different from the one demonstrated in the book. After you finish with a chapter, think of an alternative application that might use the same features and see if you can build it. For instance, if the book shows you how to create an employee directory, try creating a product catalog using the same features. If you can duplicate the results, you have truly grasped the concepts and enhanced your skills.

Use Other Dreamweaver Resources

As Dreamweaver becomes increasingly popular among professional Web developers, so does the number of great resources available to help you get the most from the software. Macromedia provides support via the Macromedia Exchange and peer support is available through Web sites such as `www.dmxzone.com` and `www.dwfaq.com`.

In addition, as you develop dynamic Web pages, you will undoubtedly encounter questions regarding third-party applications such as Microsoft's ASP.NET or Active Server Pages, Sun's JavaServer Pages, or Macromedia's ColdFusion. Take advantage of the extensive online libraries that each of these companies offers for support and the unofficial support communities on the Web.

System Considerations

Prior to installing Dreamweaver, be sure that your workstation meets the minimum requirements necessary to run the application. If you need a bit more memory or a bigger hard drive, now might be the time to perform any upgrade.

In addition, take the time to get your system running in peak performance: Run Scandisk on your hard drive, go ahead and do that disk defragmentation you have been putting off, and clean up those temporary Internet files. The faster your computer runs when developing your applications, the happier you will be.

Security Considerations

Running Web applications on your local workstation can open up a completely new realm of security issues. It is extremely important that you keep your workstation up-to-date with the most current operating system updates and security patches. In Part III of the book, we will be working with SQL Server, which has recently exposed workstations to a potential threat. After installing any of the applications we use in the book, please be sure to check the manufacturer's Web site for any critical updates or security patches.

I'm being repetitive, but I'm going to say it again in clear terms: Please keep your operating system and applications up-to-date with security patches.

Words to Work By

Nobel laureate and Pulitzer Prize winner Pearl Buck once said, "To know how to do something is to enjoy it."

By picking up this book, you have taken the first step toward knowing how to build database-driven Web applications. I hope that by enhancing your understanding and skills, you will grow to enjoy building the applications as much as I do. Remember that although Web development can often be a demanding and frustrating endeavor, the result of seeing your applications in action usually makes it all worthwhile.

PART I

CHAPTER 1

CHOOSING THE RIGHT TOOLS FOR YOUR DYNAMIC APPLICATION

As a professional, your time is probably one of the most valuable commodities. If you're like most of us, projects, meetings, and all the other responsibilities included in your job description often make it difficult to fit everything you need to do within the 8 to 10 hours devoted to the workday. Add to that time spent with family, friends, and a little time for yourself and it's probable that you run out of hours in the day long before you run out of items on your to-do list.

As a fellow professional, I understand exactly what this is like. I have been accused (on more than one occasion) of biting off more than I could chew and have found myself with too few hours in the day. With that in mind, the goal of this book is to arm you with knowledge that will help you build quality Web applications by using tools that allow you to work faster and avoid time-consuming pitfalls.

So, pour yourself a fresh cup of coffee and let's get cracking!

This chapter introduces you to the tools involved in the process of serving a dynamic Web page. After completing this chapter, you should be able to do the following:

- Understand how database-driven applications are processed by a Web server
- Choose the Web server software that is appropriate for your needs
- Understand the differences between dynamic platforms and select one that is appropriate for your needs
- Select a database management system that is appropriate for your application

Understanding How Database-Driven Web Applications Work

Before we get into the nuts and bolts of building a database-driven Web application, let's do a basic review of the technology used to bring our creations to the world—namely the client browser, Web server software, application server software, and the database.

 STATIC PAGES VERSUS DYNAMIC PAGES

In this chapter, we will rely on the terms *static* and *dynamic* to define certain types of pages. Static pages are those that have the information typed directly into the document rather than relying upon a database to provide data. Dynamic, or database-driven, pages are those that rely upon a database to create content prior to displaying the page.

Before dynamic pages appeared, the process of serving up a static HTML page was a relatively simple one. As shown in Figure 1.1, the client browser requests a page from the Web server through an HTTP request that occurs when a visitor clicks a link to your site or types **http://www.yoursitename.com** into his Web browser.

After the request is received from the server, the Web server software (typically Apache HTTP Server or Microsoft's Internet Information Services) returns the requested page to the browser; the browser then decodes the HTML and displays the page in the browser. It is a very simple process that generally requires few server resources.

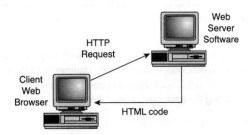

FIGURE 1.1   The process of serving a static Web page.

The process of serving dynamic pages, however, is a bit more complex. After the request from the client is made, the Web server software examines the request and determines if it is capable of serving the page or whether it needs to involve the application server software. It distinguishes between static and dynamic pages based on the extension contained in the page request. If the request ends in .htm or .html, the Web server software returns the page directly to the client. If, however, the request contains a different extension (for example, .asp, .aspx, .jsp, .cfm, or .php), the Web server software forwards the request to the appropriate application server software that has been registered to handle those requests. For instance, a page ending in .cfm would be forwarded to the ColdFusion Server Application.

After the application server software receives the request, it finds the requested page and pre-processes any code that is specific to the application. For instance, the ColdFusion Server pre-processes any code contained in tags that are part of the ColdFusion Markup Language (CFML). Other application services such as PHP would pre-process any of the PHP Hypertext PreProcessor (PHP) script contained in the page.

In addition, application servers, such as the .NET engine, JRun, and IBM's WebSphere, compile the entire page and store that compiled code in a cache that can be served over and over without additional processing. The fact that the code is already compiled when the client request is made allows platforms like JSP and ASP.NET to claim substantial performance increases over other platforms.

PRE-PROCESSING PAGES

The term *pre-processing* means that an application server will look through the requested page's code line-by-line and find any code that should be processed before the page is returned to the requesting browser. By pre-processing a page, Web developers can set if-then statements as to what information should be displayed. For instance, if you only want authenticated users to view the page content, you could build a piece of code that follows this algorithm (using the appropriate code, of course):

```
If the user is not an authenticated user
Redirect them to a different page to login
Else
Show them the content
```

Without the pre-processing step, the page would have been automatically served to anyone who requested it.

After the pre-processing is complete, the application server determines whether it should draw information from the database.

 ALL APPLICATION-SPECIFIC PAGES ARE NOT NECESSARILY DYNAMIC PAGES

Remember that just because a page ends in an extension other than .htm or .html, doesn't mean that the page will display content from a database. Static pages can contain the extension of any of the application servers and still be processed normally. It just means there will be a slight delay (usually not noticeable to the visitor) while the page is passed from the Web server software to the application server software and then back to the browser. This allows you to consistently name all your static and dynamic pages using the same extension throughout your site.

If content is required from the database, the application server software gathers the information via a block of code that uses the Structured Query Language (SQL) and stores the information in a temporary object called a recordset. This recordset can be used to validate information (for example, whether the user's name and password are valid) or can be displayed on the page (like the results from a search).

After the application server software has all of the data it requires, it converts all of the data into HTML and returns it to the client browser.

 CODING FOR EVERY BROWSER IS AS IMPORTANT AS EVER

Whether you are building static or dynamic applications, remember that you should strive to code your pages to operate in all of the major browsers (Internet Explorer and Netscape). Unless you are 100 percent positive that your clients will be using a specific browser (often the case in an intranet), you want to be sure that everyone can use the site regardless of browser they choose.

Although the process, shown in Figure 1.2, seems like an involved one, it often takes less than a second for the process to be completed and the page to be on its way to the client.

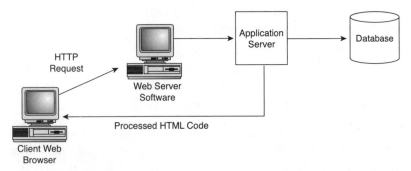

FIGURE 1.2   The process of serving a dynamic Web page.

Now that you understand the process of how a dynamic page is requested, pre-processed, and served, let's take a look at each of the applications involved in the process and examine the options available on the market.

Choosing Your Web Server Software

The first element in the process of serving a dynamic page is the Web server software. Although there is a variety of Web server applications on the market, two primarily dominate the market: Microsoft's Internet Information Services (IIS) and the Apache Software Foundation's Apache HTTP Server. Depending on the size and structure of your organization, you may already know what Web server software you are using based on the server operating system your organization uses. If, however, you are in charge of choosing the software for your organization, you need to decide which software meets your performance and price needs. There are also databases and application servers that come with their own Web server. For instance, both the Oracle Database Management system and the ColdFusion application server come with integrated Web server technology.

Internet Information Services (IIS)

IIS is Microsoft's Web server software and is available to users running Windows NT, Windows 2000, Windows Server 2003, and Windows XP Professional. IIS offers a highly configurable, easy-to-use, robust Web service capable of effortlessly handling high-traffic sites. In addition, IIS also serves as an application server for Active Server Pages (ASP) allowing IIS users to build ASP applications without having to install an additional application server. IIS, however, can serve JavaServer pages, ColdFusion pages, PHP pages, and .NET applications with the help of additional application servers.

In addition, the IIS GUI, shown in Figure 1.3, offers a variety of management features including the ability to password protect file and folder access, serve the pages of multiple sites through the use of header files, and manage the Web server via an available Web interface application.

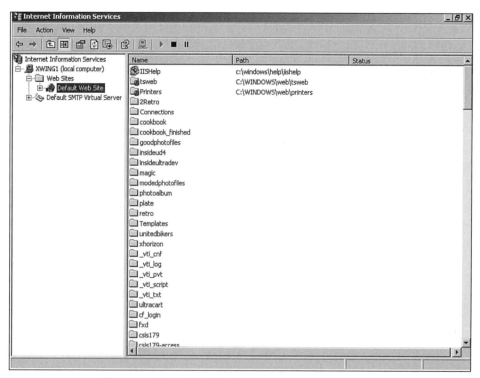

FIGURE 1.3   The IIS Management Console.

Because IIS comes free with Windows 2000, Windows Server 2003, and Windows XP Professional, it is generally the Web server of choice for companies running their Web server on the Windows NT or 2000/2003 platform.

Tip   RUNNING A WEB SERVER ON A WINDOWS 9X MACHINE

If you don't have access to a PC running Windows 2000 or XP, you can install Personal Web Server, a handy little application from Microsoft, and still be able to serve dynamic pages with limited functionality. Keep in mind, however, that you will not be able to build and test the .NET pages on your Windows 9x machine because the .NET tools are only for Windows 2000 and XP.

Also, if you are running Windows XP and plan to run a Web server, be sure that you have Windows XP Professional. Windows XP Home Edition does not have Web server capability and there is no method for adding Web services.

Although IIS isn't the fastest Web server software on the market, the only real disadvantages to IIS are the constant vigilance that is required to close security holes and the fact that IIS doesn't run on any operating system other than Windows.

Apache HTTP Server

Apache Software Foundation's Apache HTTP Server is one of the fastest Web server software applications on the market. Used by the vast majority of Web servers on the Internet, Apache is open source (which means the software is free as long as it is used according the licensing guidelines) and developed to run on UNIX, Linux, Windows, and Macintosh operating systems. Without all the frills and features of IIS, Apache is a lean, mean, Web serving machine with fewer security holes to deal with. Apache is also capable of serving Active Server Pages, JavaServer Pages, PHP pages, and ColdFusion pages with the help of third-party application servers. Although Apache is run from the command line, the Comanche add-on, shown in Figure 1.4, is an easy-to-use, graphical front-end used to configure Apache.

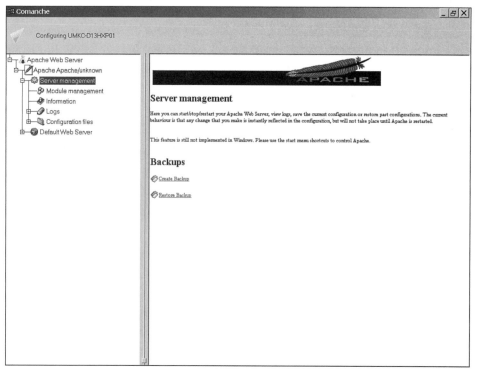

FIGURE 1.4   The Comanche graphical tool allows you to easily configure Apache HTTP Server.

Resource   **MORE INFORMATION ABOUT COMANCHE**

Comanche is developed and marketed by Covalent Technologies, Inc. For details about Comanche or to download the application, visit `http://www.covalent.net/projects/comanche/`.

About the only drawback to running Apache is the fact that there is no commercial technical support. When your server goes down in the middle of the night, there is no tech support number to call. Apache, however, has a strong peer support system on the Internet. Armed with a browser, an Internet connection, and a search engine, you can select from a variety of Web sites focused on answering Apache-related questions.

For the hands-on chapters of this book, we will be covering the installation and configuration of both IIS and Apache HTTP Server. Whichever option you choose, you should be able to complete all aspects of the exercises.

Choosing a Dynamic Application Platform

After you have your Web server software picked out, the next step is to decide on an application server. Because of the wide variety of application servers on the market and the differences in languages used to create pages for them, it's important that you do your homework prior to settling on a platform.

Some of the issues you might consider would be the operating system installed on your Web server, the access to expertise within your organization, and the budget you have for additional software. For instance, if you are unfamiliar with Java or do not have access to a Java programmer, it's unlikely that JavaServer Pages would serve as a suitable platform for your organization. If, however, you are running Windows 2000, 2003, Server on your Web server and have an understanding of the new .NET model, IIS along with the .NET services might be your best bet.

Before selecting a platform, however, do your homework and do your best to anticipate which platform will best suit your organizational needs.

ASP.NET

ASP.NET model is Microsoft's latest answer to the quest for faster, more scalable Web applications. Unlike its predecessor (ASP), ASP.NET is a compiled language, meaning that the instead of running through the code line-by-line and looking for code that should be pre-processed, the .NET pages are compiled in their entirety on the server and then stored in cache for later use. Rather than sifting through the code each time the page is called, the page is compiled one time and then simply referenced whenever it is called in the future. This is a substantial performance increase over the previous Active Server Pages. Compiled pages are much less susceptible to hacking as well, meaning that ASP.NET pages should be more secure than Active Server Pages.

These performance and security enhancements, however, do not come without hitches. First, be aware that ASP.NET is not fully compatible with ASP, so you may experience some problems when migrating your existing applications to the ASP.NET framework. Second, forget using the VBScript and JavaScript you spent the last few years refining. Instead, you'll need to hone your skills with VB.NET, JScript.NET, or C# (pronounced C Sharp), all of which are compiled languages rather than scripting languages. Don't let the prospect of learning a new language overwhelm you, though. Although it is important for you to understand the code of your applications and tweak them when necessary, the goal of this book is to show you how to let tools like Dreamweaver build the code for you.

MORE INFORMATION ABOUT ASP.NET

For details about ASP.NET and sample applications that demonstrate how the .NET model works, check out Microsoft's ASP.NET Web site at `http://www.asp.net/`.

ColdFusion

Macromedia offers a dynamic environment in the ColdFusion Server application that uses the ColdFusion Markup Language (CFML) to indicate which code should be pre-processed. CFML is unique in the fact that rather than embedding additional code within the HTML, it simply extends HTML by giving you additional tags that the ColdFusion server can interpret and convert to HTML. This means that developers who are familiar with HTML tags only need to learn the additional CFML tags before they can begin creating ColdFusion pages.

The fact that CFML is one of the easiest extension languages to learn makes it an attractive environment for developers who are not necessarily programmers but are familiar with the workings of HTML. In addition, CFML is capable of supporting objects created in both C++ and Java, making it an extremely robust language.

The cons to using ColdFusion Server (shown in Figure 1.5) are rare. ColdFusion has an excellent support structure in the form of both corporate technical support and from the numerous peer-support groups out there. About the only downside is the fact that the ColdFusion server costs, whereas other platforms such as Active Server Pages, ASP.NET, and JavaServer Pages all offer free application servers. The cost, however, is often justified by the excellent technical support available and the powerful development environment provided in the ColdFusion Studio and Dreamweaver.

MORE INFORMATION ABOUT COLDFUSION

For details about ColdFusion, check out Macromedia's ColdFusion Web site at `http://www.macromedia.com/software/coldfusion/`.

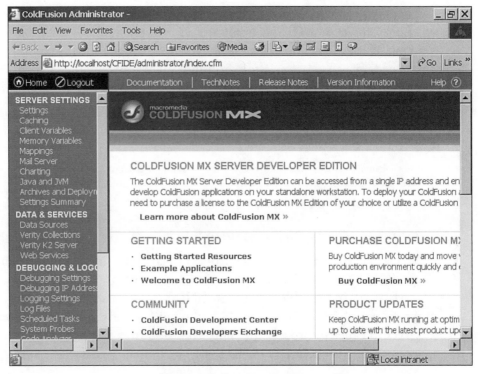

FIGURE 1.5   The ColdFusion Server.

Other Platforms

Although this book uses ASP.NET and ColdFusion to demonstrate the process of building dynamic Web applications, there are several other options available when it comes to application server software. Although we won't cover these platforms in our hands-on chapters, it's beneficial to understand what alternatives are available and why they may or may not suit your organizational needs.

Active Server Pages (ASP)

One of the most popular dynamic platforms in use on the Web today is the Active Server Pages environment, also known as ASP. ASP pages contain scripting code written in either JavaScript or VBScript that the application server pre-processes prior to serving the requested page. Because VBScript and JavaScript are very easy languages to learn, ASP has grown rapidly in its popularity among Web developers. In addition, since Microsoft's IIS serves as an application server for ASP pages, ASP is often the dynamic platform of choice for Web developers using servers with the Windows operating system.

There is an end in sight, however, for the ASP platform. With the release of Microsoft's new .NET infrastructure, it is likely that ASP's days are limited as a viable Web platform. Because ASP.NET extends the functionality of ASP using less code, it is likely that more and more developers will switch from ASP to ASP.NET over the next couple of years.

Resource   More Information About Active Server Pages

For information about Microsoft's Active Server Pages, check out the MSDN section covering ASP at `http://msdn.microsoft.com/nhp/default.asp?contentid=28000522`.

PHP Hypertext PreProcessor (PHP)

Much like VBScript and JavaScript, PHP is a scripting language that can be embedded into an HTML document for preprocessing by the PHP application server. PHP is available for use on UNIX, Linux, and Windows servers and works with both Apache and IIS, although IIS users will have to configure their server in order to process the .php extension. In addition, PHP is capable of interacting with a variety of databases including Access, SQL Server, and MySQL.

Because PHP works across platforms and is free, it is rapidly becoming an attractive candidate for dynamic applications. In fact, nearly the only downside to PHP is the newness factor. Because it hasn't been adopted on a widespread basis and commercial support is not available, organizations are still resistant to try it and stick with a more costly alternative that provides support in times of emergencies.

Resource   More Information About PHP

For information about PHP, check out the PHP Groups Web site at `http://www.php.net/`.

JavaServer Pages (JSP)

The JavaServer Pages environment is uniquely different from ASP.NET, ColdFusion, or ASP in that its technology is based on Java, a compiled, object-oriented programming language. This extends the capabilities of what you can do with JSP to just about anything you can do with the Java language.

Unlike scripting languages that embed code within the HTML page, JavaServer Pages include a small program referred to as a servlet that run on the server and modify the HTML of the page before they are sent back to the browser. Just like pre-processed scripts, servlets can perform tasks such as inserting data from a database, controlling the behaviors of HTML elements, and even rewriting the HTML code completely.

One of the biggest benefits to running JSP are the Open Source JSP server applications that operate on a variety of platforms and are free to use. Currently, the Jakarta Project (a sub-project of Apache) is offering the Tomcat server for UNIX, Linux, and Win32 platforms on their Web site at `http://jakarta.apache.org`. However, support for Tomcat is often difficult to obtain and comes only in the form of peer-support. Other commercial alternatives are available through Macromedia in the form of JRun, shown in Figure 1.6, and IBM in their WebSphere application, and both offer the traditional support options common to commercial software.

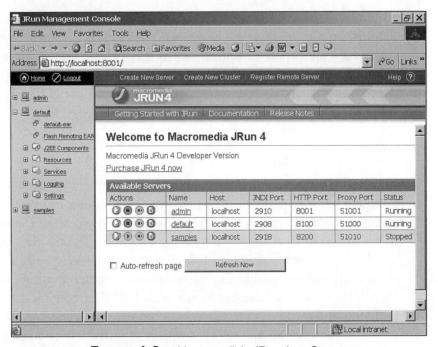

FIGURE 1.6   Macromedia's JRun Java Server.

Ironically, the fact that JSP is based in Java is also one of its biggest weaknesses because building applications with JSP requires an understanding of Java. Unlike the scripting languages and markup tags used by the other platforms, Java is a full-blown object-oriented programming language and requires substantially more training to learn.

Resource   **MORE INFORMATION ABOUT JAVASERVER PAGES**

For information about JavaServer Pages, check out the Sun Microsystems site at `http://java.sun.com/products/jsp/`.

Because it isn't possible to effectively cover every dynamic platform in the pages of this book, the hands-on chapters will focus on the ASP.NET and ColdFusion platforms. Because the ASP.NET platform is free to all Windows 2000 and XP users and the ColdFusion Server is available in a 30-day trial from Macromedia, these platforms provide us with an inexpensive method of demonstrating how easy it can be to build dynamic Web applications with Dreamweaver.

Selecting a Database Management System

After you have selected your Web server software and application server, the final decision to make is the choice of database management system. Currently, there is a wide variety of options when it comes to databases, ranging from free to very costly and limited to very robust. Which application you choose should depend on the type of Web application you are building, the availability of software in your organization, and (of course) your budget.

Microsoft Access

Access is Microsoft's entry-level database management system (DBMS). Because it is included with many of the Microsoft Office suites, it is often readily available on corporate desktops. For small businesses, its low cost as a stand-alone application also makes it an attractive option. In addition, Access' easy-to-use graphical user interface, shown in Figure 1.7, allows users to easily build databases without the complex command-line interfaces offered by other applications. As a result, Web developers who have experience with HTML, but are just beginning their foray into the realm of dynamic sites, often turn to Access for their DBMS of choice, because cheap and easy are usually an attractive combination.

As with all good things, however, Access does have its downsides. Because Microsoft considers Access to be a *personal* database management system, there are limitations as to how large any single database can grow and how many users can connect with a database at the same time. With Access 2000 and XP, Microsoft states that there is a limit of a maximum of 255 concurrent connections to a database at the same time and a maximum database size of 2 gigabytes.

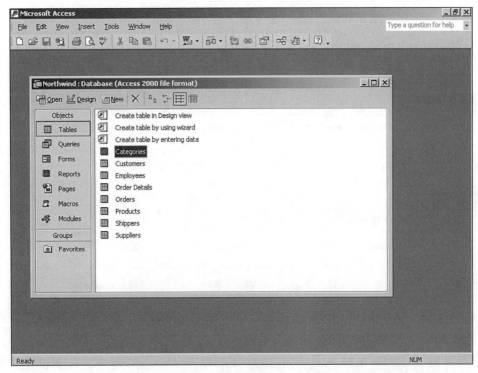

FIGURE 1.7   Microsoft Access' graphical user interface.

 CONCURRENT USERS ARE NOT NECESSARILY CONCURRENT CONNECTIONS

A concurrent connection is not the same thing as a concurrent user. *Concurrent connections* mean that more than one user at a time is interacting with the database (adding, editing, or deleting information) at the same time. Keep in mind, however, that just because a user is filling out a form that will eventually be included in the database does not mean they are using a database connection. They do not connect to the database until they submit the form and the data is entered into the database. For this reason, your site could have thousands of *concurrent users* (users who are interacting with the site at the same time) and still have only a few concurrent connections at a time.

Remember, however, the more reliant on a database your site becomes the more concurrent connections you will have.

Although 255 concurrent connections and 2 gigabytes of data may sound like quite a bit, many Web developers (myself included) will tell you that the chances of Access performing less than 255 concurrent connections is unrealistic in the real world of Web development. If each of the concurrent connections were with a separate table, this might be possible, but with users interacting with the same tables, the more realistic number becomes 10 to 20. With that in mind, Access can still serve as a suitable database option for a small to medium site. As the site grows, however, the Web developer needs to explore options for upgrading the database to a database management system more suited for higher traffic.

Resource | **MORE INFORMATION ABOUT MICROSOFT ACCESS**

For details about Access and sample databases that demonstrate its capabilities, visit the Access home page at http://www.microsoft.com/office/access/default.asp.

Microsoft SQL Server

Database administrators often refer to Microsoft's SQL Server as Access' big brother. Although this analogy is true in the fact that an Access database can "grow up" into a SQL Server database, the two database management systems are really quite different.

As we discussed in the last section, Microsoft views Access as a personal database management system, so restrictions keep it from serving the database needs of an entire enterprise. SQL Server, shown in Figure 1.8, was designed specifically for handling the needs of large organizations.

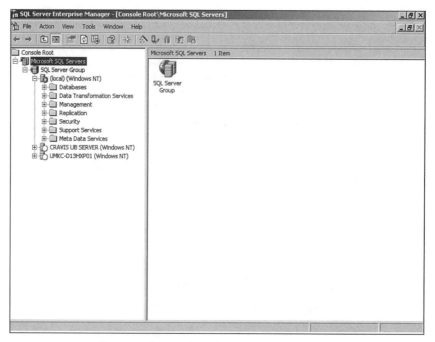

FIGURE 1.8   SQL Server's Enterprise Manager.

SQL Server databases are not restricted in their growth potential (except by the size of the server's hard drive), and the number of concurrent connections to a SQL Server database far exceeds those of an Access database. By default, SQL Server allows 1,024 concurrent connections, but this can be tuned by the server administrator to allow up to 4,096 concurrent connections.

Note   **DATABASE LIMITATIONS VERSUS SERVER LIMITATIONS**

Remember that just because a database management system claims to be able to allow 4,096 connections at the same time (that means 4,096 pages are adding, editing, or deleting records from the database at the *exact* same time) doesn't mean that your Web application can survive that kind of load. Although your database may be able to handle the connections, if your server isn't tuned for tip-top performance, you might find your hardware sending up the surrender flag before your database management system does.

Along with SQL Server's power, however, come a few negatives. First, SQL Server is limited to use on a Windows server. Although there are ways for UNIX and Linux machines to access SQL Server via virtual machines (a topic that would require a book of its own), it is a cumbersome process to use SQL Server in an environment other than Windows.

The second negative to SQL Server is the cost. This issue is what usually makes SQL Server an unlikely candidate for small- and medium-sized businesses. For those businesses that can afford the approximate $2000 price tag, they often find themselves in a bind as their organization grows. Microsoft licenses SQL Server on a per processor basis. This means that as traffic to your site grows and you upgrade your hardware to meet the demands of your visitors, you might find yourself having to purchase a second, third, or even fourth license for SQL Server as you add processors to your server.

Note   **UPGRADING FROM ACCESS TO SQL SERVER**

The nice thing about Access and SQL Server both being Microsoft products is it is relatively easy to upgrade an existing Access database and all its data to a SQL Server database. This allows small- to medium-sized businesses to start with a low-cost, easy-to-maintain, Access database and then upgrade to SQL Server as their site outgrows Access.

Resource   **MORE INFORMATION ABOUT SQL SERVER**

For more information about SQL Server and to download a free 90-day trial of the software, visit
`http://www.microsoft.com/sql/`.

Other Database Management Systems

You might be wondering why I am dumping the rest of the database management systems into an "other" category. I don't go into detail about each of the following database management systems but they are just as valuable as Access or SQL Server. The applications that follow are viable database tools and power some of the largest sites on the Web. Because this book demonstrates the use of Access and SQL Server, there is not the space to cover every database management system on the market that can fuel a dynamic site. I do, however, want to briefly introduce each of the applications and provide some pros and cons that you should be aware of.

MySQL

MySQL has been garnering respect from Web developers for the past few years due to its portability, excellent reputation with regard to performance, and the fact that it's an Open Source application. This combination means that MySQL can be used on a wide variety of platforms for free (in most cases). With those offerings in mind, you might be asking why on Earth anyone would go with another, more costly option.

Up until recently, MySQL lacked some of the functionality of the commercial database management systems and rendered it undesirable to some Web developers. For instance, until version 3.23.34, MySQL did not support transactions, which essentially allows the database management system to treat a group of commands issued at one time as one single command. *Transactions* are often used when a Web developer would rather have all the commands processed or (in the case of a problem) none processed. An example is a situation where a visitor to your site orders five items and the power to the server is lost in the middle of processing the order. The Web developer would usually rather that the visitor resubmit the entire order rather than process whatever was entered into the database prior to the power failure and then ask the visitor to re-submit the rest of the order.

The other issue that is sometimes viewed as a disadvantage to MySQL is the lack of commercial support. Although the MySQL community has one of the strongest peer-support groups of any database management system, lack of a single point of support (for example, a support phone number) has steered organizations toward commercial alternatives, even if they are more costly.

As MySQL continues to grow and features are added, it is clear that it will develop into a powerful tool for Web developers.

MORE INFORMATION ABOUT MySQL

If you would like more information on MySQL, check out its Web page at `http://www.mysql.com`.

DB2

Another database management system that is gaining popularity is IBM's DB2. DB2 is based on the Java programming language, making it the ideal choice for those choosing JavaServer Pages as their dynamic platform.

DB2 is not limited to the JSP platform, however. Because of the flexible nature of the Java language, DB2 can also communicate with pages built on platforms such as ASP.NET, Active Server Pages, and ColdFusion.

The drawbacks to DB2 come in the form of cost and support. Although not as expensive as Oracle, DB2 still remains more expensive than SQL Server. In addition, the number of companies and professionals using DB2 remains much smaller than those using SQL Server or Oracle, so peer support is not as readily available.

INFORMATION ABOUT DB2

If you would like more information on DB2, check out the DB2 Web page at `http://www-3.ibm.com/software/data/db2/`.

Oracle

Generally regarded as the most powerful database management system on the market, Oracle offers a robust combination of speed and security. In addition, Oracle offers a wide variety of options ranging from a Personal edition to an Enterprise edition, all of which run on both the UNIX and Windows platforms.

These features, however, are not without a robust price tag. The application itself can cost thousands of dollars not to mention the costs of learning this complex application, resulting in a substantial hit to the corporate budget.

MORE INFORMATION ABOUT ORACLE

If you would like more information on the variety of Oracle database management systems, check out the Oracle Web page at `http://www.oracle.com/ip/deploy/database/`.

PostgreSQL

PostgreSQL (PgSQL) is the relative newcomer to the realm of database management systems. As an open source option, however, PostgreSQL is quickly being adopted as a powerful, inexpensive replacement for more costly database management systems. Although not quite as popular as MySQL, PgSQL offers similar functionality and speed as MySQL in an Open License package. Although PgSQL is available on the UNIX, Linux, and Windows platforms, Windows users have to pay for a version of PgSQL developed by dbExperts.

Resource   MORE INFORMATION ABOUT POSTGRESQL

If you would like more information about PostgreSQL, visit its Web site at `http://www.postgresq dbexperts.net`.

Because of the widespread availability of Microsoft Access and the 90-day free trial of Microsoft SQL Server, the hands-on chapters of this book use Access and SQL Server to demonstrate the process of building a database back-end for your dynamic applications. The skills and practices discussed in developing a database, however, are easily transferred to any of the other database management systems.

Summary

In this chapter, you were introduced to the process used by a Web server to serve dynamic pages. We also covered the most popular Web server software currently on the market, several application server options, and ended with a discussion on the various database management systems and their pros and cons. Armed with the information in this chapter, you should be able to identify the right combination of the three that will serve the needs of your organization and your Web applications.

In the next chapter, we will look at the differences between applications that are developed for the Web and those that are built for intranet use. In addition, we will take a look at what issues you should be aware of when building an application of either type.

CHAPTER 2

CHOOSING YOUR APPLICATION TYPE

Now that you have your database and platform selected, it's time to take a good look at your application and determine whether it will be accessible publicly on the Web, privately on a corporate intranet, or privately via an organizational extranet. There are various factors to take into account when designing each of these applications and this chapter examines those factors and helps you make a decision as to the best environment for your data.

By the end of this chapter, you should feel comfortable with the following:

- Understanding the differences between the World Wide Web, an intranet, and an extranet
- Identifying the issues that are present when designing applications for all of these environments
- Planning an application specific to any or all of these environments
- Understanding how Web applications, intranet applications, and extranet applications can function together

NOTE WHICH COMES FIRST...THE PLATFORM OR THE APPLICATION?

Much like the old chicken and egg question, there is often discussion about which issue should be considered first—platform or application type. There are some who say you should always understand what type of application you are building before you start worrying about what platform you are going to build on or what kind of hosting servers you need. Others, however, believe that knowing what kind of resources (for example, servers, platform software, and so on) you have to work with helps you understand what type of applications you are capable of producing. For the purpose of this book, we're going to proceed by choosing our platform and database first and then discuss what applications we're going to work with.

Web, Intranet, and Extranet Applications

As you are probably already aware, the World Wide Web has been serving up Web pages to the surfers of the world since 1989. Over this period, companies, organizations, and private individuals have contributed to the content of the Web by building sites that range from powerful eCommerce applications to small family Web sites. One thing that all of these applications have in common is that, unless security measures have been taken to restrict access, they are accessible to all users of the Web (see Figure 2.1).

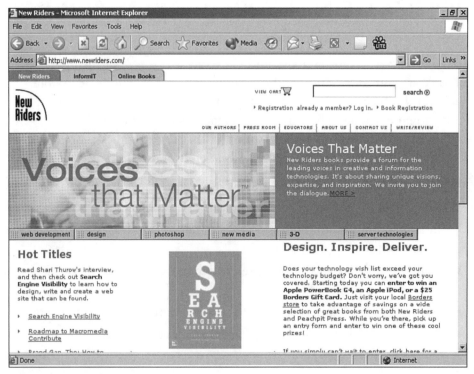

FIGURE 2.1   Typical Web sites are available to anyone who has a browser and an Internet connection.

Many organizations, however, are seeking ways to enhance the way they do business by not only harnessing the public power of the Web, but also determining how to use the technology that fuels the Web for more private purposes. Over the past decade, the terms *intranet* and *extranet* have been adopted into the vocabulary of Web developers to describe different ways of harnessing the functionality of the Web while reducing security concerns.

A NOTE ON THE LINGO

Because Web applications, intranet applications, and extranet applications tend to rely on the same technology to run, it is sometimes easy to confuse the three. Understanding the difference, however, can assist you in developing the application that best suits your needs.

A Web application is accessible to anyone who has access to the World Wide Web and the appropriate permission to access the files. Visitors use a *Web brows*er to view the pages and administrators use a *Web server application* to publish the pages.

Intranet applications, on the other hand, are usually not accessible via the World Wide Web, but instead are part of a closed local area network (LAN). Even though it may look like a Web application because users access the pages using their Web browser and administrators may publish the application using a Web server application, an intranet application is technically *not* a Web application because it is not published on nor is it accessible via the World Wide Web.

Extranet applications often consist of a hybrid of the Web applications and intranet applications. By accessing the front end of the application via a Web application, users can then access a secure area of a network that is part of an intranet.

Understanding Web Applications

As more and more consumers are becoming Web savvy, companies have begun designing an organizational Web site as more than just a way to give visitors information about their company. Organizations that used to have static, informational Web sites now have interactive features that allow their visitors to take virtual tours of their facilities, custom order products, pay online using a credit card, and track purchases right to their front door. Many of these new applications evolved by combining the informational aspects of the Web with the power of a database to form dynamic applications that are more functional and easier to maintain than their predecessors.

ARE DYNAMIC APPLICATIONS REALLY EASIER TO MAINTAIN THAN STATIC ONES?

Dynamic applications are easier to maintain than static pages, but I use *easier* as a relative term to the amount of work that would be required to produce the same result with static pages. For instance, suppose my company has a product catalog of 1,200 products. With a dynamic Web application, I could allow my visitors to browse that catalog by building a search page, results page, and details page (three pages total). Basically, with three pages and a database, I could avoid building those three pages for all 1,200 products (3,600 pages total).

The fact that I have to design the database, populate it with data, and then build the front page for my Web site might mean more time in the development process, but after it is developed, I can add a product to my site just by adding a new record to my database. Because my application is dynamic, the information then becomes part of what my Web visitor sees without additional work. In the long run, this becomes a much less time-consuming way of maintaining a large site and, thus, becomes *easier*.

Dynamic applications on the Web, however, are not without their downfalls. Usually, sites with more powerful and interactive applications require more resources, ranging from more powerful (and more costly) servers, more expensive development software, increased bandwidth requirements, and a higher level of user support. In addition, secure applications and those that engage in eCommerce require enhanced security and a higher level of product testing and intrusion detection than was required by previous, more basic applications. As a result, although the advantages of the evolving Web are enormous, the cost of developing, implementing, and maintaining a dynamic Web application grows.

 IS A WEB APPLICATION DIFFERENT THAN A WEB SITE?

The terms *Web application* and *Web site* are often used interchangeably, although I don't agree that they are the same. When I think of a Web site, I think of a collection of informational pages placed on the Web for the viewing pleasure of the world—basically, a static site that can only be viewed and never interacted with.

A Web application, on the other hand, brings both the informational aspect of a Web site together with the interactive elements of a software application to form an environment where information is not only given to the visitor, but collected from them as well.

This distinction is what leads me to refer to database-driven Web sites as *Web applications*.

Understanding Intranet Applications

If you think about it, Web sites are a lot like articles in a daily newspaper. Basically, they are available to everyone who is willing to pay a fee to get access to them. If you don't want to pay, you can head down to your local library and access them for free. The only problem with this, however, is that not all organizations want all of their information to be available to everyone. In fact, information like research and development documentation, marketing plans, and customer information are all examples of information that organizations go to great lengths to protect.

The question, then, becomes this: How can an organization distribute and discuss private information freely within its organizational structure without making the information public on the Web? In many cases, the answer has come in the form of a corporate intranet.

The term *intranet* describes a system that uses the same group of technologies that fuel the Internet on a corporate-wide basis. Essentially, an intranet is a mini-version of the Internet that can include Web services, organization-wide email, chat applications, and just about any service that is offered on the Internet. The major difference is that it is only accessible by members of the host organization from within the confines of the corporate network.

THE CREATION OF THE TERM "INTRANET"

We have Steve Telleen, Ph.D. to thank for the term *intranet*. Steve coined the phrase in 1994 while describing how Amdahl Corporation could use Web technology to communicate internally.

To implement an intranet, the organization must begin by building an internal network of computers based on the TCP/IP protocol that is used to power the Internet.

THE WEB IS NOT THE SAME THINGS AS THE INTERNET

Remember, the World Wide Web is only one element of the Internet and the terms are not interchangeable. The Internet is made up of elements that also include email protocols and file transfer protocols.

The most visible tool that companies usually integrate into their intranet is an internal Web application. To accomplish this, the organization usually builds a host server that runs Web server software and, if necessary, an application server such as ASP.NET or ColdFusion Server. As shown in Figure 2.2, this machine behaves exactly like a Web server but is not directly connected to the Web. The server is, however, connected to the internal TCP/IP network of computers and only those computers on the internal network are capable of requesting pages from the server and interacting with it.

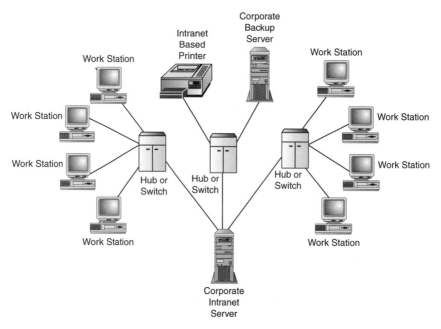

FIGURE 2.2   The organizational view of an intranet.

When an employee wants to access the intranet, she simply types the machine and page address into her browser and interacts with the server in the same manner as any Web page.

 REQUESTING A DOCUMENT FROM AN INTRANET SERVER

When you want to access a Web page, you follow a certain protocol to request the document from a specific server. For instance, if you want to access the main page of Amazon.com, you type in the domain name that is associated with Amazon's Web server, **http://www.amazon.com**, and you are presented with the page that has been specified as the default page of the site.

Requesting a document from an intranet server is very similar, except you simply use the name of the server. For instance, suppose your organization has named its intranet server Zeus. To access the Web services on that computer, you would simply type **http://zeus** into your browser and the Web services installed on Zeus would take over. You could also access the server by using the IP address assigned to the computer. In that case, you might type something like **http://134.104.198.12** into your browser.

The benefits of an intranet come from the fact that, when properly implemented, an organization can freely share information that should not be available to the public. Using the intranet, departments like Research and Development can share their innovations with Marketing and Sales with less of a concern that one of their competitors might be able to view their data.

Intranets, however, are not necessarily for every organization. Because they depend upon heightened security to ensure that prying outside eyes have no access to them, they require very careful development and testing prior to being released. In addition, technicians vigilantly explore possible security flaws and determine ways to eliminate them. This testing, development, and maintenance can become costly for an organization in the form of hardware, software, and human resources.

Understanding Extranet Applications

Although the term *extranet* sounds as though it is the opposite of an intranet, it is not. Although an intranet is designed at restricting access to those who are outside the organization, an extranet, shown in Figure 2.3, works to extend access to information to users who, though not part of the organization's network, need access to private information.

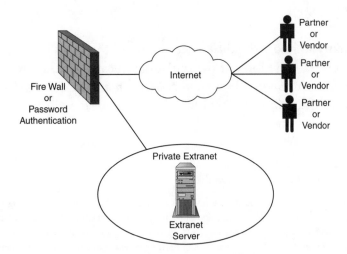

FIGURE 2.3   An extranet provides private access to parties outside of the corporate intranet.

For instance, suppose your company maintains an inventory database of all the products it offers. This database is part of your company's intranet and access to it is limited to the computers on your network. To assure that an item is never out of inventory, however, the company would like to create a secured section of the intranet that allows properly authenticated vendors to view inventories and update pricing. To accomplish this, the organization has to make its network accessible to machines that are not part of the organizational network. To accomplish this, software and hardware solutions known as firewalls are implemented that restrict access to the network based on the computer's IP address or a username/password combination. Using these tools, an outside vendor can have access to the organizational network and perform the necessary tasks.

Opening up the network to the outside world, however, increases the risk of security breaches and requires an even higher level of vigilance on the part of network administrators. In addition, Web developers who create the applications designed for use on an extranet must be sure that there are no potential security issues with their code.

Designing the Right Application for Your Needs

Now that you know the differences between the types of Web applications, it's time to take a close look at the type of applications you intend to build and determine which model best encompasses them. To do this, let's take a look at three basic questions that should help you analyze your project and understand its ideal environment.

 ARE THREE QUESTIONS ENOUGH?

The questions will address designing the right application for your needs—specifically, some of the most common issues that are universal to choosing an application type. In reality, there are hundreds of questions that your organization needs to address with respect to your specific needs. These three questions, however, will hopefully spark many more questions on your part, which will help you better understand what type of application is right for you.

What Is the Nature of Your Application?

Basically, what do you intend your application to accomplish? If your site is intended to offer your products to consumers on a retail basis, a Web application is best. If, however, you plan to sell your products on a wholesale basis to a select group of vendors, it might be a better idea to create an extranet that each vendor can access with authenticated credentials. Finally, if your goal is to enhance the internal communications within your organization, an intranet might be better than a Web site intended to provide corporate information to the public.

Who Are Your Anticipated Users?

After you know the intended purpose of your application, it's a good idea to understand who your intended audience is. Knowing *who* your audience is and how you expect them to interact with your site is not enough, however. To ensure that your users can properly interact with the site, you should also know what tools the users have at their disposal.

For instance, if you are building a Web application, it is shortsighted to build an application that only functions in Internet Explorer if you know that Netscape users will be visiting your site. In addition, client-side elements such as screen resolution, access speeds, and the use of third-party applications (like Macromedia Flash Player or Adobe Acrobat) should all be factors in how you develop your application for the Web.

Intranet developers usually have a much easier time identifying their target audience, because the audience usually consists of the employees of the organization. Because many organizations tend to standardize which operating systems, software, and browsers are used on client machines, intranet developers can usually tailor their applications to their users without worrying about the absence of a browser plug-in or slow loading pages due to dial-up connections.

Extranet developers, on the other hand, often have to balance the issues of knowing who their users are but not having control over the software that is used to access the system. Because the extranet client is located on another network, it is entirely possible that the client's organizational policies regarding computers, software, and browsers differ from the company hosting the extranet.

Because of the wide variety of technologies and the fact that software configurations vary from machine to machine, developers for the Web, intranets, and extranets have to be careful to ensure that their target audience is capable of accessing all aspects of the application.

What Type of Security Do You Require?

Another very important issue to consider when developing your application is the level of security required to protect your data. Although Web applications generally require a lower level of security than intranet or extranet applications, the addition of components such as user accounts with personal information, eCommerce transactions, and pay subscription services require additional security to ensure that your information is secure. To secure Web applications, tools such as database-driven user authentication, Secure Socket Layer (SSL) certificates, and challenged-response are available.

Although intranet developers may use some of the same tools that Web developers use in securing their applications, they also rely on an additional set of security tools to lock their applications. Approaches such as IP blocking (where all machines with IP addresses other than those that fall within the range used by the organization are blocked), hardware and software firewalls, and digital signature certificates all help the developer ensure that the information is only available for internal use.

Extranet developers face the additional task of securing the information located on the extranet without compromising the integrity of the intranet security. For this reason, extranet developers often use a combination of the tools used by both Web developers and intranet developers to ensure that their users can log on and view the information but have limited access to the data included in the extranet.

Planning Your Application

In Chapter 1, "Choosing the Right Tools for Your Dynamic Application," we discussed the platform and database requirements of your anticipated application. At this point, you should have a feel for whether the application will be part of a Web site, intranet, or extranet. Armed with this information, it's time to get down to the nitty-gritty and start planning the details.

Server Requirements

Now that you know what platform you will be using and your anticipated audience size, it's time to start thinking about your server requirements. Depending on whether you are part of an organization or a freelance consultant, your options in choosing a server will be very different.

Organizational Hosting

If you are part of a large organization, it's possible that you have servers available for your use. The question is whether those servers can meet your usage demands, have the appropriate Web server and application server installed, meet your security needs, and allow you access to the appropriate database files.

For example, suppose your Human Resources (HR) department has requested that you build a database-driven application that allows its employees to log in and update employee records. HR only wants this information visible from within the organization and would like the data stored in a SQL Server database. The first thing you might want to determine is whether your organization has a server available that is not connected to the Web so you can restrict access on an organizational basis. If there is a server available, you then check to see what platforms it is capable of hosting so you can determine what language the application needs to be coded in.

Let's suppose that the server exists and it is running Microsoft IIS and is capable of running Active Server Pages and ASP.NET pages. Because you now have chosen an environment (an intranet), a Web server (IIS), and a platform (ASP or ASP.NET), the final step is to determine whether a server is available that is currently running SQL Server where the HR database can reside. With all those pieces in place, you now are ready to start development on the actual application. If, however, any of those pieces is not in place, it's likely that you will have to discuss alternative options with Human Resources and proceed from there.

Remote Hosting

Hosting an application on a commercial host outside your organization can present issues of its own. For smaller businesses, it is more cost effective to let the hosting company shoulder the cost of maintaining and upgrading server hardware. The disadvantage to remote hosting, however, is that you have little control over the servers if and when they go down. However, there are a lot of good hosts on the market and a little research goes a long way in finding one.

Before you settle on a host, it's a good idea to check out the host Web site and see what options are offered. Some elements that you might look for include the following:

- **Service guarantee.** Find out whether the host guarantees that services will be continually available. Many hosts offer a 99 percent uptime guarantee. This means that your server will be up 99 percent of the month or they generally refund that month's server fee. Remember, that the host must perform maintenance, which includes rebooting the server occasionally, so a 100 percent uptime guarantee may be a bit unreasonable.

- **Server hardware.** Before settling on a host, be sure to ask for details regarding the server where your application will be hosted. Questions like the age of the server, processor speed, amount of memory, and anticipated update schedules will keep your site from being hosted on an antiquated machine that doesn't meet your needs.

- **Operating system.** Determine what operating system the host offers. If you are planning to develop an application using ASP.NET or ASP, you more than likely need a host that is running Windows servers. Other platforms such as PHP, ColdFusion, or JSP can be run on either a Windows or UNIX server as long as the appropriate software is installed.

- **Cost.** Be very careful when researching the cost of a remote host. Many organizations are tempted by discount hosts who end up offering terrible service and no customer support. Also, be wary of extra charges for services like customer support or restoring your data from tape.

- **Supported components.** Will your application require components such as ASPEmail, a CGI-BIN, or PERL? Most reputable hosts will tell you up front exactly what components are available for your use.

- **Database support.** Determine what databases the host provides support for. Most hosts that use Windows servers provide support for Access databases using ODBC or OLE connections for all their plans. If you require a SQL Server database, you may have to pay for a higher-level usage plan or purchase the use of the database *a la carte*.

- **Support options.** Before selecting a host, I highly recommend contacting the host's customer support department to see how quickly you receive assistance. A good quality host can often be identified by how willing they are to provide customer support in a timely manner.

- **Shared servers.** Be aware that many remote hosts place more than one Web site on a single server. Although this usually is not a problem, if one site on the server uses faulty code, it is possible that it could bring the server and all the sites on it to its knees. If your organization requires a separate server, be aware that there are hosts that offer private servers. The cost, however, is at a premium.

- **Usage load.** Most remote hosts allot a monthly bandwidth limitation for each site on their servers. These limitations are in place to keep high-bandwidth sites from monopolizing the server resources and diminishing the bandwidth that is allotted to the host. Be wary of hosts that offer "no bandwidth restrictions." Although this may sound great for your site, it also sounds great to the site trading MP3s that is hosted on the same server. Because the MP3 site is hogging all the bandwidth and server resources, it's likely that your site will suffer performance issues.

- **Data recovery.** It is important that you know if your host is responsible for backing up your data and on what schedule (nightly, weekly, and so on) the data is backed up. In addition, determine what procedure you need to follow to have data restored and whether there is a restoration fee involved.

Software Requirements for Your Users

When planning your application, it's a good idea to try to anticipate any browser plug-ins, ActiveX controls, or third-party software that your visitors might need to interact with your site. Applications such as Adobe Acrobat Reader, Macromedia Flash Player, Apple QuickTime, and RealNetwork's Real Player are all examples of applications that developers often use to enhance the content stored on their Web site, intranet, or extranet.

The nice thing about these applications is they are generally easy for your visitors to install and can enhance your site with sound, video, and the ability to display documents on any platform. However, by integrating these applications into your project, you rely upon the developing companies to produce software that is free of bugs and doesn't interfere with the functionality of your application.

Bridging the Gap Between Web Applications and Intranet/Extranet Applications

If you are going to be developing multiple applications for your organization, it's likely that you are going to want to allow them to interact with one another. For instance, vendors might want to gather information from your organizational Web site and then log on to your extranet, whereas your staff members would be interested in accessing both your organizational intranet and your Web site. Allowing users to move easily from one application to another is often a lofty goal with various security issues in the way. To minimize potential security risks, it's important that you consider the crossover traffic when developing your applications.

Summary

In this chapter, you were introduced to the three most common types of applications. With the information from this chapter, you should be able to decide whether your project would serve your organization best as a Web application, intranet application, or extranet application.

In the next section of the book, we will begin the hands-on material and start the process of building a complete intranet application from the ground up. Chapter 3, "Building a Database for Dynamic Applications," focuses on developing the database that will serve as the back end for our application.

PART II

Creating Intranet-Strength Applications with MS Access, ASP.NET/ColdFusion, and Dreamweaver MX 2004

BUILDING A DATABASE FOR DYNAMIC APPLICATIONS

Building a database from scratch is no easy task and building a database to use with a Web site, intranet, or extranet raises additional issues. The goal of this chapter is to walk you through the process of building a database that we can later use when developing our intranet application. The chapter will also introduce you to Microsoft Access, a relational database management system, and help you identify and avoid potential pitfalls that can arise when developing for the Web.

By the end of this chapter, you should be able to do the following:

- Understand the structure of a relational database
- Follow the six steps of the database design process
- Be familiar with building tables and creating relationships using access
- Understand the potential limitations when using Microsoft Access
- Have an expanded database vocabulary

WEB APPLICATIONS, INTRANET APPLICATIONS, AND EXTRANET APPLICATIONS

In Chapter 2, "Choosing Your Application Type," we spent the entire chapter examining the differences between Web, intranet, and extranet applications. One thing they all have in common, however, is this: each relies on the technology that fuels the Web. For this reason, in this chapter and those that follow, we're going to lump them all together by referring to them as *Web applications*.

Understanding the Structure of a Relational Database

Databases come in all shapes and sizes, and they range in size and complexity from a simple alphabetized box full of recipes to the most complex back-end relational database for an eCommerce site. For the most part, however, when we use the term *database* with regards to business and technology, we refer to objects created by database management systems—like Microsoft Access or SQL Server—that are installed on our home or work computers. We use these databases to store a wide variety of data such as employee information, business transactions, and product inventories.

Applications such as Access or SQL Server build their databases based on the relational model, where each database is comprised of tables that are uniquely named. Each table is then made up of records (commonly referred to as rows) and fields (also called columns) of related information. When retrieving data from a relational database, the system cares only about the data that is stored in each record; non-relational systems, on the other hand, not only consider the data but also the structure of the database, making the process of retrieving results much slower.

For example, suppose your relational database has a table similar to the one shown in Table 3.1 that stores the names, usernames, passwords, and login information for each employee in your company.

TABLE 3.1   An Example of a Table in a Relational Database

LASTNAME	FIRSTNAME	USERNAME	PASSWORD	LASTLOGIN
Johnson	Fred	johnsonf	happyday	03/15/2003
Jackson	Sara	jacksons	plowdown	02/11/2003
Martin	Eva	martine	dailyend	03/12/2003
Bellows	Dan	bellowsd	duster	03/11/2003

Because the relational model relies only on the value of the data itself, you could easily ask the system to find all the employees who have not logged in for more than 90 days.

What Is Involved in the Database Design Process?

After you are familiar with how a relational database works, you're ready to look specifically at the project at hand and determine what your database should look like and how it should behave. There are many ways to approach the development of a new database, but over the years, I have developed a six-step process that allows me to think through the database one step at a time. I have found that if I follow this process from beginning to end, I usually end up with a good database that functions as expected.

To see how well this process works, let's build a scenario and walk through the steps to see how they work. Suppose that you and I own a small consulting firm that specializes in developing database-driven Web applications for the business sector. Recently, we have been contacted by KrystalClear Technologies, a local startup company that is entering the telecommunications industry and offering residential and commercial telephone services. The company does not currently have a budget to hire an in-house database administrator and Web developer, so they have contacted our firm to explore the possibility of contracting for the development of a corporate intranet.

Although the decision makers at KrystalClear know that the functionality of the intranet must grow over time, they would like to start by having us develop four modules that would serve as the foundation for future developments. Those elements are the following:

- **A Human Resources employee management system**. This system would allow the Human Resources staff to manage information about each employee hired by KrystalClear.
- **An Information Services asset management system**. This element would allow the Information Technology staff to maintain information about the computer hardware, software, and peripherals owned by KrystalClear.

- **A departmental intranet management system.** This system would allow a liaison in each department to update his individual departmental information page. This reduces the need to have staff from Information Services make updates to the intranet any time a department needs to make a change.
- **The front-end user interface for the intranet.** This is the look and feel of the pages that the employees of KrystalClear will use on a daily basis. Although the management at KrystalClear has left this element up to your creative suggestions, they would like to be sure that the KrystalClear corporate logo is present on every page.

With that scenario in mind, let's proceed through the database design process and see what we can do.

Step 1—Think/Talk

The first step in designing a database is to consider the project you are working on and the features that your future users might want to have access to. I have found that during this step, it is extremely helpful to talk to both the management that is supervising the project and the end users who will work with the system on a daily basis to determine what they expect from the end-result and what issues they are trying to resolve.

Obviously, this is a hypothetical situation and we cannot sit down and talk with the managers and employees of KrystalClear. However, let's suppose we emailed a list of eight questions to an Intranet Coordinating Committee (a select group of employees and managers who have volunteered to work with us on the intranet project) and they have provided us with the following answers. In response to their answers, I have added some issues that we might need to consider (this is the thinking and talking part).

> **Q1:** What reason or reasons do you have for developing this application?
>
> **A1:** The purpose of developing our corporate intranet is to provide our employees with a single point of contact for information pertaining to our organization. Our intention is for any employee to be able to find directory information about other employees, learn about the internal activities of any department, and engage in activities such as requesting computer support, filling out employee benefit forms, or a variety of other activities that have previously been done via the telephone or in writing.

Thoughts about the answer: These all appear to be very good reasons for building an intranet. It appears that communication between users and departments is the highest priority.

Q2: Who are the anticipated users of the application?

A2: All employees located at our corporate offices should have access to the intranet via our local area network (LAN). Eventually, as we develop a wide area network (WAN), we would like employees at our outlying offices to be able to access the intranet as well.

Thoughts about the answer: Because the user of the intranet will currently be restricted to the LAN and not available to the outside world, external security is less of a concern than internal security. We should focus our efforts on ensuring that only the appropriate users have access to restricted areas of the system.

Q3: Are there any areas of the application that need to be secured? If so, how do you plan to designate which users are allowed to view those areas?

A3: Each departmental site will be secured in that editing it will only be allowed by the departmental manager and another departmental employee authorized by the manager. In addition, some departments, such as Human Resources, should have access to edit information that pertains to their jobs. This means that there will be sections of the Human Resources intranet site that only employees of HR will be able to access.

Thoughts about the answer: The Human Resources table that stores user details will need to have a field that specifies what department the user works for. From this, we can grant or deny access to restricted departmental information.

Q4: How many users do you anticipate accessing the system at the same time?

A4: At this time, all 125 employees should have access. We anticipate that 15 to 20 employees would be viewing information on the intranet at the same time.

Thoughts about the answer: Having 15 to 20 employees at a time viewing the data would probably result in at most 3 to 4 concurrent connections. This falls well within the restrictions on Microsoft Access, so we can use Access as our back-end database.

Q5: What is the projected growth for your company over the next five years with respect to employees?

A5: Over the next five years, we project having 400 to 500 employees; however, only 250 of those would be at the corporate office.

Thoughts about the answer: This projected growth would probably still be within the restrictions of an Access database, but we might want to recommend expansion to a SQL Server database should the company grow beyond these numbers.

Q6: If your company grows more quickly than anticipated, would be you open to upgrading the database?

A6: Yes. Unanticipated growth would most likely be caused by entrance into new markets, so we would be more than willing to fund software and hardware upgrades to meet our corporate needs.

Thoughts about the answer: An upsize to SQL Server would be relatively easy, however, the company should be notified of the hardware and licensing costs of SQL Server long before they reach the time to upsize.

Q7: You mentioned that you want each departmental manager and an additional liaison to be able to update their pages. What will be the procedure for indicating that an employee is allowed to make those changes?

A7: The departmental manager will email the Human Resources department the name of the employee selected to maintain their information. HR will then update the employee's record to indicate that she has permission.

Thoughts about the answer: The Human Resources table will need to have a field specifying whether the user is permitted to update the departmental site.

Q8: How will employees access the corporate intranet?

A8: Employees will access the intranet using their work computers. Our machines come configured with Microsoft Internet Explorer so users will use that browser to view the intranet.

Thoughts about the answer: Because all users will be on Internet Explorer, cross-browser compatibility is less of an issue than with a typical Web application. However, the company is anticipating a WAN in its future and it is not possible to project what browser remote offices might be using so we still need to code for all browsers.

As you can see, interacting with the Intranet Coordinating Committee has provided us with a wealth of information and has sparked questions of our own. After we feel our questions have been answered and we are satisfied with the amount of information that we have, it's time to move on to the next step.

Tip **PRACTICE "ACTIVE LISTENING"**

When talking with the people who will be using your new Web applications, it's a good idea to use a skill known as *active listening* where you not only listen to what they have to say, but respond to their statements with additional questions, comments, or observations. More often than not, your responses will generate more feedback on their part and provide you with additional information. Although this may sound like a no-brainer, you'd be surprised how often I have sat in on meetings where a technologist would sit quietly, listen, and take notes only to get back to his office and wonder about an issue that could have easily been asked and answered in the meeting.

Step 2—Anticipate

The second step that I use in designing a database is to put myself in the place of the end user and try to anticipate any functionality that she might need that has not already been expressed. This process is often based on the conversations from the previous step and usually draws from my experience developing similar applications for other organizations.

For instance, with regard to the departmental updates of their own pages, the committee stated that the manager of the department would send an email to a member of the human resources staff indicating which employees should have permission to update the departmental site. From this, we can anticipate that the database table that stores the employee information should have a field that indicates whether the employee has access to update the page.

By anticipating these types of features, we can build our database in a manner that will better suit the application and we can forecast potential issues and address them with the committee.

Step 3—Build

Now that you have an understanding of what the organization is seeking and have used your past experiences to anticipate additional functionality, it's time to start building the application. We'll take a detailed look at the steps of building our intranet application for KrystalClear a little later in the chapter.

Step 4—Analyze

After the database has been developed, it is a very good idea to do some testing to ensure that it behaves as performed. Even though the KrystalClear employees won't directly interact with our intranet database through the use of Access, we can use Access to test some of the functionality that we know will be part of the application.

For instance, we know that our intranet application will be using queries based on the Structured Query Language (SQL) to add, edit, and modify data located in the database. Using the SQL View of Microsoft Access, shown in Figure 3.1, we can test those queries before we ever write a line of code for our Web pages.

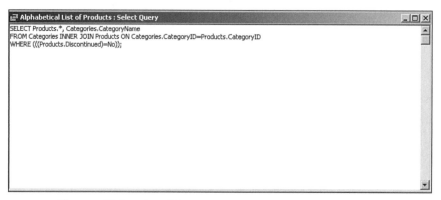

FIGURE 3.1   The SQL View of Microsoft Access is just one
tool that helps us test our application.

By running these tests, we can ensure that the data our database returns in response to the query is the information that we expected.

Step 5—Restructure

Unless you are really (and I mean *really*) good it's likely that the Analyze phase of the design process turned up some issues in your database that need to be resolved. Don't worry. No matter how long you build databases, you will probably always catch something that doesn't work correctly or needs some tweaking. During the Restructure phase, you can go back to make adjustments and resolve any issues that arise. After you make a change, however, it is important that you return to the Analyze phase and ensure that the changes you made did not cause problems with any other element of your database. After three or four iterations through the Analyze/Restructure phases, your database will be functioning properly and you'll be ready to move on to the last step.

TESTING YOUR CHANGES

Be sure you test every change that is made during the Restructuring phase. Any modifications to the system require that you go back to Step 4 and restart until you are able to get through Step 5 with no changes.

Step 6—Deploy

Much like soldiers who are prepared for battle, at this point, your database should be ready to be deployed into action. This usually means the database structure and relationships have been thoroughly tested and everything functions as anticipated to begin the development of the Web pages that will interact with it.

Because we haven't begun developing our intranet database yet, let's take a few steps back to the Build phase and get cracking on our development.

A Brief Introduction to Access

In case you are not very familiar with the workings of Microsoft Access, let's take a few minutes to go over the basic tools available in the Access interface.

 LEARNING ACCESS

Although we will be walking through the process of building a database in Access, if you are not familiar with the menus and features, it is a good idea for you to start with a book that focuses strictly on Access. There are several good books on learning Access including *Microsoft Access 2000—Illustrated Complete* (Course Technology, 2001) by Lisa Friedrichsen and Elizabeth Eisner and *Microsoft Access Version 2002 Step by Step* (Microsoft Press, 2001) by Online Training Solutions Inc.

To start our brief tour, open the application on your local computer and let's walk through the fundamental objects created within Access.

The Database Window

The Database window, shown in Figure 3.2, provides an easy-to-use interface to create, edit, and delete database objects. An Access database is more than just a bunch of data stuffed into a single file.

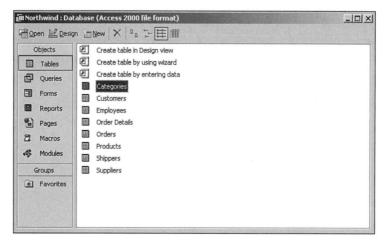

FIGURE 3.2   The Database window provides access to the various database objects that can be created and manipulated from within Access.

Instead, an Access database is a collection of objects that store your data, represent the data in different views, and contain information about how each of the objects should interact with one another.

Tables

A table is the fundamental building block of any database because it is where the data is stored. The table consists of fields and records—fields specify the nature of the information that is being stored and rows contain a single record of data. For instance, in Figure 3.3, the first row contains information about Nancy Davolio. The fields show us that the table contains her employee ID, last name, first name, address, telephone number, and so on.

Using the table view of Access, you can add records to a table, edit the data, or remove the record altogether.

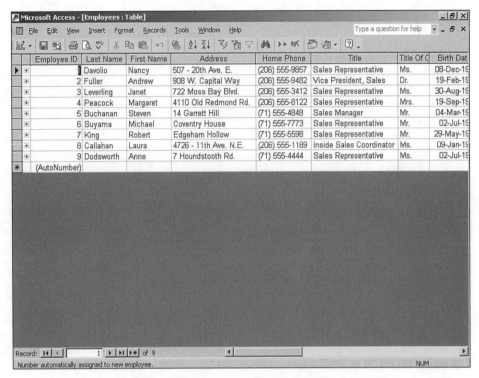

FIGURE 3.3   The table view allows us to see the rows and
columns that make up our table.

Queries

As the number of records in your table grows, so will the difficulty in finding
and editing data located within it. Think of a query as a better way of organiz-
ing the data contained in your table for a specific purpose.

For instance, suppose you have a table that contains quite a few records, similar to the one shown in Figure 3.4, but you only want to see the records of people who live in Tennessee.

To accomplish this, you can build a query that scans the data and only returns
the information that meets the criteria. As shown in Figure 3.5, designing a
query that (in plain language) says, "Show me all the records where the state
field has TN in it," will accomplish your goal.

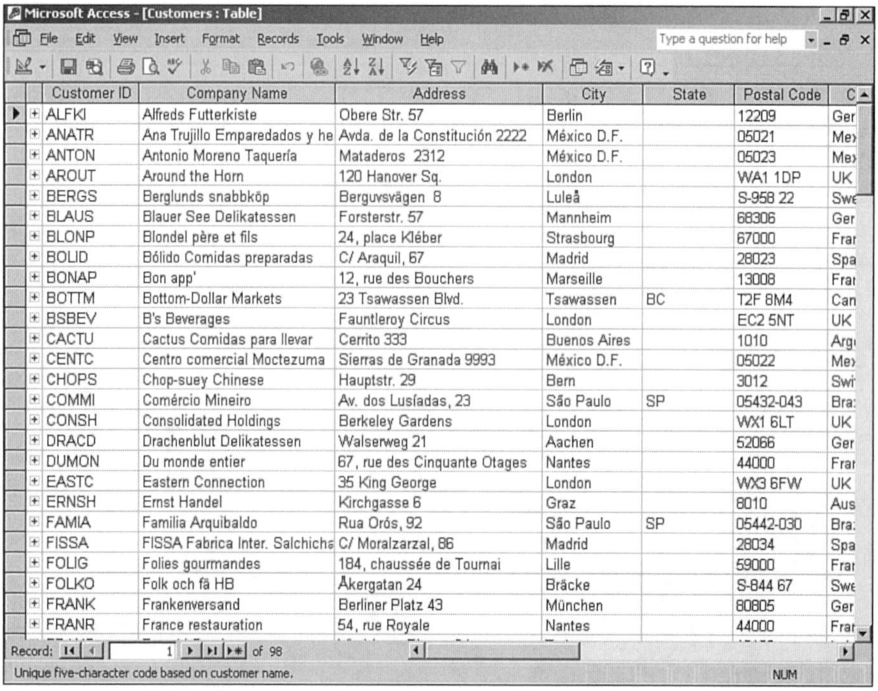

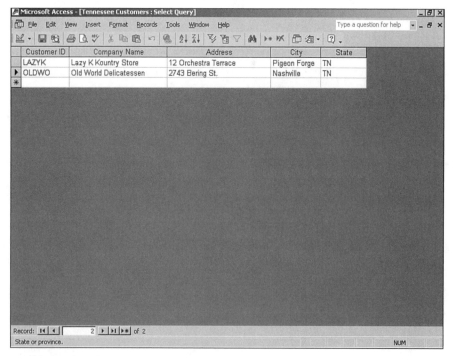

FIGURE 3.4   The table view can sometimes make it difficult to find the data you are looking for.

FIGURE 3.5   A query can help you quickly find the data you are seeking.

Forms

Entering data into your database can quickly become an eye-straining task. Staring at all those columns, rows, and gridlines definitely isn't the most visually appealing way to populate your database. The alternative to entering data directly into the table is to build a custom form that is easier on the eyes. A simple form, shown in Figure 3.6, allows you to enter the demographic data for each of your users.

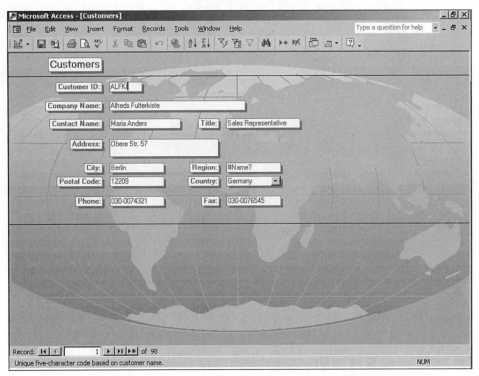

FIGURE 3.6   A form can make it easier to input and update data.

When a database is used strictly as the back end of a Web application, the database forms are not used much because the Web pages you build to interact with the tables serve as your forms.

Reports

Although a query is a much more manageable way of viewing your data, it still leaves something to desire visually. Reports, on the other hand, allow you to customize the way your data is presented in printable format. Reports draw their information from a table or a query and organize the information into an attractive layout that you can customize. A sample report, shown in Figure 3.7, represents the query of users in Kentucky in a format that is more visually appealing.

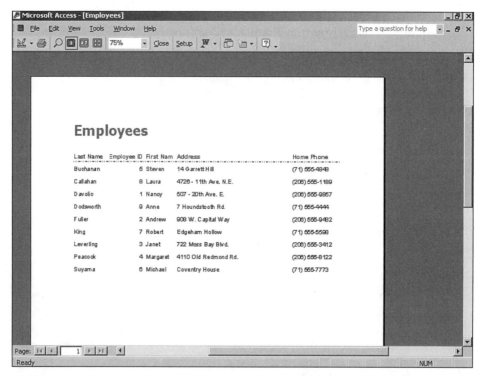

FIGURE 3.7   Reports provide a custom view of your data that is easily printed.

Pages

One of the newer features within Access is the Data Access Page component. Data Access Pages are Active Server Pages that allow you to display your forms on the Web. Through these pages, you can interact with your database in a manner similar to a small Web application.

Relationships

Although technically not an object that is stored within an Access database, the Relationships tool, shown in Figure 3.8, is an extremely important feature within Access and certainly deserves an introduction.

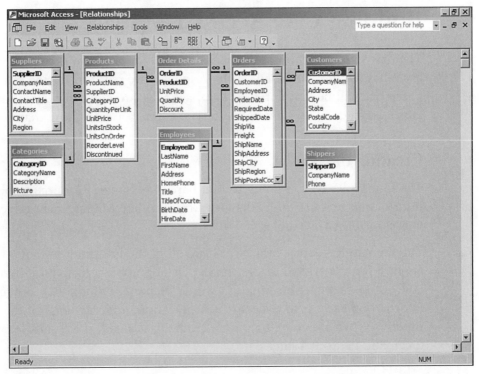

FIGURE 3.8   The Relationships window helps you avoid storing duplicate data.

One of the biggest goals in constructing a database is to avoid storing duplicate data. If you have duplicate data located within your database, and one piece of data is updated and the other is not, information within your database is now incorrect. To avoid storing duplicate data, you build tables that relate to one another. For instance, suppose that in addition to your users table you add a purchases table that stores all of the items that each user buys, the quantity he purchased, and the date the transaction was completed. Without a relationship and a set of rules to maintain referential integrity, you could potentially add records to the purchases table without relating those records to the person who purchased them. The result would be orphaned data. As you will see when we build our own database, creating relationships within Access is a very easy process that will ensure your database functions smoothly.

Building Our Access Database

The first step in building our client's intranet application is to build the database that will fuel it. Based on the responses we received during our planning phase, we will be building four database tables to store our data. After the tables are created, we can define relationships between those that need them.

Creating the Tables

The four tables we are going to build are the Human Resources table, the Information Services table, the Departmental Site Management table, and the Username/Password table.

The Human Resources table will store all of the information that KrystalClear might have in a typical employee file. Demographic information like name, address, and contact information would be present along with organizational information such as title, department, location, and the name of the employee's supervisor. We are going to start with the basics and, if KrystalClear wants to, it can add fields at a later date.

EXERCISE 3.1   Creating the Human Resources Table

1. Open Microsoft Access on your workstation.
2. From the menu bar, select File, New.
3. In the New File panel, shown in Figure 3.9, select a Blank Database.
4. Using the File New Database dialog box, create a folder called KrystalClear in your My Documents folder. As shown in Figure 3.10, name the file kc_corporation_0493.mdb and click Create.
5. In the database window, click the Tables category and then choose Create Table in Design View.

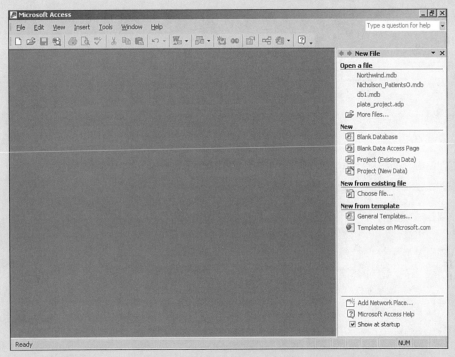

FIGURE 3.9   Choose to create a blank database from the New File panel.

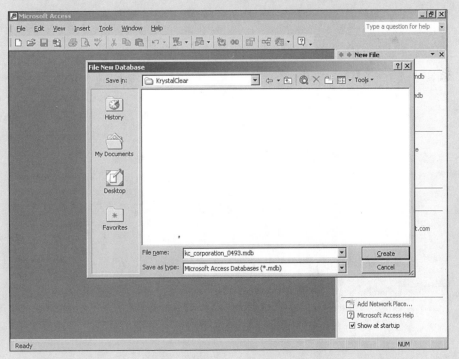

FIGURE 3.10   For security reasons, give your database file a unique name.

6. In the Design view, add the data using the parameters shown in Table 3.2.

TABLE 3.2   Sample Data for Human Resources Table

FIELD NAME	DATA TYPE	FIELD SIZE	REQUIRED	ALLOW ZERO LENGTH	INDEXED
EmployeeID	Text	11	Yes	No	Yes (No Duplicates)
LastName	Text	50	No	Yes	No
FirstName	Text	50	No	Yes	No
HomeAdd	Text	50	No	Yes	No
City	Text	25	No	Yes	No
HomeState	Text	2	No	Yes	No
Zip	Text	10	No	Yes	No
HomePhone	Text	50	No	Yes	No
Title	Text	50	No	Yes	No
Department	Text	50	No	Yes	No
Extension	Text	10	No	Yes	No
HireDate	Date/ Time	N/A	No	N/A	No
EditPages	Yes/No	N/A	No		No

You should now have a table that looks like the one in Figure 3.11.

7. Right-click on the gray box to the left of EmployeeID and choose Primary Key from the context menu. By indicating that EmployeeID is a primary key, no two records will be allowed to have the same Employee ID. This ensures that no duplicate entries are added to the database.

8. Save the table as tbHR and close the table.

NAMING CONVENTIONS

It is a good idea to get into the habit of applying naming conventions to your database objects. For instance, by naming the table tbHR, we can quickly identify this object as a table by the tb prefix. It doesn't seem as important when looking at the table name from within Access, but when you are staring at 300 lines of code and trying to identify whether your code is correct, it makes things a lot easier. In addition, avoid using spaces in your filenames and field names. There are issues that can arise from within your SQL queries if you use spaces. Instead, run the characters together and use capital letters to signify where a space might occur (as in LastName). If you really want to make it easier to identify your tables when searching through your code, you can add a prefix to the column name that matches the table name. For instance, the LastName column in the tbHR table would be named HRLastName.

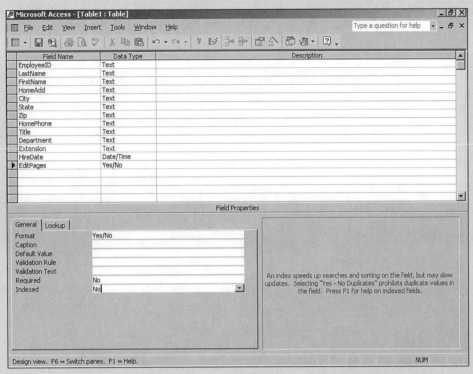

FIGURE 3.11   The structure of the Human Resources table.

We now have a table that contains the fields for our employees. For the most part, the fields pertain to their contact information and company status. The EditPages field, however, was created in response to our communication with KrystalClear. This field allows Human Resources to indicate who has access to edit pages. When combined with the Department field, not only do we know whether that employee can edit pages, but for what department.

The next step is to create the table that allows Information Services to assign an asset (for example, computer, phone, or pager) to a specific employee.

Exercise 3.2   Building the Information Services Table

1. In the Database window, select the Tables category and choose Create Table in Design View.

2. In Design view, add the data using the parameters shown in Table 3.3.

Table 3.3   Sample Data for Information Services Table

Field Name	Data Type	Field Size	Required	Allow Zero Length	Indexed
AssetID	AutoNumber	Long Integer	N/A	N/A	Yes (No Duplicates)
EmployeeID	Text	11	No	Yes	No
AssetType	Text	25	No	Yes	No
AssetBrand	Text	25	No	Yes	No
AssetModel	Text	50	No	Yes	No
AssetSerial	Text	50	No	Yes	No
Date Assigned	Date/Time	N/A	No	N/A	No
Date Returned	Date/Time	N/A	No	N/A	No
ReturnReason	Memo	N/A	No	Yes	No

You should now have a table that looks like the one in Figure 3.12.

Looking over the table, you should see a group of fields that have unique names, data types that match the data that will be stored in the records, and appropriate field lengths. Be careful when setting your field lengths because the sum of your field sizes directly affects the size of your database. It's a good idea to estimate as closely as possible how many characters are going to be necessary for a field. Although you don't want to devote too many characters and increase the size of your database, you also don't want to chop off pieces of data (which Access will do if the data submitted is too large for the field size).

In addition to the field name, data type, and size, we have also indicated that none of the fields in the database should be required fields and only the AssetID field should be an AutoNumber field. When building dynamic applications, it is better to use a technique called *form verification* to ensure that the information the user has entered meets your requirements. If you choose to allow the database to determine if a field is required, when the missing data is encountered, a very cryptic error message is displayed in the browser (which has a tendency to freak out users). If, however, you use form validation, you can customize your error message with a clear, polite message that lets the user know what is wrong and how she can remedy it.

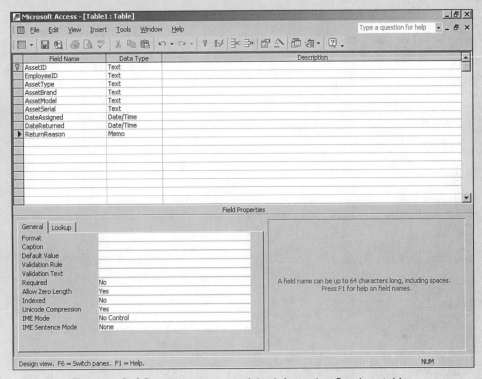

FIGURE 3.12   The structure of the Information Services table.

3. Right-click the gray box to the left of AssetID and choose Primary Key from the context menu.

4. Save the table as tbIS and close it.

The third table that we are going to create allows each department to update information contained in its departmental intranet site.

EXERCISE 3.3   Creating the Tables for Departmental Site Management

1. In the Database window, select the Tables category and choose Create Table in Design View.

2. In the Design view, add the data using the parameters shown in Table 3.4.

TABLE 3.4   Sample Data for Departmental Site Management Table

FIELD NAME	DATA TYPE	FIELD SIZE	REQUIRED	ALLOW ZERO LENGTH	INDEXED
PageID	AutoNumber	Long Integer	N/A	N/A	Yes (No Duplicates)
Department	Text	50	No	Yes	No
PageTitle	Text	100	No	Yes	No
NavLink1Text	Text	50	No	Yes	No
NavLink1URL	Text	50	No	Yes	No
NavLink2Text	Text	50	No	Yes	No
NavLink2URL	Text	50	No	Yes	No
NavLink3Text	Text	50	No	Yes	No
NavLink3URL	Text	50	No	Yes	No
MainPageData	Memo	N/A	No	Yes	No
LastUpdated	Date/Time	N/A	No	N/A	No

You should now have a table that looks like the one in Figure 3.13.

3. Right-click the gray box to the left of PageID and choose Primary Key from the context menu.

4. Save the table as tbPageMgmt and close it.

The last table we need to create stores the usernames and passwords that allow the users to log in and out of the intranet. We store this information in a separate table so that the employee can have her own username and password without it being a visible part of her employee record.

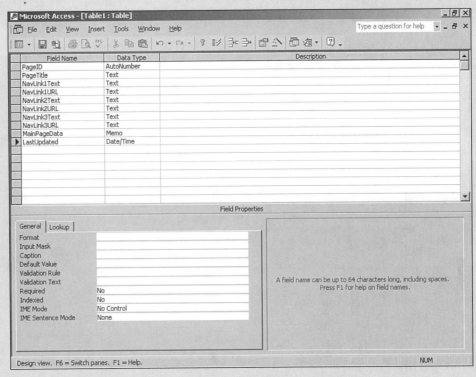

FIGURE 3.13   The structure of the Departmental Site Management table.

EXERCISE 3.4   Creating Username/Password Tables

1. In the Database window, select the Tables category and choose Create Table in Design View.

2. In the Design view, add the data using the parameters shown in Table 3.5.

TABLE 3.5   Sample Data for Username/Password Table

FIELD NAME	DATA TYPE	FIELD SIZE	REQUIRED	ALLOW ZERO LENGTH	INDEXED
UserID	AutoNumber	Long Integer	N/A	N/A	Yes (No Duplicates)
EmployeeID	Text	11	No	Yes	No
Username	Text	50	No	Yes	No
Password	Text	50	No	Yes	No
LastLogin	Date/Time	N/A	No	N/A	No

You should now have a table that looks like the one in Figure 3.14.

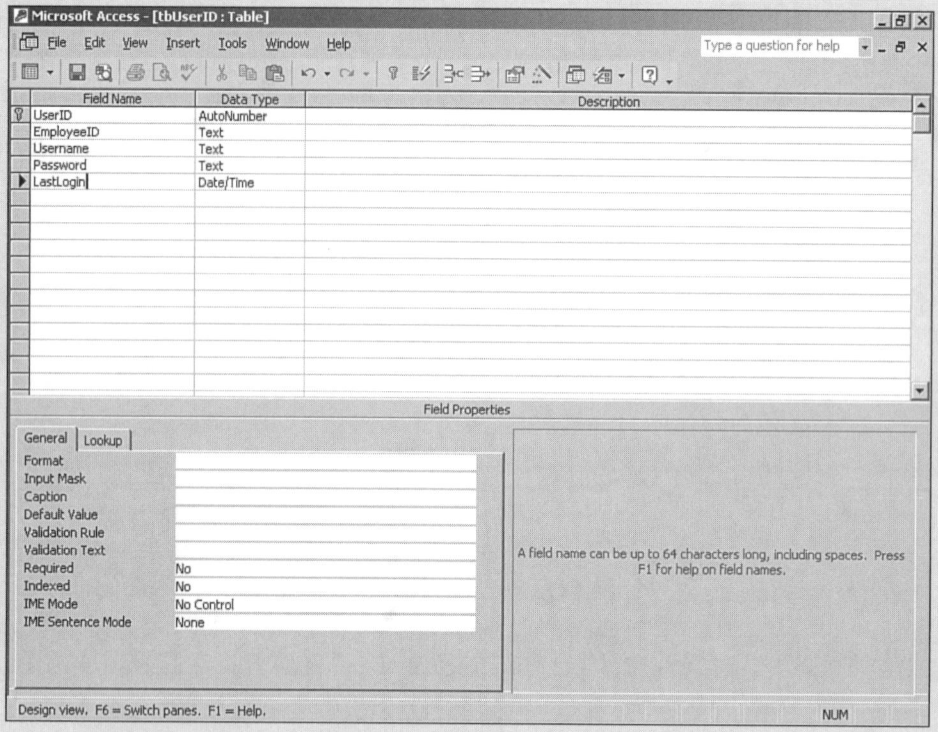

FIGURE 3.14   The structure of the Username/Password table.

3. Right-click the gray box to the left of UserID and choose Primary Key from the context menu.

4. Save the table as tbUserID and close it.

Building Relationships Between Tables

The final step in building our database is to create the necessary relationships between our tables. Because each asset must be assigned to a user that exists in the HR table, we will create a relationship between those two tables. In addition, because a username and password can only be assigned to an employee with a record in the HR database, we will create a relationship between those two tables as well.

EXERCISE 3.5   Building Relationships Between Tables

1. With the kc_corporation_0493 database open, choose Tools, Relationships from the menu bar.

2. In the Show Table dialog box, shown in Figure 3.15, click on each of the four tables and click the Add button.

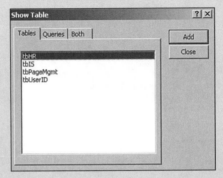

FIGURE 3.15   The Show Table dialog box allows you to specify which tables you would like to create relationships for.

3. Click the Close button on the Show Table dialog box. You should now see the four tables within the Relationships window. Expand each of the boxes so that you can see all the field names. To do this, click on the bottom border of the box and drag the mouse down. The windows should now look like Figure 3.16.

4. Click the EmployeeID field in the tbIS box and drag it onto the EmployeeID field in the tbHR box.

5. In the Edit Relationships dialog box, shown in Figure 3.17, check the Enforce Referential Integrity check box and then check the Cascade Update Related Fields and Cascade Delete Related Records. Click the Create button.

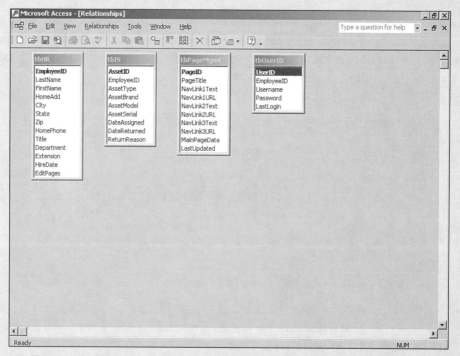

FIGURE 3.16   The Relationships window before adding the relationships.

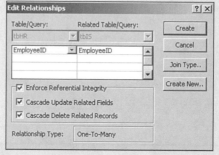

FIGURE 3.17   The Edit Relationships dialog box allows you to enforce referential integrity.

By creating this relationship, we are creating what is called a *one-to-many relationship*. This means that the one record in the HR database (the employee) can have many records in the IS database (for example, a phone, a computer, or a pager). In addition, by applying referential integrity to the relationship, we ensure that when an employee leaves the company and is deleted from the HR database, his records in the IS database are deleted as well. This avoids having orphaned records in the IS database.

6. Click and drag the EmployeeID field in the tbUserID box onto the EmployeeID field in the tbHR box.

7. Select all three check boxes again and click the Create button. As shown in Figure 3.18, you should now have two relationships between three of your tables.

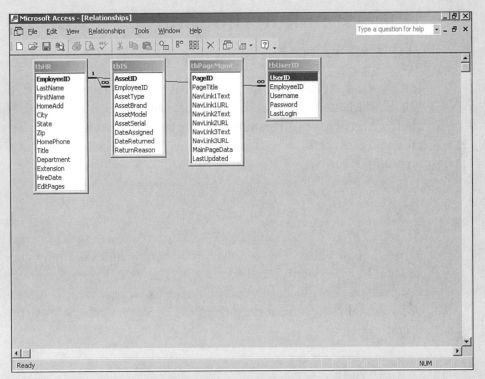

FIGURE 3.18   The relationships have been created.

8. Close the Relationships window and save the layout when prompted.

Congratulations! You have just created the back-end database for our upcoming intranet project. Before we break out Dreamweaver and start laying down code, there are a few more issues that we need to cover regarding Microsoft Access.

Understanding the Limitations of an Access Database

In Chapter 1, "Choosing the Right Tools for Your Dynamic Application," we briefly touched on the pros and cons of using Access as your database of choice. Just in case you skimmed over that part, I think it is important to reiterate some of Access' limitations and provide some additional information regarding security.

Size

Access 2000 and Access 2002 (XP) are limited in size to 2GB, whereas Access 97 is limited to 1GB. This file size restriction includes not only your data, but your table, query, report and form objects as well. Keep in mind that every time you create a new object in your database, like a new table or query, the amount of data it takes to store the structure of that object counts toward your total overall file size.

Concurrent Users

Microsoft lists 255 as the maximum number of concurrent users to an Access database. This means that only 255 users can actively interact with the database at the same time. This might be theoretically true in Microsoft's labs under the ideal circumstances, but the reality of working with an Access database is that performance falls off sharply when more than 25 or 30 concurrent requests are made. This means that although Access remains suitable for small Web applications, those that experience growth where they are experiencing more than 25 concurrent connections should consider upgrading to a more robust database.

Security

Security can be an issue with applications that are available via the Web if you name your database something that can be easily guessed and it is placed in a path that can be easily guessed. For instance, if KrystalClear built a database-driven Web site, named the database krystalcleardatabase.mdb, and placed it in the database folder on its Web server, the data would be at risk. Because the name and path are easily guessed (www.krystalclearcommunications.com/database/Krystalcleardatabase.mdb), someone could simply build a link to that URL in his own Web page, right-click the link, choose Save Target As, and download the contents of the database for viewing on his desktop.

Although this scenario may seem unbelievable to you, there are plenty of hackers who enjoy seeing if they can find access points to information that powers Web sites. For this reason, be sure to name your database something no one would guess and place it in a folder that has a name no one would guess.

ADDITIONAL STEPS TO LOCK DOWN YOUR ACCESS DATABASE

A few additional things you can do to further secure your Access database include setting a username and password within your database. Then, to open the database and view the contents, a valid username and password must be provided. To allow your dynamic application to access the database, you can pass the username/password combination in either your ODBC connection or custom connection string.

Macromedia also documents a security method that entails storing your database in a folder above the root directory and renaming your database. This method, documented at `http://www.macromedia.com/devn et/mx/dreamweaver/extreme/dw_extreme001_02.html`, however, relies on a bug in Windows NT and 2000 which could be closed by Microsoft in future security updates.

Expanding Your Database Vocabulary

Now that you have walked through the process of building an Access database from scratch, a few more terms that will help you in the coming chapters as we connect our database to our Web application. I'll cover these briefly because they will be covered in later chapters in full detail.

Database Connections

A database connection is a string of code that is stored in your Web pages that tells the page where the database is located, what type of database it is, and in what manner the pages should connect to the database.

Note   **LEARNING ACCESS**

Be aware that as you begin learning about database connections, the technical jargon can really make your head spin. When discussing the topic, abbreviations like DSN, ODBC, ADO, OLEDB, and RDO are tossed around. Don't worry. They eventually start to make sense and then you'll know you have been sucked into the world of dynamic applications.

Structured Query Language

The Structured Query Language is a programming language that is used to interact with databases. A string of code written in SQL is commonly referred to as a SQL query and these queries can be used to select, insert, update, and delete data from a database using your database connection. Although most SQL commands work for a wide variety of databases, there are some differences that occur between vendors and applications. For a good introduction to SQL, check out *Teach Yourself SQL in 10 Minutes* (Sams, 2001) by Ben Forta. It's a great primer on the Structured Query Language.

Tip   **SEEKWULL OR ES CUE EL?**

During a conversation with your fellow tech-heads, if you ever feel like you are in over your head and want to change the topic, just mention the pronunciation of SQL. As the acronym for Structure Query Language, many hardcore database administrators insist on the correct pronunciation of Es Cue El. It has been my observation, however, that as the popularity of SQL has grown, so has the acceptance of the SeeKwull pronunciation. Either way, you'll be wrong in someone's eyes and right in someone else's—and it makes for fun water cooler conversations.

Summary

In this chapter, you learned the basics of a relational database and what is involved in the design process of building a database from scratch. We put this understanding into use by designing the database that we will use to design the organizational intranet for our hypothetical client.

In the next chapter, we will focus on configuring your machine to act as a test server so we can later build the applications that have been requested. Chapter 4, "Configuring Your Workstation for Application Development," will show you how to configure IIS, ASP.NET, and ColdFusion servers on your local workstation.

CONFIGURING YOUR WORKSTATION FOR APPLICATION DEVELOPMENT

The next step in building the application for your new client, KrystalClear, is to configure your local workstation so that you can build and test your pages prior to making them live on the corporate intranet. As you learned in Chapter 1, "Choosing the Right Tools for Your Dynamic Application," there are several different elements involved in the production of an intranet or Web application. Because of this, you need to be sure that each element is installed and configured properly prior to developing and testing your applications.

By the end of this chapter, you should have the following:

- A Web server application installed and configured on your local workstation
- The ASP.NET and/or ColdFusion application server installed and configured
- A directory structure created for the intranet application on both your local workstation and the test or production server
- A functional connection to your Access database

BEFORE YOU START...

Prior to configuring your workstation, it's a good idea to be sure that you have Dreamweaver properly installed and that your workstation is functioning optimally. Because your machine will soon be serving as a limited-functionality Web server, you should defragment your drives and unload any memory-intensive applications that might be running in the background. Doing this allows you to more effectively gauge the performance of your applications and identify areas that need to be tweaked.

Configuring Your Web Server Software

The first step in setting up your local workstation is to configure your Web server software so that your machine is capable of serving Web pages. If you think your workstation is already set up for this, simply open a browser and type **http://localhost** or **http://127.0.0.1** in the address bar and see if anything is returned. If you receive a page that states the page cannot be displayed, you need to walk through the exercise in this section to install and configure your Web server software.

If, however, you receive a functional Web page, it's likely that your machine is already configured to serve HTML pages. Even if your machine is already configured, if you aren't familiar with the use of Microsoft's Internet Information Services (IIS) Management Console, it would probably still be a good idea to walk through the following exercise to familiarize yourself with the controls.

Exercise 4.1   Installing and Starting the IIS

1. If you type in the **http://localhost** address and receive a 404-Page cannot be found error, it is possible IIS is not installed on your machine. To determine if IIS is installed, open the Control Panel and double-click the Add or Remove Programs icon.

2. In the Add or Remove Programs panel, click the Add/Remove Windows Components icon.

3. After Windows builds the list of Windows components, double-click the IIS component. As shown in Figure 4.1, you can see which of the sub-components are already installed on your machine.

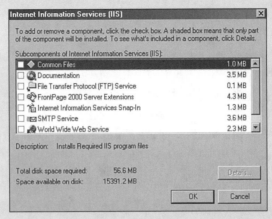

FIGURE 4.1   The IIS dialog box displays what subcomponents have already been installed.

4. If no subcomponents have been installed, check the boxes next to Common Files, Documentation, Internet Information Services Snap-In, and World Wide Web Service. The IIS dialog box should now look like Figure 4.2.

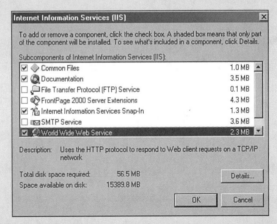

FIGURE 4.2   The IIS dialog box with the appropriate services checked.

5. Click OK to apply the changes to IIS. Click Next in the Windows Component Wizard to update the changes to your workstation

6. When the update is complete, click Finish to close the Windows Components Wizard.

7. Close the Add or Remove Programs dialog box and open the Computer

Management console by right-clicking the My Computer icon and choosing Manage from the context menu.

8. In the Computer Management Console, click the plus sign next to the Services and Applications category and then click the plus sign next to Internet Information Services.

9. With the Internet Information Services category expanded, click the Web Sites subcategory and click the Default Web Site element. As shown in Figure 4.3, you see all the folder and files that are currently located in the wwwroot folder created by IIS.

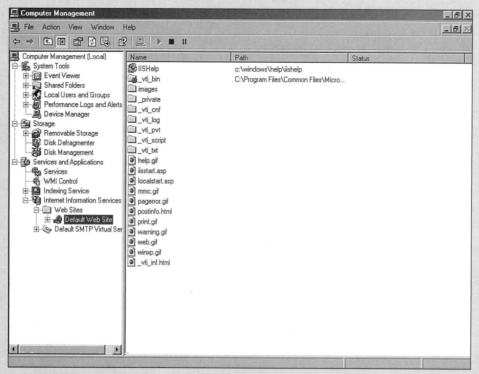

FIGURE 4.3   The files and folders that exist by default in the wwwroot folder.

10. With the Default Web Site selected in the left panel, click the Start Item button on the button bar that looks like a triangle. This starts the IIS service and allows visitors to access the contents of your wwwroot folder using their Web browser.

11. Close the Computer Management console.

12. Open your browser and type **http://127.0.0.1** in your address bar. You should see a default Web page being served and not get an error.

WINDOWS XP HOME EDITION USERS

If you are working through this book at home and have the Home Edition of Windows XP installed on your computer, you will need to upgrade to the Professional Edition of Windows XP to continue with the exercises using your workstation as a test server. Unfortunately, Microsoft does not include the Internet Information Services in the Home Edition and does not offer any way of installing IIS.

Installing and Configuring Your Web Application Server

After your machine is capable of serving standard HTML pages, the next step is to install and configure your Web application server. If you recall from Chapter 1, those pages that contain code beyond the standard HTML code require a Web application server to process the code and interact with the back-end database. In the case of the intranet application, this section demonstrates how to configure your workstation using either the ASP.NET or ColdFusion platform. Feel free to choose either one as the development environment for the application. If you want to learn how to build the intranet application in both environments, this is possible, because the ASP.NET and ColdFusion application engines can be located on the same machine with no adverse effects.

Configuring a Workstation for ASP.NET Applications

In the past, serving Active Server Pages required nothing beyond IIS because IIS was pre-configured to work with the ASP engine. To serve pages using the new .NET infrastructure, however, Windows 2000 and XP users must download the framework package from Microsoft that will install the proper files. If you are using Windows Server 2003, the ASP.NET Framework is included and installed by default.

EXERCISE 4.2   Downloading and Installing the .NET Framework

1. Installing the .NET framework on your workstation is a matter of simply downloading the installation file from Microsoft running the setup program. To download the executable, visit `http://msdn.microsoft.com/netframework/downloads/` and choose to download the latest version of the .NET framework. Be sure to download the redistributable rather than the SDK.

2. After the executable is downloaded, double-click the icon and follow the instructions to complete the installation. As shown in Figure 4.4, the installation wizard walks you through the entire process.

FIGURE 4.4   The installation wizard makes installing the .NET framework simple.

3. When the installation is complete, open Microsoft Notepad and type the following code in the new document:

```
<script language="vb" runat="server">
Sub Page_Load()
time.text=Hour(Now) & ":" & Minute(Now)
End Sub
</script>
<html>
<body>
The ASP.NET framework reports the time to be  <asp:label id="time"
runat="server" />
</body>
</html>
```

4. Save the document to the C:\Inetpub\wwwroot path with the filename of test.aspx. .NET applications use the .aspx extension to distinguish themselves from previous versions of Active Server Pages, which used the .asp extension.

5. After saving the file, open your browser and type **http://localhost/ test.aspx** in the address bar. As shown in Figure 4.5, your text .NET page should now be displayed properly in the browser.

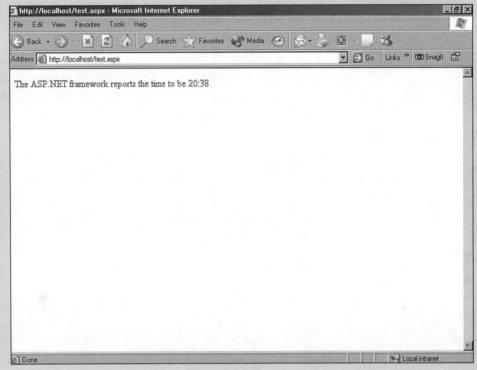

FIGURE 4.5   With IIS functional and the .NET framework installed, pages using the .aspx extension can be processed.

Configuring a Workstation for ColdFusion Applications

An alternative to developing pages using ASP.NET is to create them on the ColdFusion platform. Similar to ASP.NET pages, those pages that use the .cfm extension require the ColdFusion Server to process them before being sent to the client browser.

If you do not currently own the ColdFusion Server, but would like to try out its functionality, you can download a free 30-day trial of the software by visiting www.macromedia.com/downloads.

EXERCISE 4.3   Installing a ColdFusion Server Application

1. If you have downloaded the 30-day trial of ColdFusion, double-click on the downloaded executable and proceed with the trial installation. If, however, you have access to the full version of ColdFusion or any Macromedia application (which usually include the 30-day trial on the CD), simply insert the CD-ROM and choose to install the ColdFusion Server. Follow the steps of the ColdFusion Server Installer and configure IIS as your external Web server.

2. After you have completed the installation of the ColdFusion Server, open Notepad and type the following code into the document:

```
<html>
<body>
The ColdFusion server reports the time to be
<cfoutput>
    #timeformat(now(),'hh:mm:ss')#
</cfoutput>
</body>
</html>
```

3. Save the document to the C:\Inetpub\wwwroot path with the filename of test.cfm. ColdFusion documents use the .cfm extension to differentiate themselves from other types of Web documents.

4. After saving the file, open your browser and type **http://localhost/test.cfm** in the address bar. As shown in Figure 4.6, your text ColdFusion page should now be displayed properly in the browser.

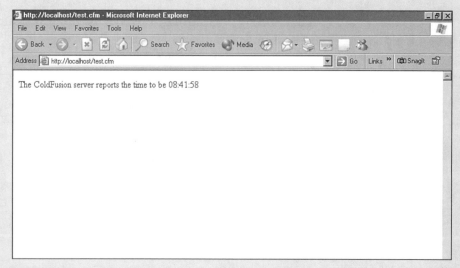

FIGURE 4.6   The ColdFusion Server is properly processing pages.

Creating a Directory Structure for Your Application

Now that you have your workstation configured properly, it's time to start thinking about the directory structure for the intranet project. To properly categorize our files for easy identification, we need to create a root folder for the application files and subfolders for elements such as image files, media, and so on.

When IIS was installed on your machine, one of the changes Windows made was to create a new folder with the path of C:\Inetpub\wwwroot. When page requests are sent to your machine, IIS looks in this folder (or any subfolders that are specified) and serves the file if it exists. If the file doesn't exist, IIS does not look outside the boundaries of this folder, but instead returns a 404-Page could not be displayed error. By designating this specific folder (and its subfolders) as the only place Web visitors can request files from, IIS maintains the security of the rest of the information on your server and keeps prying eyes out of your other files and folders.

Note   MAINTAINING YOUR WEB APPLICATIONS IN SEPARATE FOLDERS

It is a good idea not to dump all your application files and folders directly into the wwwroot folder, but instead to create subfolders for each project. Because Dreamweaver maintains site information about each project, if you lump everything together into one directory, you lose access to some valuable tools and run the risk of Dreamweaver performing improperly. For these reasons, be sure to create a new subfolder within your wwwroot folder for each application that you work on.

To build the intranet application on both the ASP.NET and ColdFusion platforms, you need to create two separate directories in which to store the two sets of files. Because the applications will be identical in look and feel, it is possible that both applications could share the same graphics folder; however, we will create separate folders to enhance the portability of each.

EXERCISE 4.4   Creating the Root Folder and Subfolders

1. Using Windows Explorer or My Computer, browse to the C:\Inetpub\wwwroot path and create a new folder by choosing File, New, Folder from the menu bar. Name the new folder KrystalClear-ASP.

2. Open the new folder by double-clicking it. Create two new subfolders. Name the first kc_database_0012 and the second images.

 Tip

CREATIVE NAMING FOR ACCESS DATABASES

As mentioned in Chapter 3, "Building a Database for Dynamic Applications," it's good security practice to give both your Access database and the directory it is located in unique names that would be very difficult to guess. This reduces the possibility that someone could download your database and have access to the data stored within. If you are using a remote host, it's likely that your host may have configured a private folder that does not allow file contents to be listed or files to be downloaded. In this case, this folder is the perfect place for your database.

3. Right-click the KrystalClear-ASP folder and choose Copy from the context menu. From the menu bar, choose Edit, Paste.

4. Rename the second folder KrystalClear-CF. These two new folders, shown in Figure 4.7, will serve as the locations for our intranet application.

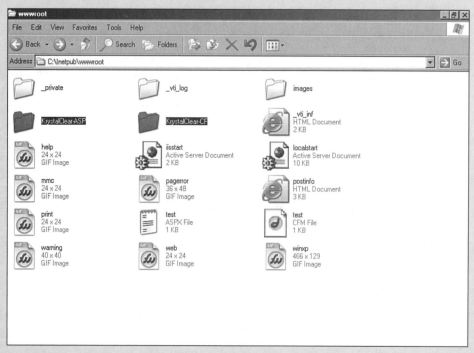

FIGURE 4.7   Two new folders have been created to house our intranet application.

5. Locate the kc_corporation_0493.mdb database that was created and saved to your My Documents folder in Chapter 3. Copy and paste the database to both kc_database_0012 folders.

Applying the Appropriate Directory Permissions

After you have the directory structure in place, the next (very important) step is to apply the proper permissions to the appropriate directories. When IIS is installed on your machine, a set of user accounts is created that allows visitors from outside your machine to access folders located on your machine. The most important account with respect to Web and intranet applications is the IUSR account. This account represents any Internet user who seeks to access resources located on your computer, and the permissions for this account specifically govern what these visitors can and cannot see.

For typical HTML pages, the read permission is adequate because the IUSR account never needs to write anything to your hard drive or execute any applications. For dynamic applications, however, visitors may be adding records to a database located on your local drive, so they would need to have write permission as well.

 THE IMPORTANCE OF FOLDER PERMISSIONS

Incorrect directory permissions are one of the most common problems that occur when developing dynamic applications. If you encounter an error that tells you your recordset must use an updateable query, that the system could not lock your file, or that the database is read-only, it is likely that you do not have your permissions set correctly. For further details on setting database permissions, check out the TechNote from Macromedia at http://www.macromedia.com/support/ultradev/ts/documents/database_permission.htm.

To ensure that visitors can interact properly with the database, you need to provide the IUSR account on your machine with read/write privileges to the database folder and its contents.

EXERCISE 4.5   Setting the Directory Permissions

THIS EXERCISE IS FOR NTFS VOLUMES ONLY

This exercise only needs to be completed if you are running an NTFS volume on the hard drive where your www-root folder is located. If you are running a FAT32 volume, you should not have to worry about permission levels on your local workstation. Keep this exercise in mind, however, when you transfer your files to your testing or production server, as the permissions may need to be adjusted on that machine.

1. Using Windows Explorer or My Computer, browse to the Krystal Clear-ASP folder and right-click the kc_database_0012 folder. From the context menu, choose Properties.

2. In the KrystalClear-ASP Properties dialog box, choose the Security tab.

TURNING OFF SIMPLE FILE SHARING IN WINDOWS XP

If you are running Windows XP and you don't see the Security tab, turn off simple file sharing by opening My Computer and choosing Tools, Folder Options from the menu bar. On the View tab, look in the Advanced Settings panel and uncheck the box next to Use Simple File Sharing. Click OK to apply the change.

3. If the IUSR account is not already listed in the Windows accounts in the folder permissions, click the Add button and enter the name of your IUSR account. Click the Add button.

IDENTIFYING YOUR IUSR ACCOUNT NAME

The IUSR account name is IUSR_ plus your computer's name. Therefore, if you have named your computer Phixius in the Network properties, your IUSR account name would be IUSR_Phixius.

4. In the Properties dialog box, shown in Figure 4.8, give the IUSR account full control over the folder and click OK.

5. Provide the ASPNET account with the same permissions on the folder that you provided to the IUSR account.

6. Follow the same steps to provide the IUSR account full control over the kc_database_0012 folder in the KrystalClear-CF folder as well.

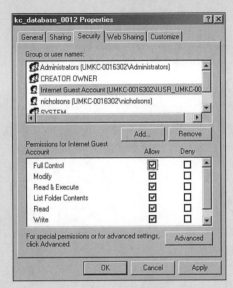

FIGURE 4.8   Give the IUSR account full control over the database folder so visitors can read and write to the database.

Establishing a Dreamweaver Site

I hope that as your experience with dynamic content grows, the number of applications that you work with will grow too. Web developers often create, manage, and update a number of different Web applications using the same software and workstation. To accommodate this, Dreamweaver MX 2004 uses a system that divides each application into its own "site." When setting up your Dreamweaver site, you provide some basic information that lets Dreamweaver know how to manage your files, what dynamic platform (if any) that the site will use, and the paths to important folders such as the location of your images.

Now that your workstation is configured to serve both static and dynamic pages and the appropriate file permissions have been set, the next step is to set up a Dreamweaver site for the intranet application.

EXERCISE 4.6   Creating an ASP.NET Site in Dreamweaver

1. Open Dreamweaver.

2. Open the Site panel by choosing Window, Files from the menu bar.

3. In the Files panel, shown in Figure 4.9, click the menu button and choose Site, New Site.

FIGURE 4.9   The Site panel allows you to manage your Dreamweaver sites.

4. Name the new site KrystalClear-ASP and click the Next button.

5. Click the radio button that indicates that you want to use a server technology and choose ASP.NET VB from the drop-down list. Click Next.

Note   VB OR C#?

Dreamweaver is capable of writing code in both VB.NET and C# so whichever language you choose for your pages depends on which language you are more comfortable with.

6. Because you will be using your workstation to test your pages, choose to edit and test locally. If you are using an operating system other than Windows and would like to build your pages on your workstation and test them remotely, you can choose to edit locally and then upload to a remote testing server.

7. Browse to the KrystalClear-ASP folder you created earlier and click the Select button. Click Next.

8. Make sure that the URL to your site is `http://localhost/`
`krystalclear-asp/` and click the Test URL button. After Windows
confirms that the root folder exists and IIS is running, it returns the
confirmation message shown in Figure 4.10. Click OK to close the confirmation popup.

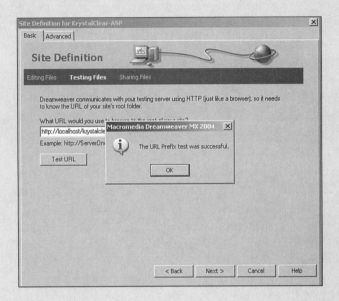

FIGURE 4.10   The Test URL functions as anticipated.

9. Click Next. Choose not to use a remote server. If you are going to use a
test server or production server that is located on your LAN or hosted
remotely, you could choose Yes and Dreamweaver provides you with
the ability to specify information about your remote server.

10. Click Next and, as shown in Figure 4.11, Dreamweaver displays
detailed information about your new site's settings.

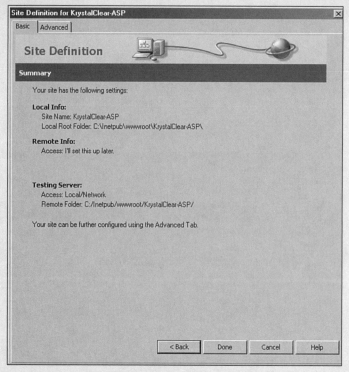

FIGURE 4.11   Your site's settings.

11. Click Done.

12. The last step you need to take in creating your ASP.NET site is to deploy the supporting files to your site's root directory. To do this, choose Site, Advanced, Deploy Supporting Files from the menu bar.

13. Next, choose Local/Network and the C:\Inetpub\wwwroot\ KrystalClear-ASP\bin\ folder and click Deploy. This process creates a bin folder in your site directory that allows the server behaviors to function properly.

14. After the files are deployed, click OK and your site is finished.

As was mentioned earlier, the intranet project is being built on both the ASP.NET and the ColdFusion platforms so you can gain exposure to the development process in both. Creating a ColdFusion site in Dreamweaver is very similar to the ASP.NET site, with just a few slight modifications.

Exercise 4.7   Creating a ColdFusion Site in Dreamweaver

1. If it is not already open, open Dreamweaver.

2. Open the Site panel by choosing Window, Site from the menu bar.

3. In the Site panel, choose Site, New Site. Dreamweaver opens the basic view of the Site definition dialog box.

4. Name the new site KrystalClear-CF and click the Next button.

5. Click the radio button that indicates that you want to use a server technology. This time, as shown in Figure 4.12, indicate that you want to use the ColdFusion technology and Click Next.

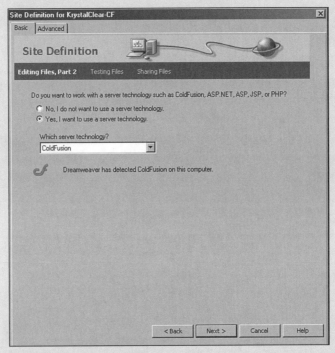

FIGURE 4.12   Choose ColdFusion as your server technology for this site.

6. Choose to edit and test locally.

7. Browse to the KrystalClear-CF folder you created earlier and click Next.

8. Make sure that the URL to your site is `http://localhost/krystalclear-cf/` and click the Test URL button.

9. Click Next. Choose not to use a remote server.

10. Click Next and Dreamweaver displays detailed information about your new site's settings.

11. Click Done and your site is complete.

Building a Connection to the Database

The next step in setting up your workstation is to create a connection between Dreamweaver MX 2004 and your database. By creating this connection, you indicate to Dreamweaver where your database is located and what driver your pages should use to access the information. The nice thing about creating a connection using Dreamweaver comes from the fact that you only have to do it once for each database in your site. After the site is established and the connection created, any pages that rely upon a connection to the database will automatically include the appropriate code to access the database.

ASP.NET

When building a site on the ASP.NET platform, you have two database connection types to choose from. The first is the traditional Open Database Connectivity (ODBC) driver, but using ODBC can slow the performance of your dynamic applications. The more attractive alternative is the OLE DB connection because it offers significant performance increases over ODBC. In addition, Microsoft is no longer making enhancements to the ODBC technology, because OLE DB has taken its place as the connectivity option of choice.

Exercise 4.8   Building a Database Connection in an ASP.NET Site

1. If it is not already open, open Dreamweaver.

2. Open the Files panel by choosing Window, Files.

3. In the Site panel, choose the KrystalClear-ASP site from the drop-down list.

4. Choose File, New from the menu bar. In the New Document dialog box, shown in Figure 4.13, choose a Dynamic Page that uses the ASP.NET VB technology. Click Create.

 NOTE   WHY CREATE A NEW PAGE?

When you open Dreamweaver for a new session of creating Web pages, it starts with a blank page. However, because that blank page has never been saved, Dreamweaver doesn't know whether it will eventually use ASP, ColdFusion, or any of the other server technologies. For this reason, before Dreamweaver will allow you to access the database-driven features, you must either save the initial blank page with the appropriate extension, open a page within a site that already contains platform-related code, or create a brand new page and specify which server technology will be used.

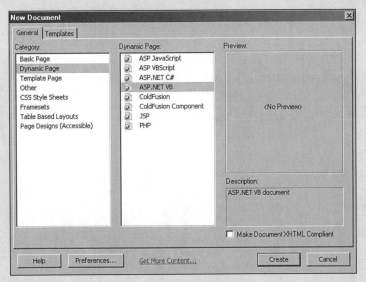

FIGURE 4.13   Create a new page that uses the ASP.NET VB technology.

5. Open the Databases panel by choosing Window, Databases from the menu bar.

6. In the Databases panel, shown in Figure 4.14, you should now see ASP.NET VB, indicating that the pages you are currently developing use the ASP.NET VB server technology.

FIGURE 4.14   The pages in your site will be developed using the ASP.NET VB language.

7. Click the plus symbol on the Databases tab and choose OLE DB Connection from the menu.

8. In the OLE DB Connection dialog box, type **connKrystalClearASP** as the Connection Name.

9. Click the Build button. In the Data Link Properties dialog box, shown in Figure 4.15, click the Provider tab and choose Microsoft Jet 4.0 OLE DB Provider. This is the provider that is used to connect to Access databases.

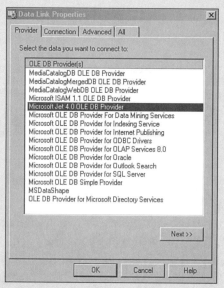

FIGURE 4.15   Choose the Jet OLE DB Provider to connect to our Access database.

10. Click Next and click the ellipsis button next to the Database Name field. Browse to the kc_corporation_0493.mdb database located in the c:\Inetpub\wwwroot\KrystalClear-ASP\kc_database_0012 folder.

11. Locate the kc_corporation_0493.mdb database that was created in your My Documents folder in Chapter 3. Copy and paste the database to both kc_database_0012 folders.

12. Click the Test Connection button and you should see the successful connection message shown in Figure 4.16.

13. Click OK to close the Data Link Properties dialog box and click OK again to complete the process of creating the database connection. In the Database panel, Dreamweaver now displays the connection to the Access database. Click OK to close the popup.

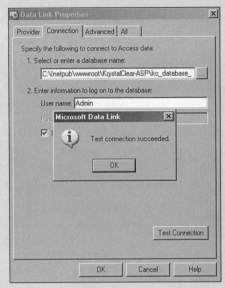

FIGURE 4.16   A connection was successfully built to the database.

ColdFusion

Creating the database connection in ColdFusion is substantially different from the method used for ASP.NET. Rather than creating the connection from within Dreamweaver, the ColdFusion architecture requires that you create the connection using the ColdFusion Administrator. In contrast to ASP.NET, however, the most recent versions of ColdFusion do not provide you with the option of creating either an ODBC connection or an OLE DB connection. Instead, the ColdFusion Administrator is used to create an ODBC connection to the database.

Exercise 4.9   Creating a Database Connection Using ColdFusion

1. Open the ColdFusion Administrator. In Windows 9x or 2000, the Administrator is access by clicking Start, Programs, Macromedia ColdFusion, Administrator. In Windows XP, the Administrator is accessed by clicking Start, All Programs, Macromedia ColdFusion, Administrator.

2. When prompted, enter the Administrator password that you chose when you installed ColdFusion.

3. In the Administrator, shown in Figure 4.17, click the Data Sources link in the left navigation menu.

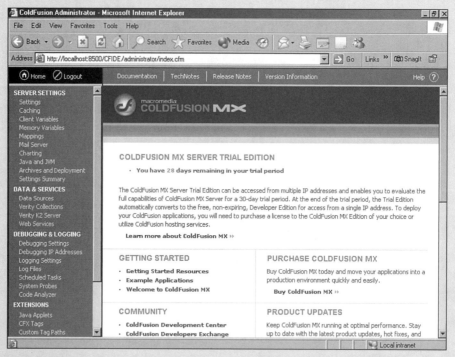

FIGURE 4.17   The ColdFusion Administrator enables you to create database connections.

4. In the Data Sources window, shown in Figure 4.18, type **connKrystalClearCF** for the Data Source Name and choose Microsoft Access as the Driver. Click the Add button.

5. In the Microsoft Access Data Source window, click the Browse Server button next to Database File and browse to the kc_corporation_0493.mdb database located in the c:\Inetpub\ wwwroot\KrystalClear-CF\kc_database_0012 folder. Click Apply.

6. Click the Submit button to create this new data source. Once the data source is created, ColdFusion Server displays a confirmation message.

7. Close the ColdFusion Administrator.

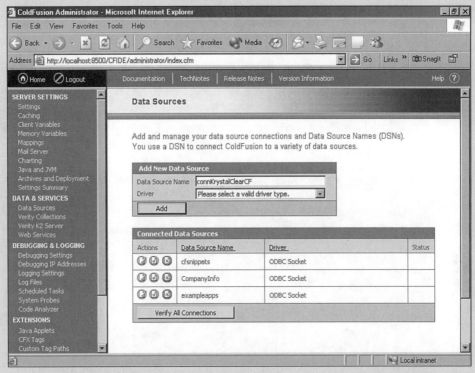

FIGURE 4.18 Name the data source and choose the appropriate driver.

Transferring the Directory Structure to Your Testing Server

After your workstation is configured to serve pages and connect to the database, the final element to consider is the method of transferring your completed pages to your test server or production server. Depending on whether you are connected to a LAN or using a server that is hosted remotely, transferring them may be as easy as saving them to the appropriate mapped drive or synchronizing the files using Dreamweaver's FTP capability.

Network Server

If your workstation is connected to a company LAN, it's possible that you have a drive that is mapped to the testing or production folder specified for your project. If this is the case, transferring the folder is as easy as identifying your remote folder, creating or changing pages on your local workstation, and then instructing Dreamweaver to publish the pages.

Exercise 4.10   Transferring a File to a Server on a Local Area Network

1. Open Dreamweaver on your workstation.

2. Switch to the KrystalClear-ASP site by choosing Window, Files from the menu bar and double-clicking the KrystalClear-ASP site from the drop-down list in the Site panel.

3. Click the Advanced tab, shown in Figure 4.19, and choose Remote Info from the Category list.

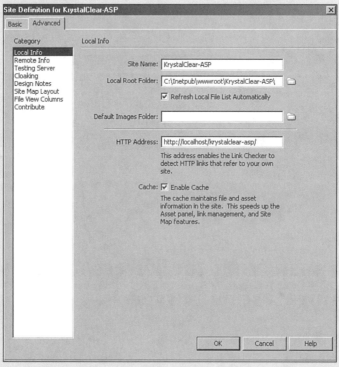

FIGURE 4.19   Choose the advanced site settings to configure access to the network server.

4. Using the Access drop-down list, choose Local/Network. As shown in Figure 4.20, you are now able to browse to a remote folder located on your testing or production server.

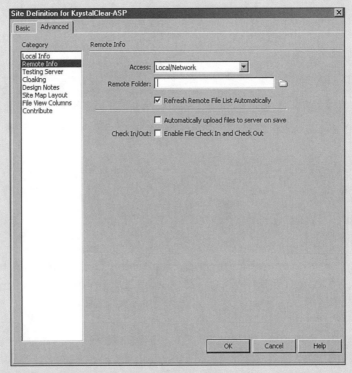

FIGURE 4.20   Choosing Local/Network as your Access type allows you to specify the location of the folder on your server.

5. Browse to the location of the appropriate folder on your server and click OK to apply the changes.

6. After you have designed and tested the pages on your local workstation, you can copy the files to your server by using the Synchronize function included in Dreamweaver. To synchronize your files, open the Files panel and select any files that you would like copied to the server. You can also transfer files one at a time by using the Put command from the Site menu.

7. From the Files panel options menu, choose Site, Synchronize.

8. In the Synchronize Files dialog box, shown in Figure 4.21, choose to synchronize on the selected files and choose to put newer files to the remote server. You can see what files will be replaced prior to actually replacing them by clicking the Preview button.

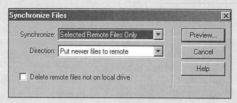

FIGURE 4.21   The Synchronize Files dialog box allows you to specify which files will be put on the server.

9. Click OK if the changes are appropriate.

File Transfer Protocol (FTP)

If you are not connected to a LAN or the server you want to use is hosted remotely, then configuring Dreamweaver to transfer files using FTP takes a few more steps. After your site is configured, however, updating pages on the server is as easy as a few clicks of your mouse.

 REMOTE SERVER VERIFICATION

If you are using a remote host, be sure that your host supports the ColdFusion platform and/or the ASP.NET platform. While many hosts offer these services, there are a lot of hosts out there (especially budget hosts) that don't.

Exercise 4.11   Synchronizing Files Using FTP

1. Open Dreamweaver on your workstation.
2. Switch to the KrystalClear-CF site by choosing Window, Site from the menu bar and double-clicking the KrystalClear-CF site from the drop-down list in the Site panel.
3. Click the Advanced tab and choose Remote Info from the Category list.
4. Using the Access drop-down list, choose FTP. As shown in Figure 4.22, you can now enter the server and account information for your FTP connection.
5. Type in the name of your FTP host and type the username and password associated with your account.
6. Click OK to save the settings. To test your connection, click the Test button.

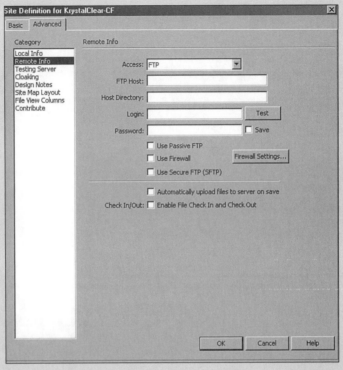

FIGURE 4.22 Choosing FTP as your access type allows you to enter the information to connect to your remote host.

7. To upload your files to the server, select any file and click the Put Files button from the Site panel button bar. When asked if you want to upload dependent files (which include any graphics or media included in the page), choose Yes.

Summary

In this chapter, you learned how to configure your workstation for use in developing dynamic Web applications. At this point, your computer is ready to create and test the dynamic pages necessary to complete the intranet application requested by KrystalClear.

In the next chapter, we will develop the first module requested by KrystalClear—the Human Resources Employee Management module. Chapter 5, "Creating the Human Resources Management System," will show you step-by-step how to build each element of the Human Resources module using both the ASP.NET and ColdFusion platforms.

CREATING THE HUMAN RESOURCES MANAGEMENT SYSTEM

The first element of the intranet application that KrystalClear has asked you to build is the Human Resources Management System. According to the information provided by KrystalClear, the Human Resources department would like to be able to create a new record for an employee when he is hired that contains information such as his name, contact information, departmental information, and other data that relates to his tenure at KrystalClear. In addition, the Human Resources staff needs to be able to update employee information when it changes and remove employees from the database when they are no longer with the company. To ensure that the information is easy to find, they have also asked for a feature that allows them to search for employees by name and department.

By the end of this chapter, you will have built the following:

- A set of pages that allows the Human Resources staff to add employees to the database
- A set of pages that allows the Human Resources staff to search for employees

- A set of pages that allows the Human Resources staff to delete records of individuals that are no longer with the company
- A set of pages who allows the Human Resources staff to edit employee records as they change
- A menu page that makes the application easy to use

Reviewing the Database Table Structure

Before we get into the practical details of building the pages we need for the Human Resources application, let's take a few moments and look back over the database tables that we created earlier in Chapter 3, "Building a Database for Dynamic Applications." By understanding the structure of the tables, why we created the specific fields, and how they relate to the intranet application, you'll have a better understanding of how your pages interact with the database.

The database table used in the Human Resources module of the intranet is tbHR table. The structure of the tbHR table, shown in Figure 5.1, consists of thirteen fields that include the EmployeeID, basic directory information, departmental data, the employee's hire date, and whether the employee is permitted to edit his departmental intranet pages.

KrystalClear uses each employee's Social Security Number (SSN) or Tax Identification Number for his EmployeeID. Because SSNs are unique, other tables in the database use this identifier to track records such as the network UserID and any corporate assets that are assigned to the employee. Because this field is indexed with no duplicates allowed, there can never be two records in the HR database with the same SSN.

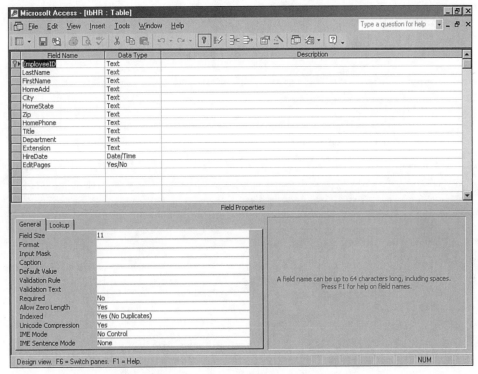

FIGURE 5.1 The structure of the tbHR table.

Creating the HR Page Template

Before we begin building pages, let's start by building a template page that we can use as a boilerplate for all of the pages that will be part of the HR application. This template includes features such as the KrystalClear logo, the intranet header, and the intranet footer. As you will see, using a Dreamweaver template provides us with the ability to update a group of pages simply by updating the template they are based on.

Resource **LEARNING MORE ABOUT DREAMWEAVER TEMPLATES**

If you want to learn more about how to use templates effectively, check out *Dreamweaver MX Templates* (New Riders, 2003) by Brad Halstead and Murray Summers.

In addition, by building a template first, we don't have to manually insert each of these elements into every page we build for Human Resources, which saves quite a bit of time in the end.

Exercise 5.1(a)   Creating the Template Page for ASP.NET

1. Before building the template page, you need to download the support files, which include the appropriate images for the intranet site. You can download the support files from http://www.krystalclear communication.com/downloads.

2. After you have downloaded the support files, unzip their contents to the images folder of your KrystalClear-ASP site.

3. Open Dreamweaver and select the KrystalClear-ASP site by choosing Window, Site from the menu bar and then selecting KrystalClear-ASP from the site drop-down list.

Note **WHAT IF THE SITE PANEL IS NOT VISIBLE?**

If you want to open the Site panel, but it is not visible in the right pane, make sure that the Files panel is active. If you see Files and it has an arrow pointing to the right, the panel is available but not active. Click the arrow and the panel will become active.

4. Choose File, New from the menu bar and select a Dynamic page based on the ASP.NET VB platform. Click Create. Save the new page to your KrystalClear-ASP folder and name it intranet_template.aspx.

5. Place your cursor on the page and insert a table by choosing Insert, Table from the menu bar. In the Insert Table dialog box, shown in Figure 5.2, create a table that has 3 rows and 1 column and a width of 750 pixels. Set the border to 1 and the cell padding and cell spacing to 0. For the Header type, choose None and click OK.

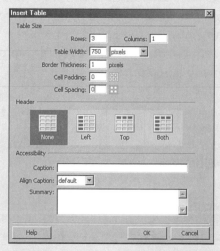

FIGURE 5.2   Use the Insert Table dialog box to add a new table to the template page.

6. With the table selected, set the border color to #000099 by typing the value into the Brdr Color field of the Property inspector.

7. Place your cursor in the top row of the new table and add the Human Resources intranet logo by choosing Insert, Image from the menu bar. If you downloaded the support files, the image should be located in the images subfolder of your site and is named kc_logo_intranet_hr.jpg.

8. Place the cursor in the bottom row of the table and insert the intranet footer. The file is located in the images folder of your site and is named kc_footer_intranet.jpg.

9. Place the cursor in the middle cell and insert another table. This table should have 1 row, 2 columns, a width of 100%, and a border, cell padding, and cell spacing of 0. Choose no header and click OK.

10. Place the cursor in the left column of the new table and set the column width to 150 by typing the value in the W field of the Property inspector. Change the background of this cell to #000099 by typing the value in the Bg field of the Property inspector.

11. In the left cell, insert another table with 2 rows, 1 column, a width of 150 pixels, and a border of 0. Set the cell padding and spacing to 1. Choose no header and click OK.

12. Place your cursor in the right cell of the table (the white cell) and select the cell by clicking the `<td>` tag in the Tag selector. From the menu bar, choose Insert, Template Objects, Editable Region. When notified that Dreamweaver will convert the page to a template, click OK.

13. Name the new editable region erMainData and click OK. When completed, your page should look like Figure 5.3.

14. Save the page as a template by choosing File, Save As Template from the menu bar. In the Save As Template dialog box, choose the KrystalClear-ASP site and type **intranet_template_hr.dwt** in the Save As field. Click Save.

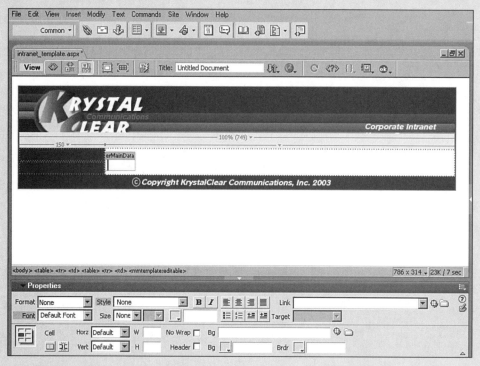

FIGURE 5.3   The template page with the header, footer, and tables in place.

Exercise 5.1(b)   Creating the Template Page for ColdFusion

1. Before building the template page, you need to download the support files, which include the appropriate images for the intranet site. You can download the support files from www.krystalclear communication.com/downloads.

2. After you have downloaded the support files, unzip their contents to the images folder of your KrystalClear-CF site.

3. Open Dreamweaver and select the KrystalClear-CF site by choosing Window, Site from the menu bar and selecting KrystalClear-CF from the site drop-down list.

4. Choose File, New from the menu bar and select a Dynamic page based on the ColdFusion platform. Click Create. Save the new page to your KrystalClear-CF folder and name it intranet_template.cfm.

5. Place your cursor on the page and insert a table by choosing Insert, Table from the menu bar. In the Insert Table dialog box, shown in Figure 5.2, create a table that has 3 rows and 1 column and a width of 750 pixels. Set the border to 1 and the cell padding and cell spacing to 0. Click OK.

6. With the table selected, set the border color to #000099 by typing the value into the Brdr Color field of the Property inspector.

7. Place your cursor in the top row of the new table and add the Human Resources intranet logo by choosing Insert, Image from the menu bar. If you downloaded the support files, the image should be located in the images subfolder of your site and is named kc_logo_intranet_hr.jpg.

8. Place the cursor in the bottom row of the table and insert the intranet footer. The file is located in the images folder of your site and is named kc_footer_intranet.jpg.

9. Place the cursor in the middle cell and insert another table. This table should have 1 row, 2 columns, a width of 100%, and a border, cell padding, and cell spacing of 0.

10. Place the cursor in the left column of the new table and set the column width to 150 by typing the value in the W field of the Property inspector. Change the background of this cell to #000099 by typing the value in the Bg field of the Property inspector. Set the vertical alignment of this cell to Top in the Vert field of the Property inspector.

11. In the left cell, insert another table with 2 rows, 1 column, a width of 150 pixels, and a border of 0. Set the cell padding and spacing to 1.

12. Place your cursor in the right cell of the table (the white cell) and select the cell by clicking the <td> tag in the Tag selector. From the menu bar, choose Insert, Template Objects, Editable Region. When notified that Dreamweaver will convert the page to a template, click OK.

13. Name the new editable region erMainData and click OK.

14. Save the page as a template by choosing File, Save As Template from the menu bar. In the Save As Template dialog box, choose the KrystalClear-CF site and type **intranet_template_hr.dwt** in the Save As field. Click Save.

Creating Pages for Adding New Employees

Now that you have a template for the HR pages, let's look at the first element of the corporate intranet that KrystalClear has requested. The Human Resources staff has requested a module that allows them to easily add a new employee to their system.

To accomplish this, we need to create two pages. The first page uses a simple HTML form and the Insert Record server behavior to create a new record in the tbHR table and add the new employee's information. After the record is created, the staff member is redirected to a second page where she receives a confirmation that the addition of the new employee was completed successfully.

Exercise 5.2(a)   Creating Pages That Add a New Employee in ASP.NET

1. From the menu bar, choose File, New. In the New Document window, click the Templates tab. Select the KrystalClear-ASP site in the Templates For panel and then choose intranet_template_hr. Click Create. Save the page as add_new_employee.aspx.

2. In the new page, replace the Untitled Document text in the Title field of the Document toolbar with Human Resources – Add New Employee.

3. Because this page is generated from a Dreamweaver template, the only area that we can edit is the erMainData editable region. Place your cursor in the erMainData region and click the Align Center button on the Property inspector.

4. Type **Add New Employee** and press Enter. Highlight the new text and click the Style drop-down list in the Property inspector. From the drop-down list, choose New CSS Style.

   In the New CSS Style dialog box, name the style **.HeaderText** and choose to make a custom style and define it in a new style sheet file. Click OK.

6. Save the style sheet to the KrystalClear-ASP folder with the name krystalclearss.css.

7. In the CSS Style Definition dialog box, shown in Figure 5.4, choose the Type category and set the Font to Arial, the size to 14 pixels, and the Weight to Bold. Click OK. Apply this new style to the Add New Employee text by highlighting it and choosing the style from the Property inspector.

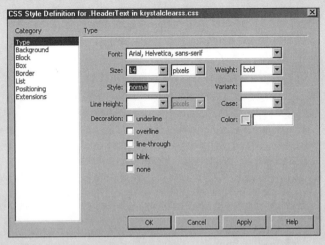

FIGURE 5.4   The CSS Style Definition dialog box allows you to easily create custom style sheets for your Dreamweaver site.

8. The next step is to add a form and table that allows the Human Resources employee to enter the appropriate data. To do this, place your cursor on the line below the Add New Employee text and choose Insert, Application Objects, Insert Record, Record Insertion Form Wizard from the menu bar.

9. In the Record Insertion Form dialog box, shown in Figure 5.5, choose the connKrystalClearASP connection and the tbHR table. In the On Success, Go To field, type **employee_added.aspx**.

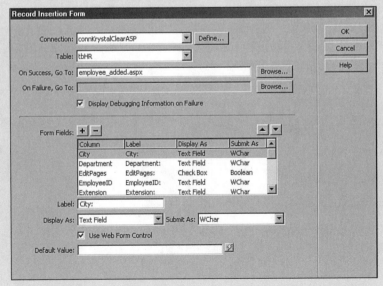

FIGURE 5.5   Choose a connection, table, and confirmation page.

10. In the Form Fields panel, use the up and down arrows to reorganize the fields into the following order:
    EmployeeID
    LastName
    FirstName
    HomeAdd
    City
    HomeState
    Zip
    HomePhone
    Department
    Title
    Extension
    HireDate
    EditPages

11. Click the EmployeeID column and notice that Dreamweaver creates a label for the corresponding text field of EmployeeID. To make the form more user friendly, go through each field and add the appropriate spaces and capitalization for each label. For instance, for the LastName field, change the label to read Last Name:.

12. Click the Department form field and change the Display As value to Menu. We want this element to appear in the form as a drop-down menu, which allows the staff member to pick from the various departments.

13. Click the Menu Properties button and in the Menu Properties dialog box, enter the labels and values shown in Table 5.1.

TABLE 5.1 The Values for Your Departmental List

ITEM LABEL	ITEM VALUE
Human Resources	HR
Marketing	Marketing
Information Services	IS

14. Click OK to close the Menu Properties dialog box and click OK on the Record Insertion Form dialog box. As shown in Figure 5.6, Dreamweaver inserts the appropriate form and form objects into your page.

15. Open the Server Behaviors panel by choosing Window, Server Behaviors from the menu bar. Notice that Dreamweaver has added the Insert Record server behavior to add the data to your table.

16. Save the page.

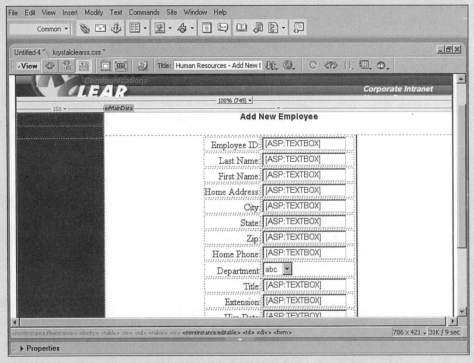

FIGURE 5.6   The data entry form has been added to the page.

17. The last step in the add employee process is to create a confirmation page. Create a new page from the HR template. Change the page title to Human Resources – Employee Added.

18. Place your cursor in the erMainData editable region and click the Align Center button on the Property inspector. Type **Thank you. The new employee has been added to the database. Please click here to return to the HR search page.**

19. Highlight the Click Here text and create a hyperlink by typing **search_employee.aspx** in the Link field of the Property inspector.

20. Save the page as employee_added.aspx.

Exercise 5.2(b)–Creating Pages That Add a New Employee in ColdFusion

1. From the menu bar, choose File, New. In the New Document window, click the Templates tab. Select the KrystalClear-CF site in the Templates For panel and then choose intranet_template_hr. Click Create. Save the page in the KrystalClear-CF folder with the name add_new_employee.cfm.

2. In the new page, replace the Untitled Document text in the Title field of the Document toolbar with Human Resources – Add New Employee.

3. Because this page is generated from a Dreamweaver template, the only area that we are able to edit is the erMainData editable region. Place your cursor in the erMainData region and click the Center button on the Property inspector.

4. Type **Add New Employee** and press Enter. Highlight the new text and click the Style drop-down list in the Property inspector. From the drop-down list, choose New CSS Style.

5. In the New CSS Style dialog box, name the style **.HeaderText** and choose to make a custom style and define it in a new style sheet file. Click OK.

6. Save the style sheet to the KrystalClear-ASP folder with the name krystalclearss.css.

7. In the CSS Style Definition dialog box, choose the Type category and set the Font to Arial, the size to 14 pixels, and the Weight to Bold. Click OK. Apply the style to the Add New Employee text by selecting it and choosing the style in the Property inspector.

8. The next step is to add a form and table that allows the Human Resources employee to enter the appropriate data. To do this, place your cursor on the line below the Add New Employee text and choose Insert, Application Objects, Insert Record, Record Insertion Form Wizard from the menu bar.

9. In the Record Insertion Form dialog box, shown in Figure 5.7, choose the connKrystalClearCF connection and the tbHR table. Leave the Username and Password fields blank. In the After Inserting, Go To field, type **employee_added.cfm**.

10. In the Form Fields panel, use the up and down arrows to reorganize the fields into the following order:
    EmployeeID
    LastName
    FirstName
    HomeAdd
    City
    HomeState

Zip
HomePhone
Department
Title
Extension
HireDate
EditPages

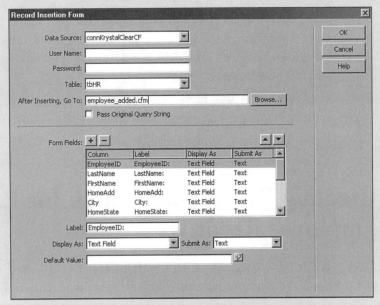

FIGURE 5.7   The Record Insertion Form dialog box allows
you to choose which fields will be added to the database.

11. Click the EmployeeID column and notice that Dreamweaver creates a
    label for the corresponding text field of EmployeeID. To make the form
    more user friendly, go through each field and add the appropriate
    spaces and capitalization for each label. For instance, for the LastName
    field, change the label to read Last Name:.

12. Click the Department text field and change the Display As value to
    Menu. We want this element to appear in the form as a drop-down
    menu that allows the staff member to pick from the various departments.

13. Click the Menu Properties button and in the Menu Properties dialog
    box, enter the labels and values shown earlier in Table 5.1.

14. Click OK to close the Menu Properties dialog box and click OK on the
    Record Insertion Form dialog box. Dreamweaver inserts the appropriate
    form and form objects into your page.

15. Open the Server Behaviors panel by choosing Window, Server Behaviors from the menu bar. Notice that Dreamweaver has added the Insert Record server behavior to add the data to your table.

16. Save the page.

17. The last step in the add employee process is to create a confirmation page. Create a new page from the HR template. Change the page title to Human Resources – Employee Added.

18. Place your cursor in the erMainData editable region and click the Align Center button on the Property inspector. Type **Thank you. The new employee has been added to the database. Please click here to return to the HR search page.**

19. Highlight the Click Here text and create a hyperlink by typing **search_employee.cfm** in the Link field of the Property inspector.

20. Save the page as employee_added.cfm.

Creating Pages That Search for Existing Employee Records

After records have been added to the database, the HR staff needs an easy way to find them. To accomplish this, KrystalClear has requested a simple search feature that allows the user of the module to search for an employee based on her first name, last name, and department. After the employee has submitted his search criteria, he will see a results page that contains the first name, last name, and department of each record that matches. In addition, the results page will contain a link to a page where the staff member can edit the employee information and update the record.

Search Page

The purpose of the search page is to collect the information that the user wants to compare with the records in the database. In the case of the HR module, the search page consists of a simple HTML form made of up two text boxes, a drop-down menu, and the submit button. The two text boxes allow the user to type in a first name and/or a last name and the menu allows the user to select the department where the employee works. The drop-down list with the departments also contains an entry that, when selected, allows the staff member to search every department within the organization. After the user clicks the

Submit button, the contents of the form are then compared with the records stored in the database and any matches are displayed.

Exercise 5.3 (a)   Building a Search Page in ASP.NET

1. Create a new page from the HR template by choosing File, New and selecting the Template tab. Change the page title to Human Resources – Search Employee Database. Save the page as search_employee.aspx.

2. Place your cursor in the erMainData editable region and click the Align Center button on the Property inspector. Type **Search Employee Database** and press Enter. Highlight the text and apply the HeaderText style by choosing it in the Property inspector.

3. Attach the krystalclearss.css style sheet the document by choosing Attach Style Sheet from the Style dropdown on the Property inspector.

4. Place your cursor on the line below the Search Employee Database text and type **Click here to add a new employee** and press Enter. Create a new Style in the Property inspector named **.BodyText**. Set the Font to Arial, the size to 12, and the weight and style to Normal. Apply this style to the new line of text.

5. Select the Click Here text and link this text to add_new_employee.aspx by typing the value in the Link field of the Property inspector.

6. Place your cursor on the line below the Add New Employee text and switch to the Code and Design view so that you can see both the page layout and the underlying code by choosing View, Code and Design View from the menu bar. As shown in Figure 5.8, your cursor is now between a `<p>` tag and a `</p>` tag. Delete the ` ` code.

7. We need to insert an ASP.NET form tag. To do this, type **<form runat="server">** and notice that Dreamweaver helps out by adding the `</form>` tag. This form tag is different from a traditional form tag in that all the contents are submitted back to the same page, rather than transferred to a different page for processing.

8. Place your cursor inside the form in the Design view and insert a table that contains 4 rows, 2 columns, and is 300 pixels wide. Set the border, cell padding, and cell spacing to 1.

9. In the upper-left cell, type **Last Name:**. In the cell directly below that, type **First Name:**. In the third cell down, type **Department:**. Highlight the three cells and reformat it to the BodyText style.

10. Highlight the four cells in the left column and click the Align Right button on the Property inspector. Set the width to 50% by typing the value in the W field of the Property inspector.

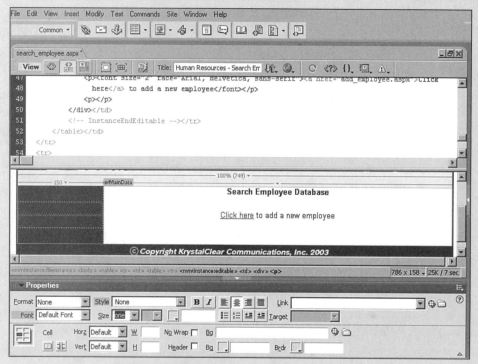

FIGURE 5.8   The split code and design view.

11. Place your cursor in the upper-right cell and choose Insert, ASP.NET Objects, asp:textbox from the menu bar. In the Tag Editor, set the ID to be tfLastName and click OK.

12. In the cell below the text field, add a second asp:textbox and name it tfFirstName.

13. In the cell below that text field, add a list by choosing Insert, ASP.NET Objects, asp:dropdownlist. Name the list **lsDepartment**.

14. We need to add the values to our list. In the code window, place your cursor between the `<asp:dropdownlist ID="lsDepartment" runat="server">` and the `</asp:dropdownlist>` tags. Type the following code string:

```
<asp:ListItem Value="%" Text="All Departments">
<asp:ListItem Value="HR" Text="Human Resources">
<asp:ListItem Value="Marketing" Text="Marketing">
<asp:ListItem Value="IS" Text="Information Services">
```

Dreamweaver should automatically add a `</asp:ListItem>` tag after each of these tags and when completed, your code should look like this:

```
<asp:dropdownlist ID="lsDepartment" runat="server">
<asp:ListItem Value="%" Text="All Departments"></asp:ListItem>
<asp:ListItem Value="HR" Text="Human Resources"></asp:ListItem>
<asp:ListItem Value="Marketing" Text="Marketing"></asp:ListItem>
<asp:ListItem Value="IS" Text="Information Services"></asp:ListItem>
</asp:dropdownlist>
```

 WHY USE THE % SIGN?

Notice that we include a label for All Departments in this list. By choosing this value, the staff member does not have to know which department the employee works in to find the record. The % sign is a value that is passed to the code that tells the SQL Statement to search for all records regardless of what value is entered into the Department field.

15. Switch to the Design view by choosing View, Design.

16. Place your cursor in the lower-right cell and insert a submit button by choosing Insert, ASP.NET Objects, asp:button from the menu bar. Set the button ID to btSubmit and type **Search** in the Text field. Click OK. With the button in place, your page should now look like Figure 5.9.

17. Save the page.

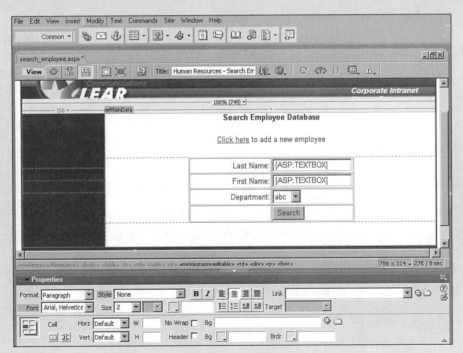

FIGURE 5.9   The search form has been created.

Creating a search page in ColdFusion is a bit different from ASP.NET because we don't have the .NET objects to work with. Instead, we can use the standard HTML tags to build our form, table, and form objects.

Exercise 5.3(b)   Building a Search Page in ColdFusion

1. Create a new page from the HR template by choosing File, New and selecting the Template tab. Change the page title to Human Resources – Search Employee Database. Save the page as search_employee.cfm.

2. Place your cursor in the erMainData editable region and click the Align Center button on the Property inspector. Type **Search Employee Database** and press Enter. Create a new Style in the Property inspector named **.BodyText**. Set the Font to Arial, the size to 12, and the weight and style to Normal. Apply this style to the new line of text.

3. Select the Click Here text and link this text to add_new_employee.cfm by typing the value in the Link field of the Property inspector.

4. Place your cursor on the line below the Search Employee Database text and type **Click here to add a new employee** and press Enter. Highlight the new text and reformat it to the BodyText style. Link this text to add_new_employee.cfm by typing the value in the Link field of the Property inspector.

5. Place your cursor on the line below the Add New Employee text and insert a form by choosing Insert, Form, Form from the menu bar. Name the form fmSearch by typing **employee_search_results.cfm** in the Action field of the Property inspector.

6. With your cursor inside the form, insert a table that contains 4 rows, 2 columns, and is 300 pixels wide. Set the border, cell padding, and cell spacing to 1. With the table in place, your page should now look like Figure 5.10.

7. In the upper-left cell, type **Last Name:**. In the cell directly below that, type **First Name:**. In the third cell down, type **Department:**. Highlight the three cells and reformat them to Arial, size 2.

8. Highlight the four cells in the left column and click the Align Right button on the Property inspector. Set the width to 50% by typing the value in the W field of the Property inspector.

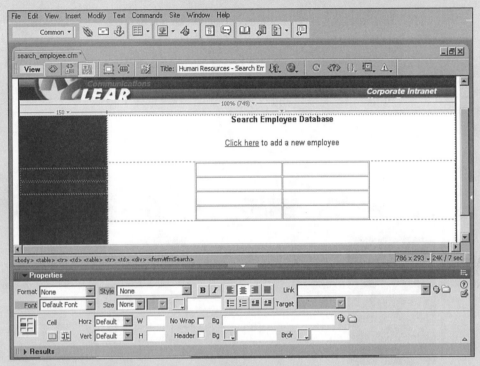

FIGURE 5.10   Your page with the search form and table in place.

9. Place your cursor in the upper-right cell and choose Insert, Form, Text Field from the menu bar. Name the text field tfLastName.

10. In the cell below the text field, add a second text field and name it tfFirstName.

11. In the cell below that text field, add a list by choosing Insert, Form, List/Menu. Name the list **lsDepartment**. Click the List Values button on the Property inspector and add the values shown in Table 5.2.

TABLE 5.2   The Values for Your New Departmental List

ITEM LABEL	ITEM VALUE
All Departments	%
Human Resources	HR
Marketing	Marketing
Information Services	IS

12. In the Property inspector, choose All Departments in the Initially Selected field.

13. Place your cursor in the lower-right cell and insert a submit button by choosing Insert, Form, Button from the menu bar. Rename the button **btSubmit**. Your page should now look like Figure 5.11

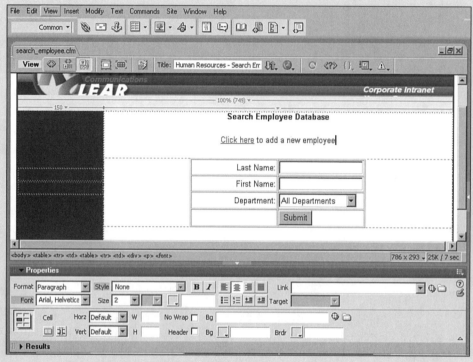

FIGURE 5.11   The search form has been created.

14. Save the page.

Results Page

The results page uses a series of dynamic elements to provide the user with the information he requested. For instance, the first thing the results page does when loaded is collect the search criteria that was passed from the search form. After the results page knows the search criteria, it uses a SQL query to sort through the database to find all records that match. These records are then placed in a temporary container called a recordset (also called a dataset in the ASP.NET environment). The information stored in the recordset can then be displayed on the page so that the HR staff member can choose the record that matches her needs.

Displaying the search results in ASP.NET is a relatively simple process because of the included DataGrid server behavior that places the records on the page in a series of rows and columns.

Exercise 5.4(a)   Displaying the Search Results in ASP.NET

1. Open the search_employee.aspx page and place your cursor inside the form, just to the right of the table that contains the search elements and press Enter.

2. Before we can display the search results on the page, we need to apply a server behavior that collects the information that was passed from the search page and compares it with the information stored in the database. Open the Server Behaviors panel and click the plus sign. From the menu, choose DataSet.

3. In the DataSet dialog box, shown in Figure 5.12, set the DataSet Name as dsResults and choose the connKrystalClearASP connection and the tbHR table.

4. If we were looking to display all the records in a table or wanted to compare the database contents with just one form parameter, we could use the Simple view. Our search page, however, uses three search parameters (last name, first name, and department), so we have to use the Advanced view instead. Click the Advanced button to switch to the Advanced view.

5. In the Database Items field of the Advanced view, click the plus sign next to Tables and then click the plus sign next to tbHR to display the fields that are located in that table. Select the Department field and click the Select button. Notice that Dreamweaver updates the SQL query in

the SQL field to retrieve only the fields that have been indicated. Add the EmployeeID, FirstName, and LastName fields to the query by selecting each field and clicking the Select button.

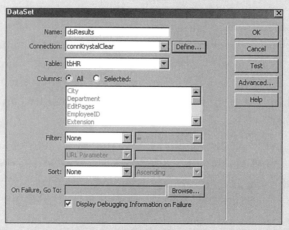

FIGURE 5.12   The DataSet dialog box allows you to build custom SQL queries that retrieve records from the database.

6. Now that the SQL query knows which table to look in and which fields to search, we need to indicate that it should compare the data that was submitted via the HTML form and only return those records that match. To do this, click the plus sign in the Parameters section. In the Add Parameter dialog box, shown in Figure 5.13, type **@FirstName** and set the type to VarChar.

FIGURE 5.13   The Add Parameter dialog box allows you to build custom parameters for your SQL queries.

7. Click the Build button to build the value of the parameter and type **tfFirstName** as the value name. Set the source to a Form Variable and type **%** as the default value. By typing **%**, if the staff member leaves that field blank, the results page will not exclude any records based on that field.

8. Click OK to close the Build Value dialog box and click OK to close the Add Parameter dialog box.

Note

BE CAREFUL WHEN EDITING PARAMETERS

If you come back and edit your parameters, be aware the Dreamweaver does not keep your original value name if the value name differs from the database column. For instance, our database column is named FirstName, but our form element is named tfFirstName. If you go back in and edit the @FirstName parameter, Dreamweaver will set the value name back to FirstName, which can cause problems if you don't correct it.

9. Following the same steps, build two additional parameters. For the second, use the parameter name @LastName, the build value name of tfLastName, the build source as Form Variable, and the default value as %. For the third, use the parameter name @Department, the build value name of lsDepartment, the build source as Form Variable, and the default value as %. With your parameters in place, the DataSet dialog box should look like Figure 5.14.

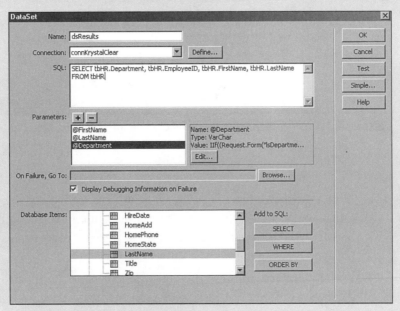

FIGURE 5.14   The basics of the SQL query have been entered.

10. If you look at the existing statement in the SQL field, it basically says, "Get the value of the EmployeeID, FirstName, LastName, and Department fields from the tbHR table." We need to add a statement, however, that limits the results to only those that match the custom parameter we created. To do this, add the following text on the line below the FROM statement:

```
WHERE tbHR.FirstName LIKE ? AND tbHR.LastName LIKE ? AND
tbHR.Department LIKE ?
```

The ? symbol is used as a placeholder for the parameters. After your SQL Statement is completed, the DataSet dialog box should look like Figure 5.15.

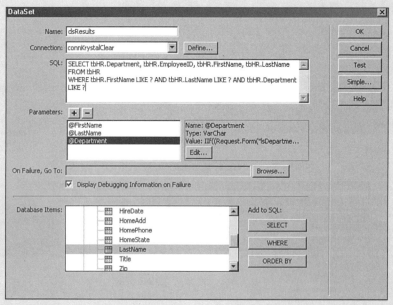

FIGURE 5.15   Your SQL query is complete and the dataset is ready to be created.

11. Click OK to create the dataset.

12. Now that the dataset is built, we just have to display the search results on the page. Place your cursor on a new line in the search form. On the Server Behaviors panel, click the plus sign and choose DataGrid from the menu.

13. In the DataGrid dialog box, type **dgResults** as the ID and choose the dsResults dataset. Choose to display the first 10 records and include the navigation links to previous and next pages.

14. To allow the HR staff members to edit existing employee records, we need to add a column to the datagrid. Click any of the column titles and then click the plus sign next to Columns and choose Hyperlink from the menu.

15. In the Hyperlink Column dialog box, type **Edit** as the Title and click the Static Text radio button. In the Static Text field, type **Edit**. Select the Data Field radio button and choose EmployeeID from the drop-down list.

16. Click the Browse button next to the Format String field and type **edit_employee.aspx** in the File Name field. Click OK and you'll notice that Dreamweaver has reformatted the URL to include the employee's EmployeeID. When the link is clicked, not only will the staff member be directed to the edit page, but information about which employee she wishes to edit is passed as well. Click OK.

17. Using the up and down arrows, reorganize the fields so they are in the following order:

    EmployeeID
    FirstName
    LastName
    Department
    Edit

18. Click OK to close the DataGrid dialog box and, as shown in Figure 5.16, Dreamweaver adds a placeholder datagrid to the page.

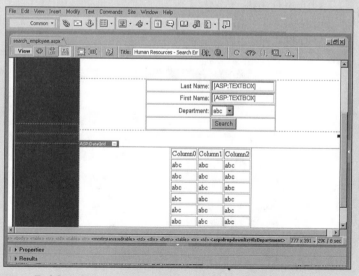

FIGURE 5.16 The datagrid placeholder has been added to your page.

19. Save this page.

Displaying the search results using the ColdFusion platform is a bit different from ASP.NET. ColdFusion uses a similar method to gather the data from the database, but does not have a datagrid behavior to automatically display it. Instead, we need to build a table with the appropriate headers and insert the data binding placeholders where the information will be displayed. After that is completed, we can use Dreamweaver's Repeat Region server behavior to loop through and display all records in the recordset.

Exercise 5.4(b)   Displaying the Search Results in ColdFusion

1. Create a new page based on the Human Resources template and change the page title to Human Resources – Employee Search Results.

2. Place your cursor in the erMainData editable region and click the Align Center button in the Property inspector. Type Employee Search Results and press Enter.

3. Highlight the text and reformat it using the BodyText style.

4. Before we can display the search results on the page, we need to apply a server behavior that collects the information that was passed from the search page and compares it with the information stored in the database. Open the Server Behaviors panel and click the plus sign. From the menu, choose RecordSet(Query).

5. In the Recordset dialog box, shown in Figure 5.17, set the recordset name as rsResults and choose the connKrystalClearCF connection and the tbHR table.

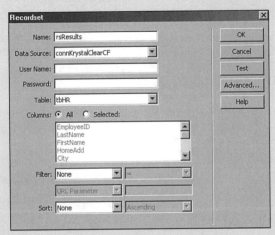

FIGURE 5.17   The Recordset dialog box allows you to retrieve records from your database.

6. Click the Advanced button to switch to the Advanced view.

7. In the Database Items field of the Advanced view, click the plus sign next to Tables and then click the plus sign next to tbHR to display the fields that are located in that table. MF Select the Department field and click the Select button. Notice that Dreamweaver updates the SQL query in the SQL field to retrieve only the fields that have been indicated. Add the EmployeeID, FirstName, and LastName fields to the query by selecting each field and clicking the Select button.

8. Now that the SQL query knows which table to look in and which fields to search, we need to indicate that it should compare the data that was submitted via the HTML form and only return those records that match. To do this, click the plus sign in the Page Parameters panel. In the Add Parameter dialog box, shown in Figure 5.18, type the name of the parameter **Form.tfFirstName** and set the default value to %.

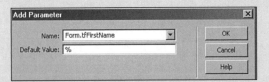

FIGURE 5.18   The Add Parameter dialog box allows you to build custom parameters for your SLQ queries.

By naming the parameter Form.tfFirstName, we are indicating that the parameter should adopt the value that was passed by the form via the URL that was contained in the text field named tfFirstName. Click OK to close the Add Parameter dialog box.

9. Following the same steps, build two additional parameters. For the first, use the parameter name Form.tfLastName with the default value as %. For the second, use the parameter name Form.lsDepartment with the default value as %. With your parameters in place, the Recordset dialog box should look like Figure 5.19.

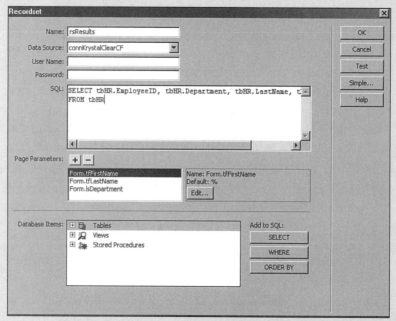

FIGURE 5.19   The fundamental elements of your SQL Query.

10. If you look at the existing statement in the SQL field, it basically says, "Get the value of the EmployeeID, FirstName, LastName, and Department fields from the tbHR table." We need to add a statement, however, that limits the results to only those that match the custom parameter we created. To do this, add the following text on the line below the FROM statement:

```
WHERE LastName LIKE '#Form.tfLastName#' AND FirstName LIKE
'#Form.tfFirstName#' AND Department LIKE '#Form.lsDepartment#'
```

The `#Form.tfLastName#` is used as a placeholder for the parameters. After your SQL Statement is completed, the Recordset dialog box should look like Figure 5.20.

11. Now that the recordset is built, we only have to display the search results on the page. Place your cursor on the line below the Employee Search Results line and insert a new table that has 2 rows, 5 columns, and a width of 425 pixels. Set the border, cell padding, and cell spacing to 1.

12. In the top-left cell, type **Employee ID**. Press Tab and type **Last Name**. Press Tab again and type **First Name**. Press Tab one more time and type **Department** in the next cell. Leave the top-right cell blank.

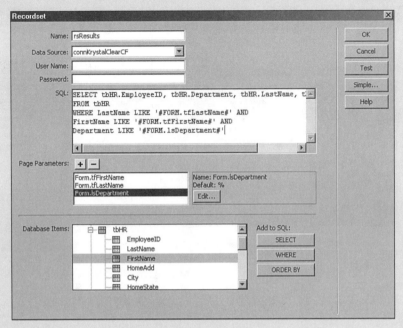

FIGURE 5.20   The SQL query is complete and the recordset is ready to be built.

13. Select the top row of the table by placing your cursor over the left border of the top-left cell and clicking. In the Property inspector, choose Arial, size 2, Bold, and click the Align Center button. In the W field of the Property inspector, type **20%**.

14. Open the Bindings panel by choosing Window, Bindings from the menu bar. Click the plus sign next to the rsResults recordset to display the fields that are available. Drag the EmployeeID and drop it in the lower-left cell under the Employee ID header cell. Drag the LastName field under the Last Name header and the FirstName field under the First Name header and drag the Department field into the cell under the Department header. Finally, in the bottom-right cell, type **Edit**. Your page should now look like Figure 5.21.

STRETCHED OUT PAGE?

Don't worry that the data placeholders stretched out your page. At production time, your pages will return to normal after the data is filled in.

FIGURE 5.21   The column headers, data placeholders, and text are in place.

15. Select the bottom row of the table and reformat it to the BodyText style and click the Align Center button.

16. The next step is to indicate that Dreamweaver should loop through all the fields in the recordset and display them all on the page. With the bottom row selected, activate the Server Behaviors panel and click the plus sign. From the menu, choose Repeat Region.

17. In the Repeat Regions dialog box, shown in Figure 5.22, choose the rsResults recordset and have the page display all records. Click OK to close the dialog box.

FIGURE 5.22   Using the Repeat Region dialog box, you can have your pages display all data in the recordset.

18. The last step is to modify the Edit text so that it is an active hyperlink that, when clicked, redirects the staff member to a page where she can edit the selected employee record. Highlight the Edit text and type **edit_employee.cfm** in the Link field of the Property inspector. Click the folder icon next to the Link field.

19. In the Select File dialog box, click the Parameters button. Enter **EmployeeID** as the name of the parameter and click in the Value field. Click the lightning bolt icon in the far right of the Value field and choose EmployeeID in the Dynamic Data dialog box. Click OK to close the Dynamic Data dialog box and click OK to close the Parameters dialog box. Finally, click OK again to close the Select File dialog box.

20. Save this page as employee_search_results.cfm.

Creating Pages to Edit Existing Employee Records

Now that the HR staff has a way to enter new employee records and search for them, the next step is to provide them with a way to edit the information as it changes. To accomplish this, the module requires two additional pages. The first page creates a recordset and then populates an HTML form with the information contained in the record. This allows the user to see what information is already stored in the database. Using the form, the user can then change any values and submit the changes to the database. Upon updating the information, the user is then presented with a confirmation message.

Recall that when we created the search feature we built a link that, when clicked, takes the user to the edit page. This link also passed information specific to which record is supposed to be available for editing. After the edit page receives the information about that specific record, a new recordset is built and the data that is currently stored in that record is displayed in the HTML form through the use of dynamic elements. After the user makes the appropriate changes and clicks the Update button, Dreamweaver's Update Record server behavior applies the changes to the record and, upon completion, redirects the user to a confirmation page.

Exercise 5.5   Editing an Existing Record in ASP.NET and ColdFusion

1. Open a new page based on the HR template and change the title to Human Resources – Edit Employee. Place the cursor in the erMainData editable region and click the Align Center button on the Property inspector.

2. Type **Edit Employee** and press Enter. Attach the KrystalClear.css style sheet, highlight the text, and reformat it to the HeaderText style.

3. Before we can edit the employee record, we need to create a dataset or recordset that contains only the record we want to update. On the Server Behaviors panel, click the plus sign and choose DataSet if you are developing a page for ASP.NET or Recordset(Query) if you are developing a page for ColdFusion.

4. In the dialog box, switch to the Simple view by clicking the Simple button.

5. If you are using ASP.NET, name the dataset **dsUpdate** and choose the connKrystalClearASP connection and the tbHR table. Choose to select all the fields.

    If you are using ColdFusion, name the recordset **rsUpdate** and choose the connKrystalClearCF connection and the tbHR table. Choose to select all fields.

6. Set a filter where EmployeeID equals the URL Parameter EmployeeID. When completed, your DataSet or Recordset dialog box should look similar to Figure 5.23. Click OK to close the dialog box.

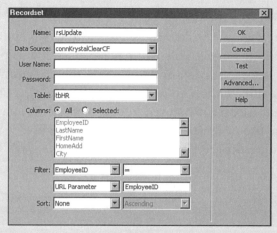

FIGURE 5.23   The proper elements for your new dataset or recordset.

7. Place your cursor on the line below the Edit Employee text and choose Insert, Application Objects, Record Update Form Wizard from the menu bar.

8. In the Record Update Form dialog box, choose the appropriate connection and the tbHR table. (ColdFusion users should leave the Username and Password fields blank.) Choose to update the record from the dsUpdate dataset or the rsUpdate recordset with the unique key column being EmployeeID.

9. For ASP.NET, in the On Success, Go To field, type **employee_updated.aspx**. For ColdFusion, in the After Updating, Go To field, type **employee_updated.cfm**.

10. In the Form Fields panel, select the EmployeeID column and click the minus symbol. This prevents a member of the HR staff from modifying the unique EmployeeID field, which helps maintain the integrity of the database.

11. Using the up and down arrows, reorganize the columns so they are in this order:

    LastName
    FirstName
    HomeAdd
    City
    HomeState
    Zip
    HomePhone
    Department
    Title
    Extension
    HireDate
    EditPages

12. When completed, the dialog box should look similar to Figure 5.24. Click OK to create the form.

13. ASP.NET users should save the page as edit_employee.aspx and ColdFusion users should save the page as edit_employee.cfm.

14. The last page we need to create is the confirmation page that indicates when a record has been successfully updated. Create a new page based on the HR template.

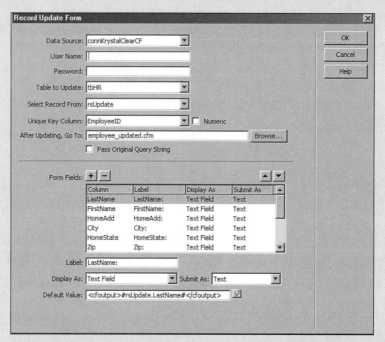

FIGURE 5.24   The completed Record Update Form dialog box.

15. Place the cursor in the erMainData editable region and type **Thank You. The employee record has been successfully updated. Click here to return to the HR employee search.** Highlight the Click Here text and create a hyperlink to search_employee.aspx or search_employee.cfm by typing the value in the Property inspector.

16. Save the page as either employee_updated.aspx or employee_updated.cfm, depending on your platform.

Testing the Application

The last step in creating the Human Resources module is to test it out. To do this, we can add a sample new employee record, search for the record, and then edit it to be sure that everything functions properly. If each element functions as expected, we can move on to the next module.

Exercise 5.6   Testing the Application in ASP.NET and ColdFusion

1. Open Internet Explorer and type **add_new_employee.aspx** or **add_new_employee.cfm** in the address bar and press Enter.

2. In the Add New Employee page, complete the fields for a sample record and click the Submit button. The application should add the information to the database and redirect you to the confirmation page.

3. On the confirmation page, click the link to the employee search page. In the employee search page, type the first name of the record you just added in the First Name field and click Submit. As shown in Figure 5.25, you should receive the record you added.

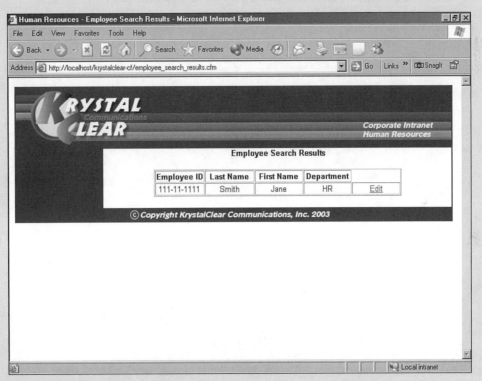

FIGURE 5.25   Your employee record is displayed.

4. Click the Edit link and you should be taken to the Edit Employee page. Change a value in employee record and click Submit. You should receive a confirmation that the record was updated.

5. To verify that the update was made, click the link to the employee search page and search for the record again. In the results page, click the link to edit the record and you should see that the change was applied.

Summary

In this chapter, you learned how to create pages that add, search for, and edit records stored in the database. To accomplish these tasks, you also learned how to build a dataset/recordset and SQL query to select records from the database. In addition, you learned how to create simple search and results pages that use a combination of HTML forms, recordsets/datasets, and server behaviors to properly display the results.

In the next chapter, we develop the Information Services Asset Management module, which demonstrates how to remove records from the database and create dynamic elements such as database-driven menus.

CHAPTER 6

CREATING THE INFORMATION SERVICES ASSET MANAGEMENT SYSTEM

KrystalClear has requested a second module for their Information Services (IS) department. IS would like an automated element that allows them to track the computers, mobile phones, and pagers that are distributed to KrystalClear employees. To accomplish this, they would like to be able to create a new entry in the database for each asset when it is delivered and then assign the asset to a specific employee when the asset is requested.

In addition to adding new assets, the IS staff would also like to be able to view the assets in inventory and easily update certain criteria such as the return date. If necessary, they would also like to be able to edit the entire record as well.

Although the principles of the IS module are very similar to those of the HR module (add, search, and edit), we will be significantly expanding on the fundamentals by adding form verification and demonstrating how to update records from within the datagrid/results table. In addition, we'll add functionality to the datagrid/results table that allows the user to filter and sort the records displayed.

By the end of this chapter, you will have built the following:

- A set of pages that allows the IS staff to add assets to the database. The forms used in these pages will include form validation.
- A set of pages that allows the IS staff to view all assets in inventory and perform a quick edit from the datagrid/results table.
- A search feature that allows the staff to filter the records that are displayed.
- A set of pages that allows the IS staff to edit the full asset record.

Reviewing the Database Table Structure

Prior to building the pages, let's take a few moments and look back over the database table we created earlier that relates specifically to the IS module. By understanding not only the structure of the tables, but also why we created the specific fields and how they relate to the other modules that make up the intranet application, you'll have a better understanding of how your pages interact with the database.

The tbIS table, shown in Figure 6.1, is composed of nine different fields.

The AssetID field is an AutoNumber field that automatically increments as a new record is added to the database. The EmployeeID field is a one-to-many relationship with the EmployeeID field in the tbHR field, which allows any user to have more than one asset in the tbIS table. For instance, if a user has a pager and a laptop computer, we can associate each of these items with the employee by adding his EmployeeID to the record for each asset. The AssetBrand, AssetModel, and AssetSerial fields record the specific make, model, and serial number of each asset. Finally, the DateAssigned, DateReturned, and ReturnReason fields allow when the asset was checked out, checked in, and what problems might exist with asset.

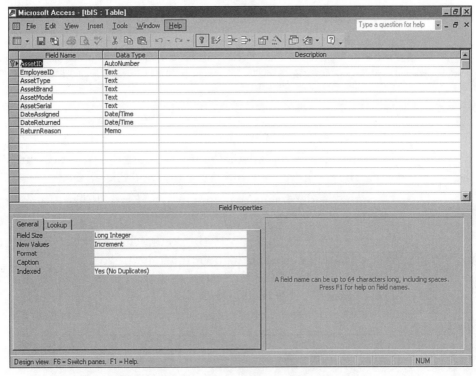

FIGURE 6.1   The structure of the tbIS table.

Creating the Information Services Page Template

Just as we did with the HR module, we also need to create a page template that represents IS. Luckily, we can reuse most of the HR template and make a minor modification so that it is suitable for the needs of IS.

Exercise 6.1(a)   Building the Template for the ASP.NET IS Module

1. In Dreamweaver, open the template created for the Human Resources module. The HR template should be located at C:\Inetpub\wwwroot\KrystalClear-ASP\Templates\ intranet_template_hr.dwt.aspx.

TEMPLATES FOLDER

When you save a template to a site for the first time, Dreamweaver creates a folder named Templates in the root directory of that site. Each time you save a template in the future, it is placed in that folder as well. Because this template stores the information about supporting files for the template, moving it or deleting it would cause pages that rely on the template to stop functioning.

2. From the menu bar, choose File, Save As Template.

3. In the Save As Template dialog box, choose the KrystalClear-ASP site, name the file intranet_template_is.dwt and click Save.

4. Click the header image that contains the KrystalClear Communications text.

5. In the Src field of the Property inspector, change the source of this image from ../images/kc_logo_intranet_hr.jpg to ../images/kc_logo_intranet_is.jpg. As shown in Figure 6.2, the image should now display the KrystalClear logo with the IS brand.

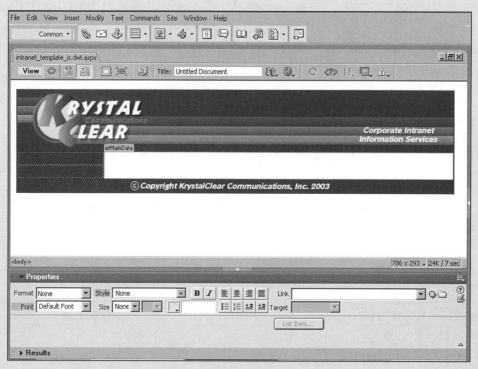

FIGURE 6.2   The template has been updated for the Information Services pages.

6. Save the page. When asked if you would like to update pages that depend on the template, allow Dreamweaver to make the updates.

Exercise 6.1(b)   Building the Template for the ColdFusion IS Module

1. In Dreamweaver, open the template created for the Human Resources module. The HR template should be located at C:\Inetpub\wwwroot\KrystalClear-CF\Templates\intranet_template_hr.dwt.cfm.

2. From the menu bar, choose File, Save As Template.

3. In the Save As Template dialog box, choose the KrystalClear-CF site, name the file **intranet_template_is.dwt,** and click Save.

4. Click on the header image that contains the KrystalClear Communications text.

5. In the Src field of the Property inspector, change the source of this image from ../images/kc_logo_intranet_hr.jpg to ../images/kc_logo_intranet_is.jpg.

6. Save the page.

Creating Pages to Add Assets to the Database

If you recall, Information Services requested a set of pages that allows them to insert a new record into the database when they receive a new asset. Just as we did in the HR module, we can use a form and a combination of form elements and the Insert Record server behavior to add the information to the database. We will also use a confirmation page to let us know that the operation succeeded.

On top of the insert record/verification that we did in the last chapter, we are going to use additional code to verify that the user completed the form properly.

Exercise 6.2(a)   Adding Assets to the Database and Validating Forms in ASP.NET

1. Before beginning the page-building process, you need to download the Dreamweaver extension for ASP.NET that allows you to verify that the forms are completed properly. The extension is called the ASP.NET Form Validation Tool Kit and is available from wwwebConcepts. To download the file, visit the Macromedia Exchange at `http://www.macromedia.com/cfusion/exchange` and search the exchange for the ASP.NET Form Validation Tool Kit.

DOWNLOADING FROM THE ebCONCEPTS WEB SITE

You can also download the extension directly from the wwwebConcepts Web site at
`http://www.ebconcepts.com/asp/extension_details.asp?MXP_ID=4`.

2. After you have downloaded the extension, close Dreamweaver and double-click the file to begin the installation process. Follow the steps of the Macromedia Extension Manager to install the extension on your computer. When the extension is installed, the Macromedia Extension Manager displays the notice shown in Figure 6.3.

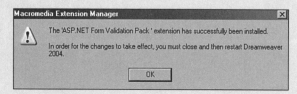

FIGURE 6.3   The Dreamweaver extension has been successfully installed.

3. From the menu bar, choose File, New. In the New Document window, click the Templates tab. Select the KrystalClear-ASP site in the Templates For panel and then choose intranet_template_IS. Click Create.

4. In the new page, replace the Untitled Document text in the Title field of the Document toolbar with Information Services – Add New Asset.

5. Place your cursor in the erMainData region and click the Align Center button on the Property inspector. Type **Add New Asset** and press Enter. Attach the krystalclearss.css style sheet, highlight the new text, and reformat it using the HeaderText style.

6. To add the asset entry form, place your cursor on the line below the Add New Asset text and choose Insert, Application Objects, Insert Record, Record Insertion Form Wizard from the menu bar.

7. In the Record Insertion Form dialog box, choose the connKrystalClearASP connection and the tbIS table. In the On Success, Go To field, type **asset_added.aspx**.

8. In the Form Fields panel, use the up and down arrows to reorganize the fields into the following order:

AssetID
EmployeeID
AssetType
AssetBrand
AssetModel
AssetSerial
DateAssigned
DateReturned
ReturnReason

9. Because this is a new asset, there are several fields that we don't need in our entry form. Using the minus button, remove the AssetID, EmployeeID, DateAssigned, DateReturned, and ReturnReason. We are removing AssetID because it is automatically assigned by the database.

10. Click the AssetType form field and change the Display As value to Menu. We want this element to appear in the form of a drop-down menu, which allows the IS staff member to pick from the various types of assets.

11. Click the Menu Properties button and in the Menu Properties dialog box, enter the labels and values shown in Table 6.1.

TABLE 6.1   The Values for Your Asset Type List

ITEM LABEL	ITEM VALUE
Pager	Pager
Digital Phone	Digital Phone
Desktop Computer	Desktop Computer
Laptop Computer	Laptop Computer

12. Click OK to close the Menu Properties dialog box and click OK on the Record Insertion Form dialog box. As shown in Figure 6.4, Dreamweaver inserts the appropriate form and form objects into your page.

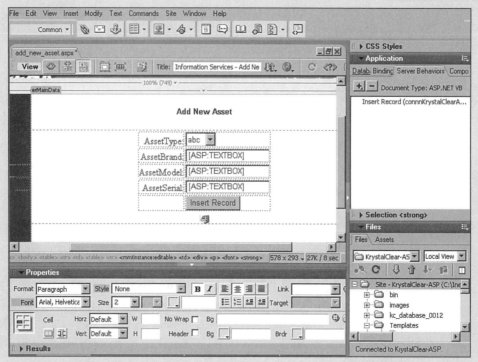

FIGURE 6.4   The data entry form has been added to the page.

13. Save the page as add_new_asset.aspx.

Next, we want to ensure that each time an asset is added to the database at bare minimum, its serial number is entered. To do this, we add a set of behaviors that check to see whether the indicated text field is blank prior to submitting the form. If it is blank, an error is generated letting the user know that she should fill in the required field.

14. Place your cursor after the Add New Asset text you typed earlier and press Enter. From the Server Behaviors panel, click the plus sign and choose WWWebConcepts, ASP.NET Form Validation. Click OK in the ASP.NET Form Validation dialog box and, as shown in Figure 6.5, Dreamweaver adds a piece of code to your page that says, "Fill in the required fields below."

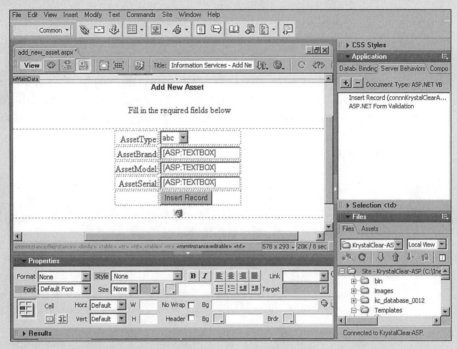

FIGURE 6.5   Validation text has been added to the page.

15. Click the ASP:Textbox located to the right of the AssetSerial label. Press the right-arrow key to move to the right of the textbox. From the Server Behaviors panel, choose WWWebConcepts, Controls, ASP.NET Required Field.

16. In the ASP.NET Required Field dialog box, type **AssetSerial** in the Control to Validate text field. This is the name of the textbox that we want to be required. In the Required Field Validator ID field, type **rfvAssetSerial**. Finally, type * in the Error Message field. The dialog box should look like Figure 6.6.

FIGURE 6.6   The ASP.NET Required Field dialog box with the proper entries.

The Control to Validate entry is the name of the text field, drop-down list, check box, or other form object that you want to be sure has a value entered in it. The Required Field Validator ID field is the new name for the object that is going to compare the values when the form is changed or submitted. For simplicity purposes, it's usually easiest to add the rfv prefix to the name of the field you want to validate. This way, you can easily identify which validator code is working for which form object. Finally, the Error Message is a custom error message that is displayed when the field is left blank. At this time, we are using the asterisk symbol because it is a commonly used indicator for required fields.

17. Click OK to close the dialog box. Dreamweaver places the asterisk placeholder next to the field to indicate that it is a required field.

18. Switch to the Split Code and Design views by clicking the Show Code and Design Views button on the button bar. In the Design view, click the AssetSerial textbox and notice that Dreamweaver highlights the corresponding code in the in the Code view. At the end of the asp:textbox tag, just before the />, type the following:

```
Onchange="ClientOnChange();"
```

The line of code should now look like this:

```
<asp:textbox id="AssetSerial" TextMode="SingleLine"
Columns="32" runat="server" Onchange="ClientOnChange();" />
```

19. Add the same OnChange code to the AssetBrand and AssetModel text boxes as well. Using this code, as the user moves from field to field, the status text of the form is updated to reflect whether there are still required fields to be filled.

20. Save the page.

21. The last step is to create a confirmation page. Create a new page from the IS template. Switch back to the Design view and change the page title to Information Services – Asset Added.

22. Place your cursor in the erMainData editable region and click the Align Center button on the Property inspector. Type **Thank you. The new asset has been added to the database. Please click here to return to the IS tracking page.**

23. Highlight the Click Here text and create a hyperlink by typing **search_asset.aspx** in the Link field of the Property inspector.

24. Save the page as asset_added.aspx.

Although the process of adding records to a table in ColdFusion is similar to the process used in ASP.NET, form validation in ColdFusion is accomplished quite differently than it is in ASP.NET. Rather than using server-side validation, ColdFusion relies on JavaScript to ensure that fields are filled in properly. This means that the validation is done on the client side.

Exercise 6.2(b)   Adding Assets to the Database and Validating Forms in ColdFusion

1. From the menu bar, choose File, New. In the New Document window, click the Templates tab. Select the KrystalClear-CF site in the Templates For panel and then choose intranet_template_IS. Click Create.

2. In the new page, replace the Untitled Document text in the Title field of the Document toolbar with Information Services – Add New Asset.

3. Place your cursor in the erMainData region and click the Center button on the Property inspector. Type **Add New Asset** and press Enter. Highlight the new text and reformat it using the HeaderText style.

4. To add the asset entry form, place your cursor on the line below the Add New Employee text and choose Insert, Application Objects, Insert Record, Record Insertion Form Wizard from the menu bar.

5. In the Record Insertion Form dialog box, choose the connKrystalClearCF connection and the tbIS table. In the On Success, Go To field, type **asset_added.cfm**.

6. Because this is a new asset, there are several fields that we don't need in our entry form. Using the minus button, remove the AssetID, EmployeeID, DateAssigned, DateReturned, and ReturnReason. We are removing AssetID because it is automatically assigned by the database.

7. Click the AssetType form field and change the Display As value to Menu. We want this element to appear in the form as a drop-down menu that allows the IS staff member to pick from the various types of assets.

8. Click the Menu Properties button and in the Menu Properties dialog box, enter the labels and values shown in Table 6.2.

TABLE 6.2   The Values for Your Asset Type List

ITEM LABEL	ITEM VALUE
Pager	Pager
Digital Phone	Digital Phone
Desktop Computer	Desktop Computer
Laptop Computer	Laptop Computer

9. Click OK to close the Menu Properties dialog box and click OK on the Record Insertion Form dialog box.

10. Save the page as add_new_asset.cfm.

Next, we want to perform some form validation that ensures the user has entered the asset's serial number. This ensures that blank entries are not added to the database and that, at bare minimum, a user must enter the serial number of the asset, which is presumed to be unique from all other assets.

11. Select the form by clicking the red border that outlines it. With the form selected, open the Behaviors panel by choosing Window, Behaviors.

12. On the Behaviors panel, click the plus sign and choose Validate Form from the drop-down menu. In the Validate Form dialog box, shown in Figure 6.7, choose the AssetSerial entry in the Named Fields panel and click the Required check box.

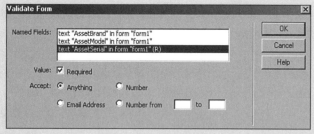

FIGURE 6.7   The Validate Form dialog box allows you to choose which fields are required.

13. Click OK to apply the JavaScript behavior. With the behavior in place, if the user attempts to submit the form without having entered something in the serial number field, he will receive and error.

14. Save the page.

15. The last step is to create a confirmation page. Create a new page from the IS template. Change the page title to Information Services – Asset Added.

16. Place your cursor in the erMainData editable region and click the Align Center button on the Property inspector. Type **Thank you. The new asset has been added to the database. Please click here to return to the IS tracking page.** Attach the krystalclearss.css and apply the BodyText style to the text.

17. Highlight the Click Here text and create a hyperlink by typing **search_asset.cfm** in the Link field of the Property inspector.

18. Save the page as asset_added.cfm.

Displaying the Asset Inventory

Now that IS staff members can add assets to the database, the next step is to provide them with a way to view all of the assets in inventory. Using a dataset/recordset or a datagrid/results table combined with the Repeat Region server behavior, we can easily display all of the records stored in the tbIS table.

Creating the Datagrid/Results Table

In the last chapter, you learned how easy it is to create a recordset based on search criteria. It is even easier to build a recordset that represents *all* the data in a table. After we have the records in a recordset, we can display them on the page with a few clicks of the mouse. Be aware, however, that dumping all the records on the page seems logical when you have 5 records in the table. The wisdom of this course of action comes into question, however, when you try to dump 5,000 records onto a single page. Doing this not only can cause your pages to stop responding, but it can irritate your users as well. For this reason, we will add controls that display only a limited number of records at a time and provide users with a way to cycle through the pages of data.

Exercise 6.3(a)   Displaying the Assets in Inventory in ASP.NET

1. In Dreamweaver, create a new page using the IS template and replace the Untitled Page text with Information Services – Asset Tracking.

2. Place your cursor in the erMainData editable region and click the Align Center button on the Property inspector. Type **Asset Tracking** and press Enter twice.

3. On the middle blank line, type **Click here to add a new asset.** Highlight the Click Here text and type **add_new_asset.aspx** in the Link field of the Property inspector. This gives a way for the IS staff to access the page for adding a new asset. After attaching the krystalclearss.css style sheet, format the first line of text as using the HeaderText style and the second line of text using the BodyText style.

4. Before we can display the assets in inventory on our page, we have to build a dataset that collects the records from the database. To do this, click the plus sign on the Server Behaviors panel and choose Dataset.

5. In the DataSet dialog box, shown in Figure 6.8, make sure you are using the Simple view and type **dsAssets** in the Name field. Choose the connKrystalClearASP connection and the tbIS table. Select only the AssetBrand, AssetID, AssetModel, AssetSerial, AssetType, and DateReturned fields and leave the Filter field set to None. Without a filter, the dataset displays the appropriate fields for every record in the table. Click OK to create the dataset.

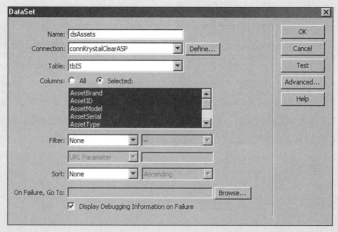

FIGURE 6.8   Create the dataset for the asset tracking module.

6. To display the contents of the dataset in the page, place your cursor on the bottom blank line, click the plus sign on the Server Behaviors dialog box, and choose DataGrid from the menu. In the DataGrid dialog box, type **dgAssets** as the ID and choose the dsAssets dataset.

7. Choose to show 25 records at a time and reorganize the columns so they are in the following order:

AssetID
AssetType
AssetBrand
AssetModel
AssetSerial
DateReturned

8. Click OK to create the datagrid and Dreamweaver places the datagrid placeholder on your page.

9. Save the page as search_asset.aspx.

Exercise 6.3(b)   Displaying the Assets in Inventory in ColdFusion

1. Create a new page using the IS template and replace the Untitled Page text with Information Services – Asset Tracking.

2. Place your cursor in the erMainData editable region and click the Align Center button on the Property inspector. Type **Asset Tracking** and press Enter twice.

3. On the first blank line, type **Click here to add a new asset.** Highlight the Click Here text and type **add_new_asset.cfm** in the Link field of the Property inspector. This gives a way for the IS staff to access the page for adding a new asset.

4. Before we can display the assets in inventory on our page, we have to build a recordset that collects the records from the database. To do this, click the plus sign on the Server Behaviors panel and choose Recordset.

5. In the Recordset dialog box, make sure you are using the simple view and type **rsAssets** in the Name field. Choose the connKrystalClearCF connection and the tbIS table. Select only the AssetID, AssetType, AssetBrand, AssetModel, and DateReturned fields and leave the Filter field set to None. Without a filter, the dataset displays the appropriate fields for every record in the table. Click OK to create the recordset.

6. Now we need to display the assets on the page. Place your cursor on the bottom blank line of your page and insert a new table that has 2 rows, 6 columns, and a width of 425 pixels. Set the border, cell padding, and cell spacing to 1.

7. In the top-left cell, type **AssetID**. Press Tab and type **AssetType**. Press Tab again and type **AssetBrand**. Press Tab again and type **AssetModel**. Press Tab again and type **AssetSerial**. Press Tab one more time and type **DateReturned** in the next cell.

8. Select the top row of the table by placing your cursor over the left border of the top-left cell and clicking. In the Property inspector, choose the HeaderText style and click the Align Center button. In the W field of the Property inspector, type **16%**.

9. Open the Bindings panel by choosing Window, Bindings from the menu bar. Click the plus sign next to the rsAssets recordset to display the fields that are available. Drag the AssetID binding and drop it in the lower-left cell under the AssetID header cell. Drag the other corresponding data bindings to the field under their header. Your page should now look like Figure 6.9.

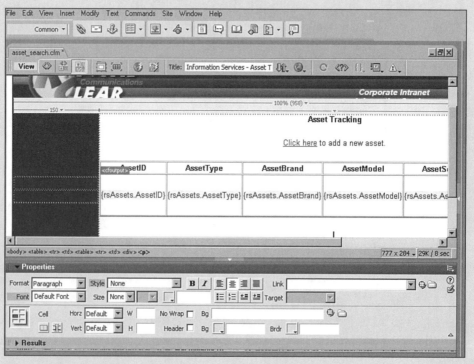

FIGURE 6.9   The page contains the table and data placeholders.

10. Select the bottom row of the table and reformat it using the BodyText style. Click the Align Center button.

11. The next step is to indicate that Dreamweaver should loop through all the fields in the recordset and display them all on the page. To do this, activate the Server Behaviors panel and click the plus sign. From the menu, choose Repeat Region.

12. In the Repeat Regions dialog box, shown in Figure 6.10, choose the rsAssets recordset and have the page display all records. Click OK to close the dialog box.

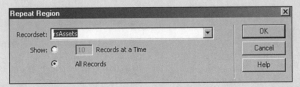

FIGURE 6.10   The Repeat Region dialog box allows you to loop through the recordset and display multiple records.

13. The last step is to create a link that, when clicked, redirects the staff member to a page where she can edit the specific asset. Select the AssetID placeholder dynamic placeholder and type **edit_asset.cfm** in the Link field of the Property inspector. Click the folder icon next to the Link field.

14. In the Select File dialog box, click the Parameters button. Enter **AssetID** as the name of the parameter and click in the Value field. Click the lightning bolt icon in the far right of the Value field and choose AssetID in the Dynamic Data dialog box. Click OK to close the Dynamic Data dialog box and Click OK to close the Parameters dialog box. Finally, click OK again to close the Select File dialog box.

15. Save this page as search_asset.cfm.

Adding a Quick Edit Field

Now that we can see all the records in the table, let's address the request of IS to be able to quickly edit certain fields. The idea here is that they want to be able to find an asset and edit the DateAssigned and DateReturned fields right there on the results page. Luckily, ASP.NET has this functionality built into the dataset server behavior. For ColdFusion, it takes a bit more development, but it is nothing that we can't accomplish.

Exercise 6.4(a)   Adding a Quick Edit Field and Edit Link to an ASP.NET Datagrid

1. Open the search_asset.aspx page and double-click DataGrid in the Server Behaviors panel.

2. The first thing we need to do is to create a set of buttons that allows the user to edit the record and apply the changes. To do this, click the plus sign in the Columns panel and choose Edit, Update, Cancel Buttons from the menu. In the dialog box, type **Edit** in the Title and choose Push Button as the button type. In the Update Table field, choose tbIS and set AssetID as the primary key. Click OK to add the field.

3. In the Columns panel, select the DateReturned field, click the Change Column Type button, and choose Free Form from the drop-down menu.

4. In the Free Form Column dialog box, shown in Figure 6.11, we need to create two different states for the field. The first state occurs when the user is simply viewing the records and she should see the value that is currently entered in the field. The second state is visible after she clicks the Edit button. This state provides the user with a text field where she can type the new value to be entered into the field.

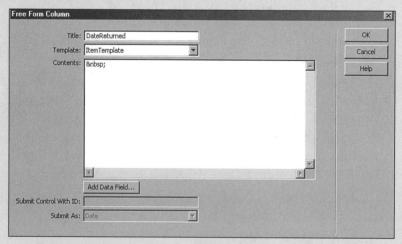

FIGURE 6.11   The Free Form dialog box allows us to modify the type of data that is displayed in the datagrid.

5. To create the first state, in the Contents field, type the following:

```
<asp:label id="DateReturned" runat="server" text=
```

Next, click the Add Data field button and add the DateReturned field to the string. Finally, at the end of the current string, type **></asp:label>**. As shown in Figure 6.12, the Contents string should now look like this:

```
<asp:label id="DateReturned" runat="server"
➥text=<%#dsAssets.FieldValue("DateReturned", Container)%>>
➥</asp:label>
```

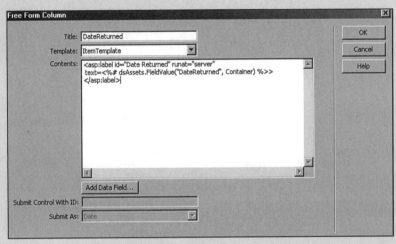

FIGURE 6.12   The Free Form Column dialog box with the custom column contents.

6. Change the Template field to EditItemTemplate. This template indicates what to display after the user clicks the Edit button. In the Contents field, type the following:

```
<asp:textbox id="DateReturned" runat="server" text=
```

Click the Add Data field button and add the DateReturned field to the string. Finally, at the end of the current string, type **></asp:textbox>**. As shown in Figure 6.13, the Contents string should now look like this:

```
<asp:textbox id="DateReturned" runat="server"
➥text=<%#dsAssets.FieldValue("DateReturned", Container)%>>
➥</asp:textbox>
```

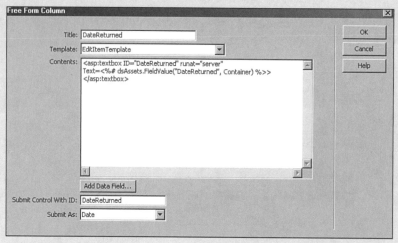

FIGURE 6.13   Build a custom string for the EditItemTemplate.

7. In the Submit Control with ID field, type **DateReturned** and choose Date in the Submit As field.

8. Click OK to close the Free Form Column dialog box.

9. The next step is to create the link to the page that allows users to edit the full record. In the DataGrid dialog box, select the AssetID column, click the Change Column Type button, and choose Hyperlink from the menu.

10. In the Hyperlink Column dialog box, set the Hyperlink Text Data Field to AssetID and the LinkedPage Data Field to AssetID.

11. Click the Browse button next to the Format String field and type **edit_asset.aspx** in the File Name field. Click OK and you'll notice that Dreamweaver has reformatted the URL to include the asset's ID. When the link is clicked, not only will the user be directed to the edit page, but information about which asset he wants to edit is passed as well. Click OK to close the dialog box.

12. Save the page

13. To complete the edit functionality of the IS pages, we need to create a page that allows the user to edit the asset and update the record in the database. In addition, we need a confirmation page that informs the user when the update has been completed successfully. Review the steps that we covered in Chapter 5, "Creating the Human Resources Management System," (Exercise 5.5[a]) and create the remaining pages on your own.

Exercise 6.4(b)   Adding a Quick Edit Field to a ColdFusion Results Table

1. Open the search_asset.cfm page. Select the data placeholder that is located under the DateReturned header and press Delete .

2. With your cursor in the empty cell, choose Insert, Form, Form from the menu bar. Name the form fmUpdate in the Property inspector.

3. With your cursor inside the form, choose Insert, Form, Text Field from the menu bar. Name the text field tfDateReturned and be sure that the text field is a Single Line element. On the Property inspector, click the lightning bolt icon next to the Init Value field. In the Dynamic Data dialog box, shown in Figure 6.14, choose the DateReturned value and click OK.

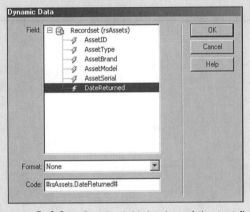

FIGURE 6.14   Set the initial value of the text field.

4. Select the new text field and click the right arrow key on your keyboard to move the cursor to the right of the text field.

5. From the menu bar, choose Insert, Form, Hidden Field. Name the new hidden field hfAssetID and click the lightning bolt icon next to the Init Value field. In the Dynamic Data dialog box, choose the AssetID and click OK.

6. We need to add a submit button for each record. Place the cursor to the right of the new hidden field and choose Insert, Form, Button from the menu bar. Name the button **btUpdate**.

   With the form, dynamic text field, dynamic hidden field, and button in place, we can now apply the Update Record server behavior, which will change the entered value for the specific record whenever the Submit button is clicked.

DON'T FORGET THAT HIDDEN FIELD

To update a record from the results table, Dreamweaver requires that you have a field in the form that contains the unique ID for the record. In our case, this is the AssetID. The field doesn't have to be hidden, but because we are already displaying it on the page elsewhere, it's convenient to place it in a hidden field.

7. On the Server Behaviors panel, click the plus sign and choose Update Record from the menu. In the Update Record dialog box, choose the connKrystalClearCF connection and the tbIS table. Ensure that the AssetID selects the record using the FORM.hfAssetID field and the DateReturned field gets a value from FORM.tfDateReturned text field. The Update Record dialog box should look like Figure 6.15.

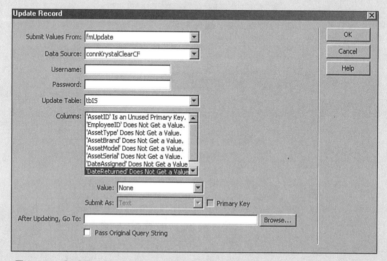

FIGURE 6.15   The Update Record dialog box configured properly.

8. Leave the After Updating, Go To field blank because we simply want the page to refresh itself after the changes have been made to the database.

9. Click OK to close the Update Record dialog box.

10. Save the page.

11. To complete the edit functionality of the IS pages, we need to create a page that allows the user to edit the asset and update the record in the database. In addition, we need a confirmation page that informs the user when the update has been completed successfully. Review the steps that we covered in Chapter 5 (Exercise 5.5[a]) and create the remaining pages on your own.

Filtering Assets with a Search Field

As the number of assets in the tbIS table grows, so will the time it takes to locate a specific record. To assist the staff in locating assets, we can add a simple search field that allows them to narrow the records that are displayed in the dataset or results table. Although it sounds complicated, it simply builds on the search capability that we already added in the Human Resources module.

Exercise 6.5(a)   Adding a Search Field to an ASP.NET Datagrid

1. The first step in creating the search element in ASP.NET is to build the form. Open the search_asset.aspx page, place your cursor after the Asset Tracking text, and press Enter.

2. With your cursor on the new line, choose Insert, Form, Form from the menu bar. This adds a form above the Add New Asset text. With the new form selected, type **fmSearch** in the Form Name field of the Property inspector.

3. Place your cursor inside the form and add a new table with 1 row, 2 columns, and a width of 400 pixels. Set the border, cell padding, and cell spacing to 0.

4. Place your cursor in the left field and type **Brand Search:**. With your cursor still in the cell and located after the Search text, choose Insert, Form, Text Field from the menu bar.

5. In the Property inspector, type **tfAssetBrand** as the name of the new text field.

6. Place your cursor in the right field of the table and choose Insert, Form, Button from the menu bar. Set the name of the button to btSearch and type **Search** in the Label field. As shown in Figure 6.16, you should now have the search field and submit buttons in your page.

Note   **WHY HTML FORM OBJECTS?**

You might be wondering why we aren't using the server-side ASP.NET form objects rather than the client-side HTML form objects. The reason comes from the fact that in ASP.NET pages, only one server-side form can be contained in each page. Because we already have a form that displays the datagrid, we have to use the client-side form objects for the search form.

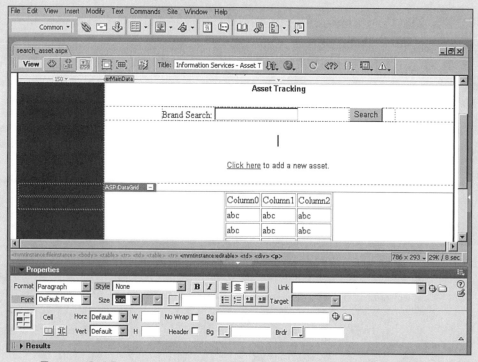

FIGURE 6.16   The Search field and button have been added to the page.

7. Now that we have the form elements in place, the next step is to modify our dataset so that it filters the results when the search feature is used. To accomplish this, double-click the dsAssets dataset in the Server Behaviors panel.

8. In the DataSet dialog box, set the Filter field to AssetBrand = Form Variable tfAssetBrand, as shown in Figure 6.17.

9. Because we want the dataset to return all rows when the Brand search is not used, we have to further modify the dataset. Click the Advanced button to switch to the advanced mode. In the SQL panel, replace the equal sign with the word LIKE. Your SQL query should now read as follows:

```
SELECT AssetID, AssetType, AssetBrand, AssetModel,
➥AssetSerial, DateReturned
FROM tbIS
WHERE AssetBrand LIKE ?
```

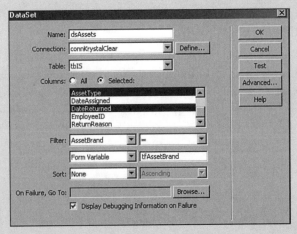

FIGURE 6.17 Modify the existing the dataset to filter the records.

10. Select the @AssetBrand parameter and click the Edit button. In the Edit Parameter dialog box, find the last set of double-quotes and place a **%** between them. This sets the default value of the parameter to all records. When the page loads and no variable is passed via the search form, all records are displayed.

11. Click OK to close the Edit Parameter dialog box and then click OK to apply the changes to the dataset.

12. Save the page.

Exercise 6.5(b) Adding a Search Field to a ColdFusion Results Table

1. Open the search_asset.cfm page, place your cursor after the Asset Tracking text, and press Enter.

2. With your cursor on the new line, choose Insert, Form from the menu bar. This adds a new form above the results table. With the new form selected, type **fmSearch** in the Form Name field of the Property inspector.

3. Place your cursor inside the form and add a new table with 1 row, 2 columns, and a width of 400 pixels. Set the border, cell padding, and cell spacing to 0.

4. Place your cursor in the left field and type **Brand Search:**. With your cursor still in the cell and located after the Search text, choose Insert, Form, Text Field from the menu bar.

5. In the Property inspector, type **tfAssetBrand** as the name of the new text field.

6. Place your cursor in the right field of the table and choose Insert, Form, Button from the menu bar. Set the name of the button to btSearch and type **Search** in the Label field. As shown in Figure 6.18, you should now have the search field and submit buttons in your page.

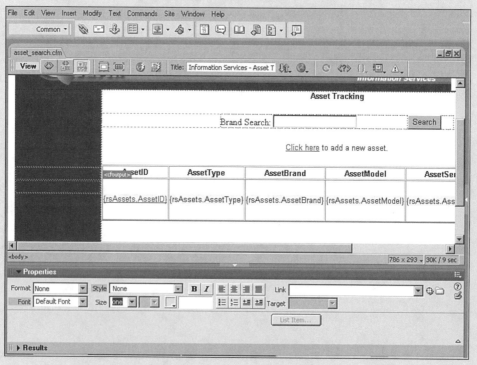

FIGURE 6.18   Your page now contains a Search field and button.

7. Now that we have the form elements in place, the next step is to modify our recordset so that it filters the results when the search feature is used. To accomplish this, double-click the rsAssets dataset in the Server Behaviors panel.

8. In the Recordset dialog box, set the Filter field to AssetBrand = Form Variable tfAssetBrand, as shown in Figure 6.19.

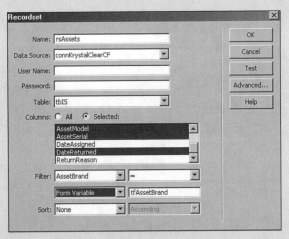

FIGURE 6.19   Modify the recordset to filter the records.

9. Because we want the recordset to return all rows when the Brand search is not used, we have to further modify the dataset. Click the Advanced button to switch to the advanced mode. In the SQL panel, replace the equal sign with the word LIKE. Your SQL query should now read as follows:

```
SELECT AssetID, ASsetType, AssetBrand, AssetModel,
➥AssetSerial, DateReturned
FROM tbIS
WHERE AssetBrand LIKE '#FORM.tfAssetBrand#'
```

10. Select the FORM.tfAssetBrand parameter and click the Edit button. In the Edit Parameter dialog box, set the default value to % and click OK.

11. Click OK to close the Edit Parameter dialog box and then click OK to apply the changes to the recordset.

12. Save the page.

Testing the Application

Again, the last step in creating this module is to try it out and make sure everything works. To test the module, we need to add a few records to the table and then test the search feature to be sure that it returns the correct results. In addition, we need to modify a record using the quick edit feature in the results. Finally, we can test the Asset ID link to guarantee that it allows the staff to edit the full record.

Exercise 6.6   Testing the Application in ASP.NET and ColdFusion

1. Open Internet Explorer and type **search_asset.cfm** if you are developing for ColdFusion or **search_asset.aspx** if you are developing for ASP.NET. The Asset Tracking page should display a list of any assets that are in the tbIS table. Because you probably don't have any assets entered yet, click the link to add a new asset.

2. In the Add New Asset page, complete the fields for a sample record and click the Submit button. The application should add the information to the database and redirect you to the confirmation page.

3. On the confirmation page, click the link to the Asset Search page. As shown in Figure 6.20, when the Asset Tracking page loads, it should display the record that you just added.

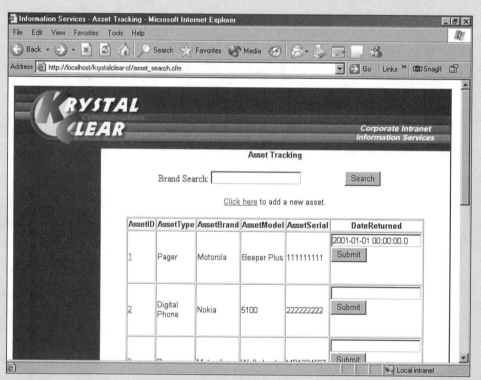

FIGURE 6.20   The asset has been added to the database.

4. Add a second record to your table with a different brand. Return to the Asset Tracking page and both assets should be visible. In the Search field, type the brand of one of the assets and click Search. As shown in Figure 6.21, the results should now only display the record that corresponds with the brand you entered.

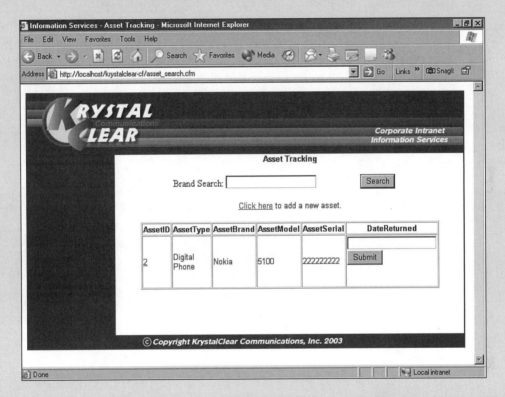

FIGURE 6.21   The results have been filtered by brand.

5. If you are developing ColdFusion pages, modify the Date Returned field and click the Submit button. The record should reflect the updated change.

6. If you are developing for ASP.NET, click the Edit button and type a new value in the Date Returned field. Click the Apply button and the record is updated.

7. Click the AssetID link for any record and ensure that you are able to edit the full record as planned.

Summary

By building this module, you learned how to expand on the functionality of a search and results page. In addition, you saw how easy it is to create a results page that allows the user to easily update a single field in the table.

In the next chapter, we will develop the Page Management module, which enhances the skills you have learned thus far by showing you how easily you can delete records from the database. In addition, the next chapter demonstrates how to apply several security measures to keep unauthorized visitors from accessing pages.

CHAPTER 7

CREATING THE DEPARTMENTAL PAGE MANAGEMENT SYSTEM

The third module that KrystalClear has asked us to design is a content management system for the departmental pages that make up the intranet. KrystalClear would like each department to have an internal site that is part of the intranet that allows the employees of the company to view information about the department and access information that is pertinent to the role each department plays in the company. In addition, KrystalClear has requested that only those designated by a manager have access to edit the pages.

To accomplish this task, we need to create a set of pages that allows the user to manage the pages that compose his departmental intranet site. These pages include a page manager that allows the user to see what pages are currently part of the site and a set of add, edit, and delete pages that allows the user to manage his site content.

In this chapter, you will do the following:

- Create a page that displays a list of departmental pages based on the what department the user is a member of
- Build a set of pages that allows the user to add, edit, and delete pages from the database
- Learn how to apply session variables to a page
- Implement a security process that only allows authorized users to edit pages

Reviewing the Database Table Structure

Let's look again at the structure of our database table before we dive into building the pages. The database table used for the Page Management module of the intranet is tbPageMgmt table. The structure of the tbPageMgmt table, shown in Figure 7.1, consists of eleven fields, which include the unique PageID, what department the pages are for, fields for hyperlinks to other pages, and a section for the main text of the page.

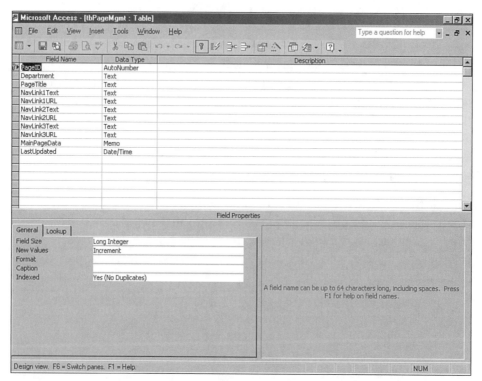

FIGURE 7.1   The structure of the tbPageMgmt table.

In addition, each record includes a timestamp that updates each time the page is updated so that users can see when the page was changed and make sure that their pages are maintained on a timely basis.

Creating the Page Management Template

As with the other modules, our first step is to create a template for the page management pages so that each page looks the same in layout and formatting. Later in the chapter, you will see how beneficial using templates can be when it comes to applying changes to a group of pages that are based on the same template.

Exercise 7.1(a)   Creating the Template Page for ASP.NET

1. In Dreamweaver, open the template created for the Human Resources module. The HR template should be located at C:\Inetpub\wwwroot\KrystalClear-ASP\Templates\intranet_template_hr.dwt.aspx.

2. From the menu bar, choose File, Save As Template.

3. In the Save As Template dialog box, choose the KrystalClear-ASP site, name the file intranet_template_pm.dwt, and click Save.

4. Click the header image that contains the KrystalClear Communications text. In the Src field of the property inspector, change the source of this image from ../images/kc_logo_intranet_hr.jpg to ../images/kc_logo_intranet_pm.jpg. As shown in Figure 7.2, the image should now display the IS logo.

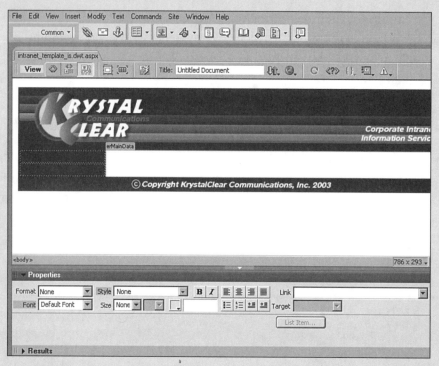

FIGURE 7.2   The template has been updated for the page manager.

5. Save the page.

Exercise 7.1(b)   Building the Template for the ColdFusion IS Module

1. In Dreamweaver, open the template created for the Human Resources module. The HR template should be located at C:\Inetpub\wwwroot\KrystalClear-CF\ Templates\intranet_template_hr.dwt.cfm.

2. From the menu bar, choose File, Save As Template.

3. In the Save As Template dialog box, choose the KrystalClear-CF site, name the file intranet_template_pm.dwt, and click Save.

4. Click the header image that contains the KrystalClear Communications text. In the Src field of the property inspector, change the source of this image from ../images/kc_logo_intranet_hr.jpg to ../images/ kc_logo_intranet_pm.jpg.

5. Save the page.

Creating the Page Manager

The main interface for the Page Management module is the page manager. Much like the asset management module, this page displays the records that exist in the table and provides links that allow the user to add and edit the pages. The Page Management module, however, includes the ability to delete pages that the staff member feels should no longer be part of the site.

One additional feature that is included in the page manager is a security protocol. If a user attempts to access the page manager but her HR profile does not indicate that she is allowed to edit pages, instead of accessing the page manager, she receives a message saying that she is not authorized. In addition, if she is approved to edit pages, the only pages displayed in the page manager are those that are part of the departmental site that she works for. In other words, the IS staff sees only those pages that are part of the IS pages and the HR staff only sees the pages that are part of their site.

Before we address the security issues, let's start by building the interface that displays the available pages.

Exercise 7.2(a)   Creating the Page Manager in ASP.NET

1. From the menu bar, choose File, New. In the New Document window, click the Templates tab. Select the KrystalClear-ASP site in the Templates For panel and then choose intranet_template_pm. Click Create.

2. In the new page, replace the Untitled Document text in the Title field of the Document toolbar with Intranet – Page Management. Save the page as page_manager.aspx.

3. Place your cursor in the erMainData region and click the Center button on the Property inspector. Type **We're sorry. You are not authorized to edit intranet pages.** Press Enter. Reformat the text using the HeaderText style.

   This text will be displayed if the user does not have the appropriate permission to use the page manager.

4. On the new line, type **Page Manager** and press Enter. Highlight the new text and reformat it using the HeaderText style.

5. On the line below the Page Manager text, type **Click here to add a new page.**, highlight the Click Here text and link it to add_page.aspx. Reformat the entire line of text using the BodyText style. Your page should now look like Figure 7.3.

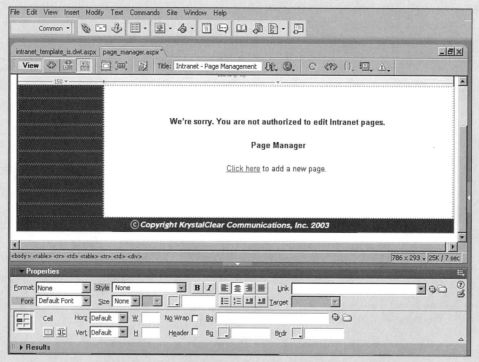

FIGURE 7.3   The page with the appropriate text included.

6. The next step is to create a dataset that contains the pages that make up the intranet. This dataset, however, is different from those that we have created in previous chapters because it limits the records it contains to those that match a value stored in a session variable (which we will create a little later). Open the Server Behaviors panel and click the plus button. Choose DataSet from the menu.

7. Choose the Simple view of the DataSet dialog box and name the dataset **dsPages**. Choose the connKrystalClearASP connection and the tbPageMgmt table. In the Columns panel, select the Department, PageID, and PageTitle fields. Create a filter that seeks records where Department equals the Session Variable sessDepartment. The RecordSet dialog box should now look like Figure 7.4.

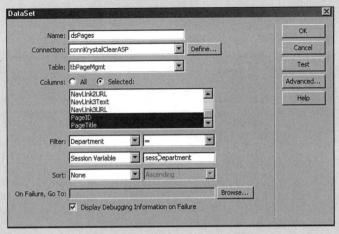

FIGURE 7.4   The dsPages dataset filters records based on a session variable.

8. Click OK to close the DataSet dialog box.

9. Now that we have the dataset, let's display the contents on the page. Place your cursor below the Page Manager text, click the plus sign on the Server Behaviors panel, and choose DataGrid.

10. In the DataGrid dialog box, set the ID to dgPages and choose the dsPages dataset. Choose to display all records and organize the columns in the following order:

PageID

Department

PageTitle

11. The next step is to turn the contents of the PageTitle field into a hyperlink that, when clicked, allows the user to edit the page. Select the PageTitle field, click the Change Column Type button, and choose Hyperlink from the menu.

12. In the Hyperlink Column dialog box, shown in Figure 7.5, change the Data Field value in the Hyperlink Text section to PageTitle and change the Data Field in the Linked Page section to PageID. Click the Browse button and type **edit_page.aspx** in the File Name field of the Select File dialog box.

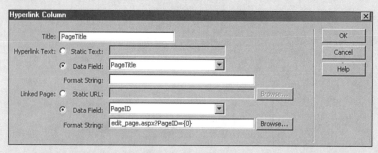

FIGURE 7.5   The dgPages datagrid displays all the pages in the dsPages dataset.

13. Click OK to close the Select File dialog box. Click OK again to close the Hyperlink Column dialog box.

14. Now that we have a link to the edit page, we need to create another link to a page that allows the user to delete the record if it should no longer be included in his site. To do this, click the plus sign in the Columns panel and choose Hyperlink from the menu.

15. In the Hyperlink Column dialog box, type **Delete** as the title and choose the Static Text radio button. Type **Delete** in the Static Text field.

16. In the Data Field drop-down list in the Linked Page section, choose PageID.

17. Click the Browse button, type **delete_page.aspx** in the File Name field, and click OK.

18. Click OK to close the Hyperlink Column dialog box and click OK one more time to close the DataGrid dialog box.

19. Save the page.

Exercise 7.2(b)   Creating the Page Manager in ColdFusion

1. From the menu bar, choose File, New. In the New Document window, click the Templates tab. Select the KrystalClear-CF site in the Templates For panel and then choose intranet_template_pm. Click Create.

2. In the new page, replace the Untitled Document text in the Title field of the Document toolbar with Page Management. Save the page as page_manager.cfm.

3. Place your cursor in the erMainData region and click the Center button on the Property inspector. Type **We're sorry. You are not authorized to edit intranet pages.** and press Enter. Reformat the text using the HeaderText style.

   This text will be displayed if the user does not have the appropriate permission to use the page manager.

4. On the new line, type **Page Manager** and press Enter. Highlight the new text and reformat it using the HeaderText style.

5. On the line below the Page Manager text, type **Click here to add a new page.**, highlight the Click Here text, and link it to add_page.cfm. Reformat the entire line of text using the BodyText style.

6. The next step is to create a recordset that contains the pages that make up the intranet. This recordset, however, is different from those that we have created in previous chapters because it limits the records it contains to those that match a value stored in a session variable (which we will create a little later). Open the Server Behaviors panel and click the plus button. Choose RecordSet from the menu.

7. Choose the Simple view of the RecordSet dialog box and name the recordset **rsPages**. Choose the connKrystalClearCF connection and the tbPageMgmt table. In the Columns panel, select the Department, PageID, and PageTitle fields. Create a filter that seeks records where Department equals the Session Variable sessDepartment. The Recordset dialog box should now look like Figure 7.6.

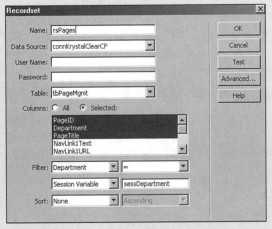

FIGURE 7.6   The rsPages recordset filters records based on a session variable.

8. Click OK to close the Recordset dialog box.

9. We need to display the assets on the page. Place your cursor on the bottom blank line of your page and insert a new table that has 2 rows, 4 columns, and a width of 425 pixels. Set the border, cell padding, and cell spacing to 1.

10. In the top-left cell, type **PageID**. Press Tab and type **Department**. Press Tab again and type **PageTitle**. Leave the top-right cell empty.

11. Select the top row of the table by placing your cursor over the left border of the top-left cell and clicking. In the Property inspector, choose the HeaderText style and click the Align Center button. In the W field of the Property inspector, type **25%**.

12. Open the Bindings panel by choosing Window, Bindings from the menu bar. Click the plus sign next to the rsPages recordset to display the fields that are available. Drag the PageID binding and drop it in the lower-left cell under the PageID header cell. Drag the other corresponding data bindings to the field under their header. Your page should now look like Figure 7.7.

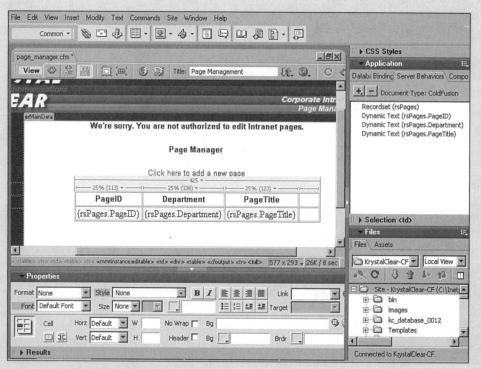

FIGURE 7.7   Your page with the table and data placeholders.

13. The next step is to turn the contents of the PageTitle field into a hyper-link that, when clicked, allows the user to edit the page. Select the PageTitle data placeholder and type **edit_page.cfm** in the Link field of the Property inspector. Click the folder icon next to the Link field and click the Parameters button.

14. In the Parameters dialog box, shown in Figure 7.8, type **PageID** in the Name field and click the lightning bolt icon in the far right of the Value field.

FIGURE 7.8   Pass the PageID through the URL to the edit page.

15. Choose PageID in the Dynamic Data dialog box and click OK. Click OK to close the Select File dialog box.

16. Now that we have a link to the edit page, we need to create one other link to a page that allows the user to delete the record if it should no longer be included in the site. To do this, type **Delete** in the lower-right cell of the table.

17. Highlight the Delete text and type **delete_page.cfm** in the Link field of the Property inspector.

18. As we did with the edit link, we need to pass the PageID to the delete page. Click the folder icon next to the Link field and create the exact same parameter that we created for the edit field.

19. Lastly, we need to repeat the region as we have done in past exercises. Select the bottom row of the table and click the plus sign on the Server Behaviors panel. From the menu, choose Repeat Region and choose to display all records from the rsPages recordset. With the links in place, your pages should look like Figure 7.9

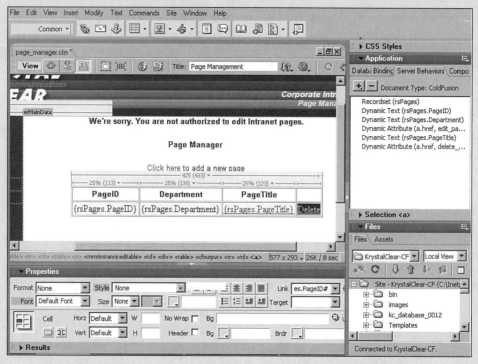

FIGURE 7.9   The page manager with the edit and delete links.

20. Save the page.

Building Add, Edit, and Delete Pages

The heart of any content management system is the ability to add, edit, and delete content from it. If users can manage their own pages, they don't have to rely on a single Web developer or the Information Services department to do the updating for them. This allows the pages to changed at the staff member's convenience, which results in pages that contain more up-to-date content.

Adding Pages to the Table

By now, you should feel comfortable with creating pages that add records to the database. With the use of Dreamweaver's Record Insertion Form application object, you can create the two pages necessary to add data to the appropriate table. Because we have covered this process in Chapter 5, "Creating the

Human Resources Management System," and Chapter 6, "Creating the Information Services Asset Management System," the exercise for creating these pages will be the short form that covers only what is unique to this module.

PREVIOUS EXERCISES ON ADDING PAGES

If you need a refresher on how to build pages that add data to the database, check out Exercises 5.2 and 6.2.

There is one unique element of our page, however, in the fact that the page populates a hidden field from the sessDepartment session variable. We do this because we don't want users creating pages for other departments, so drawing from the session variable ensures that the page is related to the appropriate department.

Exercise 7.3(a)   Creating Pages for Adding Content in ASP.NET

1. Create a new page using the Page Management template. Set the page title to Page Management – Add Page and add the **Add Page** text to the erMainData region. Save the page as add_page.aspx.

2. Using the Record Insertion Form application object, add a form to your page that adds a new record to the database. The form should include all of the fields in the tbPageMgmt table except PageID and LastUpdated and should redirect to page_added.aspx on success. Place the form fields in the following order:

PageTitle

MainPageData

NavLink1Text

NavLink1URL

NavLink2Text

NavLink2URL

NavLink3Text

NavLink3URL

Department

The Department field should display as a hidden field. With the form inserted, your page should look like Figure 7.10.

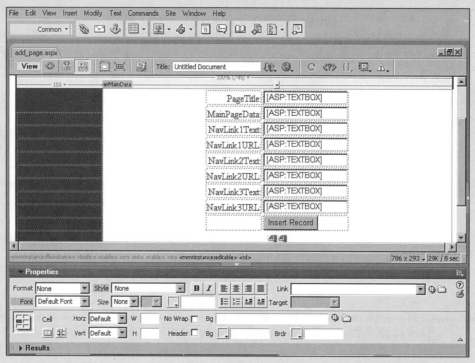

FIGURE 7.10   The page now contains the elements necessary to update a page.

3. Click the Department hidden field and type **<%# session ("sessDepartment") %>** in the Value field. This draws the value of the user's department from the session variable and allows it to be entered in the appropriate field.

4. Save the page.

5. Create an additional page that lets the user know that the page has been added to the database and includes a link back to the page manager.

6. Save it as page_added.aspx.

Exercise 7.3(b)   Creating Pages for Adding Content in ColdFusion

1. Create a new page using the Page Management template. Set the page title to Page Management – Add Page and add the **Add Page** text to the erMainData region. Save the page as add_page.cfm.

2. Using the Record Insertion Form application object, add a form to your page that adds a new record to the database. The form should include

all of the fields in the tbPageMgmt table except PageID and
LastUpdated and should redirect to page_added.cfm after inserting.
Place the form fields in the following order:

PageTitle

MainPageData

NavLink1Text

NavLink1URL

NavLink2Text

NavLink2URL

NavLink3Text

NavLink3URL

Department

The Department field should display as a hidden field.

3. Click the Department hidden field and type **<cfoutput>#Session.sess Department#</cfoutput>** in the Value field. This draws the value of the user's department from the session variable and allows it to be entered in the appropriate field.

4. Save the page.

5. Create an additional page that lets the user know that the page has been added to the database and includes a link back to the page manager.

6. Save it as page_added.cfm.

Editing Pages

Now that we can display pages in the page manager and add new pages, the next step is to provide the ability to edit the existing pages. Recall that when we created the page manager, we linked the page title so that, when clicked, users could edit that particular page. Because that link passes the PageID in the URL, our edit page can determine which page should be made available for edit.

Because we covered the building of these pages in-depth in Chapters 5 and 6, we'll just cover the basics that are unique to this application in the following exercises.

Note **PREVIOUS EXERCISES ON PAGES FOR EDITING RECORDS**

If you need a refresher on how to build pages that edit records stored in the database, check out Exercise 5.5.

Exercise 7.4(a)   Creating Pages for Editing Content in ASP.NET

1. Create a new page using the Page Management template. Set the page title to Page Management – Edit Page and add the **Edit Page** text to the erMainData region. Save the page as edit_page.aspx.

2. Create a new dataset using the Simple view. Name the dataset **dsPageUpdates** and draw all fields from the tbPageMgmt table. Set a filter on the page that only draws records where the PageID field equals the URL Parameter PageID.

3. With the dataset in place, use the Record Update Form application object to add a form to your page for editing the appropriate record. Choose to update the tbPageMgmt table and select the record from the dsPageUpdates dataset. Use the PageID field as the unique key column and redirect the user to page_updated.aspx on success. Set your form fields up according to the values shown in Table 7.1.

TABLE 7.1   The Values for Your Form Fields

COLUMN	LABEL	DISPLAY AS	SUBMIT AS
PageTitle	Page Title:	Text Field	WChar
MainPageData	Main Page Data:	Text Field	WChar
NavLink1Text	NavLink1Text:	Text Field	WChar
NavLink1URL	NavLink1URL:	Text Field	WChar
NavLink2Text	NavLink2Text:	Text Field	WChar
NavLink2URL	NavLink2URL:	Text Field	WChar
NavLink3Text	NavLink3Text:	Text Field	WChar
NavLink3URL	NavLink3URL:	Text Field	WChar
LastUpdated		Hidden Field	Date
Department		Hidden Field	WChar

4. Click the LastUpdated column and type **<%# Now() %>** in the Default Value field. This sets the field to the current date and time and updates the field with the date and time of the update.

5. Click the Department column and type **<%# session("sessDepartment") %>** in the Default Value field and click OK. This draws the value from the user's department session value and ensures that the page is associated with the correct department.

6. Save the page.

7. Create an additional page that lets the user know that the page has been added to the database and includes a link back to the page manager. Save it as page_updated.aspx.

Exercise 7.4(b)   Creating Pages for Editing Content in ColdFusion

1. Create a new page using the Page Management template. Set the page title to Page Management – Edit Page and add the **Edit Page** text to the erMainData region. Save the page as edit_page.cfm.

2. Create a new recordset using the Simple view. Name the recordset **rsPageUpdates** and draw all fields from the tbPageMgmt table. Set a filter on the page that only draws records where the PageID field equals the URL Parameter PageID.

3. With the recordset in place, use the Record Update Form application object, shown in Figure 7.11, to add a form to your page for editing the appropriate record.

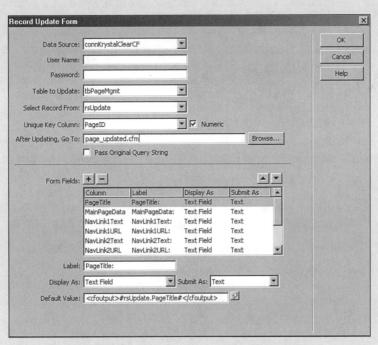

FIGURE 7.11   The Record Update Form dialog box allows you to create a form for editing your record.

4. Choose to update the tbPageMgmt table and select the record from the rsPageUpdates recordset. Use the PageID field as the unique key column and redirect the user to page_updated.cfm after updating. Set your form fields up according to the values shown in Table 7.2.

TABLE 7.2   The Values for Your Form Fields

COLUMN	LABEL	DISPLAY AS	SUBMIT AS
PageTitle	Page Title:	Text Field	Text
MainPageData	Main Page Data:	Text Field	Text
NavLink1Text	NavLink1Text:	Text Field	Text
NavLink1URL	NavLink1URL:	Text Field	Text
NavLink2Text	NavLink2Text:	Text Field	Text
NavLink2URL	NavLink2URL:	Text Field	Text
NavLink3Text	NavLink3Text:	Text Field	Text
NavLink3URL	NavLink3URL:	Text Field	Text
LastUpdated		Hidden Field	Date
Department		Hidden Field	Text

5. Click the LastUpdated column and type **#Now()#** in the Default Value field. This sets the field to the current date and time and updates the field with the date and time of the update.

6. Click the Department column and type **#Session.sessDepartment#** in the Default Value field. This draws the value from the user's department session value and ensures that the page is associated with the correct department.

7. Save the page.

8. Create an additional page that lets the user know that the page has been added to the database and includes a link back to the page manager. Save it as page_updated.cfm.

Deleting Pages

Up to this point, each of our applications has demonstrated how to add and edit content stored in the database tables. One other feature that we need to add to the page manager, however, is the ability to remove pages that are no longer necessary.

Although the process is similar to adding and editing pages, there is an extra step. Because deleting a record is permanent, we have to build a page that requires the user to confirm that he definitely wants the record removed from the database. After he makes that confirmation, the Delete Record server behavior takes over and the user receives a message confirming that the record has been removed.

Exercise 7.5(a)   Creating Pages That Delete Content in ASP.NET

1. Create a new page using the Page Management template. Set the page title to Page Management – Delete Page and add the **Delete Page** text to the erMainData region. Save the page as delete_page.aspx.

2. Create a new dataset using the Simple view. Name the dataset **dsPageDelete** and draw only the PageID and the PageTitle fields from the tbPageMgmt table. Set a filter on the page that only draws records where the PageID field equals the URL Parameter PageID.

3. Place your cursor on a new line below the Delete Page text and type **Click here to confirm the deletion of:** and press Enter.

4. Switch to the Bindings panel and click the plus sign next to the dsPageDelete dataset. Drag the PageTitle binding onto the new line just below the text you just typed.

5. Highlight the Click Here text and click the folder next to the Link field in the Property inspector. In the File Name field, type **apply_delete.aspx** and click the Parameters button. In the Parameters dialog box, add a parameter with the name PageID and set the value equal to the PageID binding by clicking the lightning bolt icon. Click OK to close the Parameters dialog box and click OK again to close the Select File dialog box.

6. Save the page.

7. Create a page from the template and type **Applying delete** in the erMainData region. Apply the Delete Record server behavior by clicking the plus sign on the Server Behaviors panel and choosing Delete Record.

8. In the Delete Record dialog box, shown in Figure 7.12, have the system check to see if the record's primary key value is defined. Choose the connKrystalClearASP connection, the tbPageMgmt table, and PageID as the primary key column. Redirect the user to page_manager.aspx after the page has been deleted.

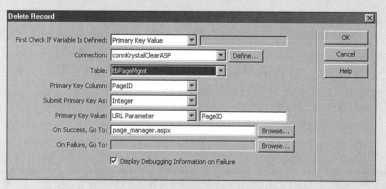

FIGURE 7.12   Configure the Delete Record dialog box.

9. Save the page as apply_delete.aspx.

Exercise 7.5(b)   Creating Pages that Delete Content in ColdFusion

1. Create a new page using the Page Management template. Set the page title to Page Management – Delete Page and add the **Delete Page** text to the erMainData region. Save the page as delete_page.cfm.

2. Create a new recordset using the Simple view. Name the recordset **rsPageDelete** and draw only the PageID and the PageTitle fields from the tbPageMgmt table. Set a filter on the page that only draws records where the PageID field equals the URL Parameter PageID.

3. Place your cursor on a new line below the Delete Page text and type **Click here to confirm the deletion of:** and press Enter.

4. Switch to the Bindings panel and click the plus sign next to the rsPageDelete dataset. Drag the PageTitle binding onto the new line just below the text you just typed. With the binding in place, your page should look like Figure 7.13.

5. Highlight the Click Here text and click the folder next to the Link field in the Property inspector. In the File Name field, type **apply_delete.cfm** and click the Parameters button. In the Parameters dialog box, add a parameter with the name PageID and set the value equal to the PageID binding by clicking the lightning bolt icon. Click OK to close the Parameters dialog box and click OK again to close the Select File dialog box.

6. Save the page.

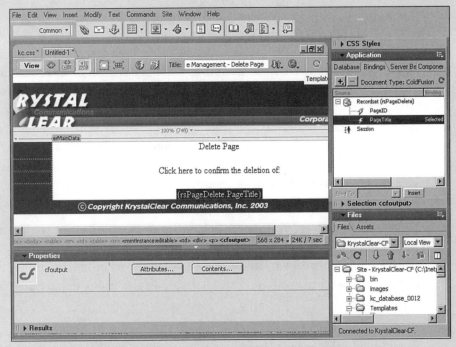

FIGURE 7.13   The beginnings of your delete confirmation page.

7. Create a page from the template and type **Applying delete** in the erMainData region. Apply the Delete Record server behavior by clicking the plus sign on the Server Behaviors panel and choosing Delete Record.

8. In the Delete Record dialog box, shown in Figure 7.14, have the system check to see if the record's primary key value is defined. Choose the connKrystalClearCF connection, the tbPageMgmt table, and PageID as the primary key column. Redirect the user to page_manager.cfm after the page has been deleted.

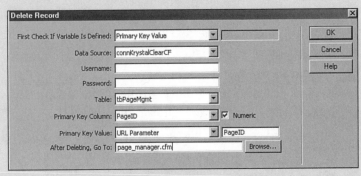

FIGURE 7.14   The Delete Record dialog box allows you to determine when a record should be deleted.

9. Save the page as apply_delete.cfm.

Securing the Pages

The last feature that we need to add to the Page Management module addresses security. KrystalClear has requested that only specific members of a department be able to make changes to the intranet pages. This means two things for us as developers. First, there must be some sort of security that keeps unauthorized staff from accessing the functions of the page manager and second, we must make certain that the departmental staff authorized to edit can only edit the pages that pertain to their department.

To accomplish this, we need to use a combination of session datasets/recordsets, session variables, and server behaviors to customize the content that is visible to the staff member. When the user logs in to the intranet, the system should set two session variables: one that carries whether the user is allowed to edit pages (sessEditPages) and one that carries the user's department name (sessDepartment).

Because these elements are session-based, they carry the data from page to page and last while the user is logged on to the intranet. With these session variables, we can determine whether the user is allowed to access the page manager and then, if the user is authorized, we can use the dataset/recordset we created earlier to customize the page and only show those records that are associated with the value stored in the sessDepartment session variable.

Exercise 7.6(a)   Securing Pages in ASP.NET

1. Open the page_manager.aspx page.

2. We're going to have Dreamweaver do some coding for us and then modify that code to meet our need. Switch to the Split Code and Design view and highlight the text that says, "We're sorry. You are not authorized to edit intranet pages."

3. On the Server Behaviors panel, click the plus sign and choose Show Region, If DataSet Is Empty. In the Show If DataSet Is Empty dialog box, choose the dsPages dataset and click OK.

   Dreamweaver adds a block of code before the highlighted text that checks to see if the recordset is empty and displays the text only if the dsPages dataset has no records. We don't really care about the recordset. We want to know if the session variable sessEditPages is empty, so we're going to modify the code a bit.

4. Find the following line of code:

```
<MM:If runat="server" Expression='<%# (dsPages.RecordCount = 0) %>'>.
```

Modify this code so it looks like the following:

```
<MM:If runat="server" Expression='<%# (session("sessEditPages") <>
➥"True") %>'>.
```

> This block of code now says, "if the sessEditPages session variable is set to anything other than 'True', show this text."

5. In the Design view, highlight the Page Manager text and everything below it. Click the plus sign on the Server Behaviors panel and choose Show Region, If Dataset Is Empty. Choose the dsPages dataset again and click OK.

6. Find the following line of code:

```
<MM:If runat="server" Expression='<%# (dsPages.RecordCount = 0) %>'>.
```

Modify this code to look like the following line of code:

```
<MM:If runat="server" Expression='<%# (session("sessEditPages") =
➥"True") %>'>.
```

> This block of code now says, "if the sessEditPages session variable is set to 'True', show this text." Basically, we have defined two regions on our page: one that is visible to authorized users and one that is visible to unauthorized users. As shown in Figure 7.15, Dreamweaver has placed MM:If tags around the two regions of code. Don't worry that the Show If Dataset Is Empty server behavior is missing from the Server Behaviors panel. Because the code is now custom code, Dreamweaver removed it from the Server Behaviors panel.

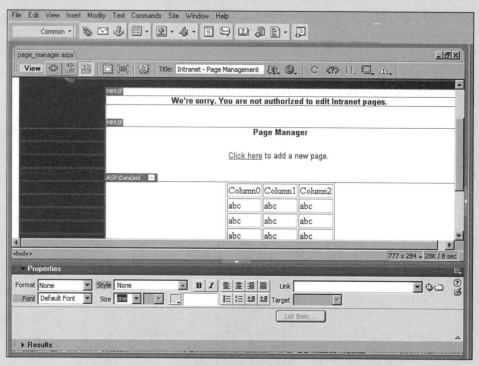

FIGURE 7.15   Because these regions are only visible under certain circumstances, they are surrounded by MM:If tags.

7. Save the page.

Exercise 7.6(b)   Securing Pages in ColdFusion

1. Open the page_manager.cfm page.

   Switch to the Split Code and Design view and insert the following block of code on the first six lines of your page:

```
<cfapplication name="KrystalClear-PM"
ClientManagement="No"
SessionManagement="Yes"
SessionTimeout="#CreateTimeSpan(0,0,30,0)#"
SetClientCookies="Yes">
<cfparam name="session.sessEditPages" default="False">
```

The first five lines of this block of code enables our page's to process session variables. The last line looks to see if the sessEditPages session variable exits and creates it with the default value of "False" if it does not already exist. If it does exist, however, this line of code does nothing.

APPLYING THIS CODE TO ALL COLDFUSION PAGES

As you will see in the next chapter, there is a way to enable session variables without having to add this code block to every page. For locking down the one page of our page manager, however, we'll go ahead and use the code block.

2. We're going to have Dreamweaver create some code for us and we'll customize it to meet our needs. Highlight the text that says, "We're sorry. You are not authorized to edit intranet pages."

3. On the Server Behaviors panel, click the plus sign and choose Show Region, If Recordset Is Empty. In the Show If Recordset Is Empty dialog box, choose the rsPages recordset and click OK.

   Dreamweaver now adds a block of code before the highlighted text that checks to see if the recordset is empty and displays the text only if the rsPages recordset has no records. We don't really care about the recordset. We want to know if the session variable sessEditPages is empty, so we're going to modify the code a bit.

4. Find the following line of code:

   ```
   <cfif rsPages.RecordCount EQ 0>
   ```

   Modify this code so it says the following:

   ```
   <cfif Session.sessEditPages NEQ "1">
   ```

   This block of code now says, "if the sessEditPages session variable is set to anything other than 'True', show this text.

5. Highlight the Page Manager" text and everything below it. Click the plus sign on the Server Behaviors panel and choose Show Region, If Recordset Is Empty. Choose the rsPages recordset again and click OK.

6. Find the following line of code:

   ```
   <cfif rsPages.RecordCount EQ 0>
   ```

   Modify this code so it says:

   ```
   <cfif Session.sessEditPages EQ "1">
   ```

This block of code now says, "if the sessEditPages session variable is set to 'True', show this text. Basically, we have defined two regions on our page: one that is visible to authorized users and one that is visible to unauthorized users. As shown in Figure 7.16, Dreamweaver has surrounded the two regions with <cfif> tags.

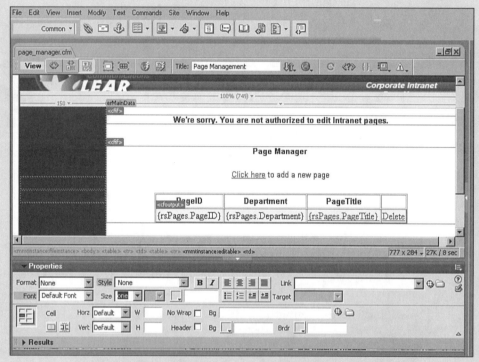

FIGURE 7.16   Because these regions are only visible under certain circumstances, they are surrounded by <cfif> tags.

7. Save the page.

Testing the Application

As with our other modules, we want to test to ensure that each element functions as expected. The page manager is a little different, however, because we have two session variables that the pages rely upon before they will function. Because we won't be integrating those session variables into the intranet application until the next chapter, we can create a single page that allows us to enter values for the session variables and test to see if everything works.

Exercise 7.7(a)   Creating a Page to Test the Application in ASP.NET

1. Create a new page based on the Page Management template. Save the page as set_session.aspx.

2. Place your cursor in the erMainData editable region and click the Align Center button on the Property inspector.

3. Switch to the Split Code view and insert a form into your page by choosing Insert, Form, Form from the menu bar. Before the > in the form tag, type **runat="server"**. Your code should now look like the following:

```
<form name="form1" method="post" action="" runat="server"></form>
```

4. Place your cursor inside the form in the Design view and insert a table into the page with 3 rows, 2 columns, and a width of 300 pixels. Set the border cell spacing and cell padding to 1.

5. Place your cursor in the top-left cell and type **sessDepartment:**. Move one cell down and type **sessEditPages:**.

6. In the top-right field, insert an asp:Textbox and set its ID to tfDepartment. Add a second asp:textbox in the cell below the first and set its ID to tfEditPages.

7. In the lower-right cell, add an asp:button. Set the button's ID to btSubmit and the Text as Set Variables. Select the button and in the Code view, add the following piece of code just before the />:

```
onClick="SetSessionVariable_Click"
```

This piece of code calls the function that sets the session variable and redirects the user to the page manager.

8. Now that we have a form in place, the next step is to create the script that builds our session variables.

9. In the Code view, create a blank line on line 2 of the code and type the following code block:

```
<script language="VB" runat="server">
Sub SetSessionVariable_Click(ByVal s As Object, ByVal e As EventArgs)
Session("sessDepartment") = Request("tfDepartment")
Session("sessEditPages") = Request("tfEditPages")
Response.Redirect("page_manager.aspx")
End Sub
</script>
```

With the code block in place, your page should look like Figure 7.17.

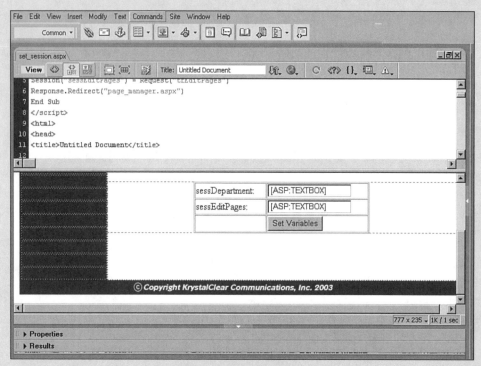

FIGURE 7.17   Your page with the session code in place.

10. Save the page.

11. To test the application, open Internet Explorer and type **http://localhost/KrystalClear-ASP/set_session.aspx** in the address bar.

12. In the set session page, type **HR** in the sessDepartment field, leave the sessEditPages field blank, and click the Set Variables button. As shown in Figure 7.18, you should be redirected to the page manager and shown the text that indicates you are not authorized.

13. Click the Back button in your browser. In the sessDepartment field, type **HR** and type **True** in the sessEditPages field (be sure that you use the proper capitalization). Now, when you click the Set Variables button, you should have access to the page manager and be able to add pages.

NETWORK LOGIN PROMPT

If you receive a request for a network login when you try to submit a username/password via the form, give the Users group on your computer Read/Execute/Write privileges to the wwwroot folder or to the root folder of you Web application and it should get rid of the network login prompt.

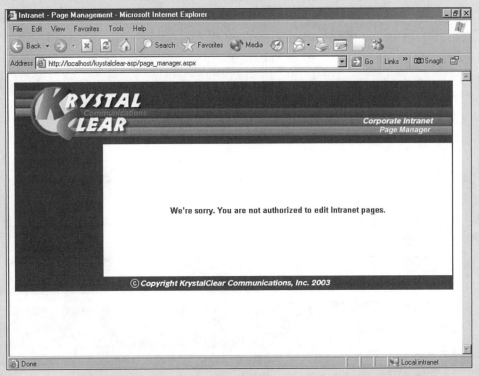

FIGURE 7.18   Because the session variable is not set to "True,"
you are shown the region for those who are not authorized.

14. Test the add, edit, and delete functionality of the module by navigating through the pages.

Exercise 7.7(b)   Creating a Page to Test the Application in ColdFusion

1. Create a new page based on the Page Management template. Save the page as set_session.cfm.

2. Place your cursor in the erMainData editable region and click the Align Center button on the Property inspector.

3. Insert a form into your page by choosing Insert, Form from the menu bar. Set the Action of the form to session_set.cfm in the Property inspector.

4. Place your cursor inside the form and insert a table into the page with 3 rows, 2 columns, and a width of 300 pixels. Set the border cell spacing and cell padding to 1.

5. Place your cursor in the top-left cell and type **sessDepartment:**. Move one cell down and type **sessEditPages:**.

6. Place your cursor in the top-right cell and choose Insert, Form, Text Field from the menu. In the Property inspector, set the name for the textbox to tfDepartment.

7. Add a second textbox in the field below the first and name it **tfEditPages**.

8. In the lower-right cell, add a button and name it btSubmit. Set the label of the button to Set Variables. Your pages should now look something like Figure 7.19.

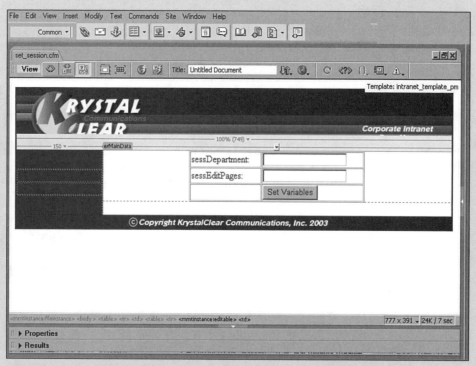

FIGURE 7.19   Your page has all the form elements to set your session variables.

9. Save the page.

10. Create a new page based on the Page Management template. In the erMainData region, type **Your session variables are set. Click here to access the page manager.**

11. Select the Click Here text and link it to page_manager.cfm.

12. In the Code view, add a new line on line 2 of your code and type the following code block:

```
<cfparam name="session.sessEditPages" default="false">
<cfparam name="session.sessDepartment" default="0">
<cfset session.sessEditPages = FORM.tfEditPages>
<cfset session.sessDepartment = FORM.tfDepartment>
```

This block of code creates the session variables and sets the values to those that were entered into the form fields.

13. Save the page as session_set.cfm.

14. To test the application, open Internet Explorer and type **http:// localhost/KrystalClear-CF/set_session.cfm** in the address bar.

15. In the set session page, type **Human Resources** in the sessDepartment field, leave the sessEditPages field blank, and click the Set Variables button. You should be redirected to the session set page where your variables are created.

16. Click the link to the page manager and you should receive the text that indicates that you are not authorized.

17. Click the Back button twice in your browser to return to the set session page. In the sessDepartment field, type **Human Resources** and type **True** in the sessEditPages field (be sure that you use the proper capitalization). Click the button to submit the form.

18. As shown in Figure 7.20, when you click the link to the page manager, you should see the page manager elements and be able to add pages.

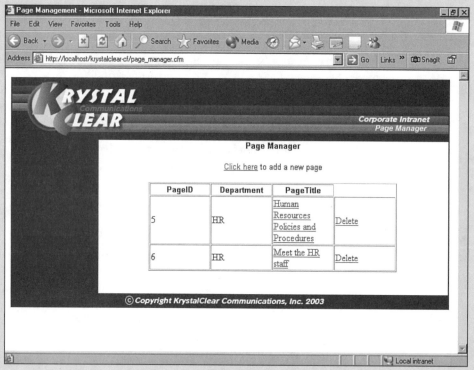

FIGURE 7.20   Because the session variable is set and matches
pages in the database, you see the page manager.

19. Test the add, edit, and delete functionality of the module by navigating through the pages.

Summary

In this chapter, you learned a bit about what it takes to build a simple content management system that allows users to add, edit, and delete pages. In addition, you learned the basics of securing a single page from unauthorized users.

In the next chapter, we will put together a front page for the intranet project and demonstrate what is involved in restricting access to an entire application. In addition, you will see how to place various elements of the modules we created in earlier chapters to use as part of the intranet.

CHAPTER 8

BUILDING THE INTRANET USER INTERFACE

Now that we have our three modules built, the next step is to build a user interface that allows the KrystalClear staff to access them. To do this, we need to create a system that allows the user to log in. The login process not only serves as an authentication tool, but also allows us to determine some information about the user, such as what department the user works in and whether he is authorized to edit departmental pages.

Based on this information, we can then build a set of pages for the intranet that contains customized content. For instance, if the user is a member of the Human Resources staff, we will only display a link to the HR employee management tool and hide the link to the IS asset management tool. In addition, if the user is authorized to edit pages, the intranet pages can display a link that allows him to access that module.

Finally, we need to create the ability to log out of the intranet so that the user can end his session.

By the end of this chapter, you will have created the following:

- A set of pages that allows the user to log in
- A front page for the intranet that displays custom content based on the user's login criteria
- A series of links to the various departmental tools that are only visible to the appropriate users
- A series of pages that allows the user to log out

Creating the Intranet Template

In order that all of our intranet pages look similar to those that we created in the earlier modules, let's build a base template that we can use for the remainder of our pages.

Exercise 8.1(a)   Creating the Template Page for ASP.NET

1. In Dreamweaver MX 2004, open the template created for the Human Resources module. The HR template should be located at C:\Inetpub\wwwroot\KrystalClear-ASP\Templates\ intranet_template_hr.dwt.aspx.

OPEN EXISTING TEMPLATE

You can also open an existing template by opening the Files panel, clicking the plus sign next to the Templates folder and double-clicking on the template name.

2. From the menu bar, choose File, Save As Template.
3. In the Save As Template dialog box, choose the KrystalClear-ASP site, name the file intranet_template_main.dwt, and click Save.
4. Click the header image that contains the KrystalClear Communications text.
5. In the Src field of the Property inspector, change the source of this image from ../images/kc_logo_intranet_hr.jpg to ../images/ kc_logo_intranet_main.jpg. As shown in Figure 8.1, the image should now display the IS logo.

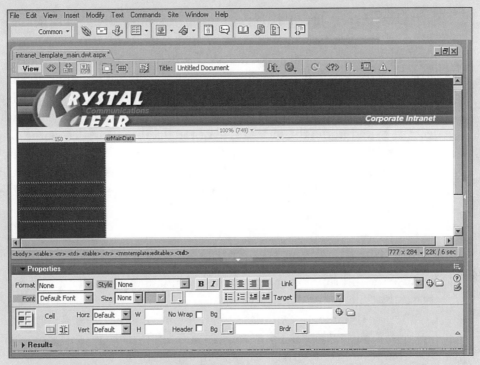

FIGURE 8.1   The template has been updated for the main intranet pages.

6. Save the page.

Exercise 8.1(b)   Building the Template for the ColdFusion IS Module

1. In Dreamweaver, open the template created for the Human Resources module. The HR template should be located at C:\Inetpub\wwwroot\ KrystalClear-CF\Templates\intranet_template_hr.dwt.cfm.

2. From the menu bar, choose File, Save As Template.

3. In the Save As Template dialog box, choose the KrystalClear-CF site, name the file intranet_template_main.dwt, and click Save.

4. Click the header image that contains the KrystalClear Communications text.

5. In the Src field of the Property inspector, change the source of this image from ../images/kc_logo_intranet_hr.jpg to ../images/ kc_logo_intranet_pm.jpg.

6. Save the page.

Logging On Users

Now that we have a page template, the next element we need to focus on is providing the KrystalClear employees with the ability to log on to the intranet. To accomplish this, we can build a form that collects the user's UserID and password. After that information is submitted, we can compare it with the records stored in the tbUserID table of the database and determine whether a record exists for the user and if the password that was submitted matches the one included in the record. If the data matches, the user is allowed to proceed into the rest of the site. If, however, the data submitted is incorrect, the user is denied access.

Analyzing the tbUserID Table

Because the information that is used to validate the login is stored in the tbUserID table, let's take a moment and look over the structure we created in Chapter 3, "Building a Database for Dynamic Applications." As shown in Figure 8.2, the tbUserID table consists of five fields that may look confusing at first glance but are relatively easy to understand.

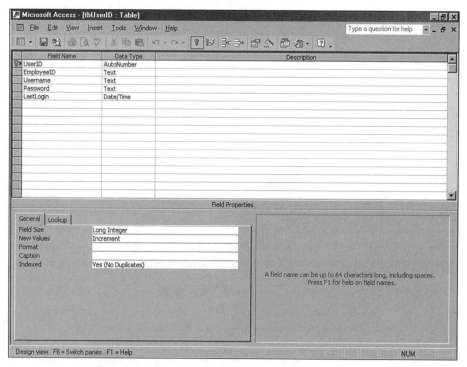

FIGURE 8.2   The structure of the tbUserID table.

The UserID field is an AutoNumber field that ensures each userID has a unique identifier. The EmployeeID corresponds with the Social Security or Tax Identification Number stored in the employee's HR record. The Username is the last name, first initial that KrystalClear uses for each employee's login. The Password field stores the user's password. Finally, the LastLogin field stores a date when the user last successfully logged in. As you will see, we can use the information stored in this field to provide the user with updates as to what has changed since her last visit.

Before we can create and test the login feature, we need to create at least one record in the tbUserID table. Remember that to have a UserID, the user *must* have a record in the tbHR table, and the EmployeeID entered in the tbUserID table *must* match an EmployeeID that already exists in the tbHR table.

Exercise 8.2   Adding Sample Users to the Database

1. Open Microsoft Access and open the kc_corporation_0493 database.

2. Open the tbHR table. You should see all the records that you added in Chapter 5, "Creating the Human Resources Management System." If you didn't enter any records in Chapter 5, create at least one record in this table by filling in the fields. In the Department field, be sure that one of your records is set to HR.

3. Take note of the EmployeeID, LastName, and FirstName fields for one of your records.

4. Close the tbHR table and open the tbUserID table. Create a new record by typing the EmployeeID that you noted in the tbHR table in the EmployeeID field. Set the Username to the user's last name and first initial. Type a password into the Password field and close the table.

5. Close Access.

BE SURE THE EMPLOYEEID IS CORRECT

Because there is a relationship between the tbUserID and tbHR tables, Access will only let you create a UserID for a record that already exists in the tbHR table. If you receive an error when trying to close the table, check to be sure that you entered the EmployeeID properly.

Creating the Login Pages

Now that we have a userID and password in the tbUserID table, we need to create the pages that allow the user to log in. The main login page consists of a form, a table, and a series of form elements. Just as our search forms did in previous chapters, when submitted, the contents of the form are compared with the records stored in the tbUserID table using a dataset/recordset. If the data submitted matches a record in the table, the user is allowed to continue using the site. If, however, the contents do not match an existing record, the user is denied access and provided with an error message.

Our login process does more than just grant access to the intranet pages, however. Because some of our modules rely upon information stored in the user's HR record, we can use this time to populate three session variables. The first session variable is the user's department, which allows us to determine what areas of the intranet the user should be able to access. The second variable is whether the user is allowed to edit the pages for his departmental intranet site. Both of these session variables can be created with the addition of a few lines of code. The final session variable stored is the date and time of the user's last login. Using this data, we can determine what information has been added to the intranet since his last visit.

The final element of the login process that we want to include is a page that confirms when the user is logged in. This page also contains a form and hidden form fields that, when submitted, updates the date field that stores the user's last login. This way, the next time the user logs in to the intranet, she will receive a completely new list of what has changed since her last login.

Exercise 8.3(a)   Creating a Login Page in ASP.NET

1. Create a new page using the Main template. Because we don't want the user to have access to any of the functionality that we will add to the template later, detach this page from the template by choosing Modify, Templates, Detach From Template from the menu bar.

2. Save the page as login.aspx.

3. Place your cursor in the main region, type **Login Page**, and press Enter. On the new line, add a new form and switch to the Split Code and Design view. Inside the form tag, type **runat="server"**. Center the new text and the form by choosing the `<td>` tag in the Tag selector and selecting Center from the Horiz menu in the Property inspector.

4. With your cursor inside the form, add a table to your page with 3 rows, 2 columns, and a width of 300 pixels. In the top-left cell, type **Username:**. In the middle-left cell, type **Password:**. Select the left column and reformat it using the BodyText style. Set the column width to 50% and click the Align Right button.

5. Place your cursor in the top-right cell and choose Insert, ASP.NET Objects, asp:textbox. Set the ID of the textbox to tfUsername and click OK. Add a second textbox in the next cell down and name it tfPassword. In the Text Mode of the second textbox, choose Password.

OPEN ASP.NET BY THE OBJECT BAR

You can also add ASP.NET objects to your page by selecting the ASP.NET option in the object bar (which is located directly underneath the menu bar) and choosing the appropriate object.

6. In the lower-right cell, insert an asp:button named btLogin. Set the text of this button to Login. With the form elements in place, your page should look like Figure 8.3.

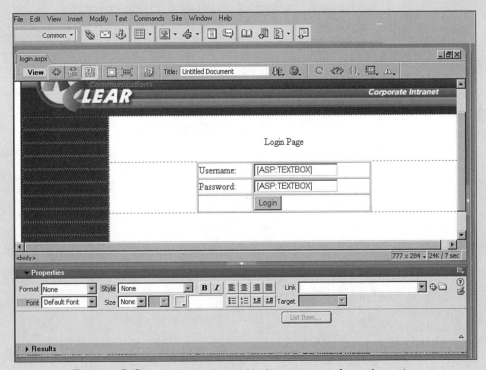

FIGURE 8.3   The login form with the necessary form elements.

7. The next step is to build a dataset that checks to see if the values submitted by the form match any records in the database. Click the plus sign on the Server Behaviors panel and choose DataSet.

8. In the DataSet dialog box, name the dataset dsLogin, choose the connKrystalClearASP connection, and the tbUserID table. Switch to the Advanced view and modify the SQL Query so it looks like this:

```
SELECT LastLogin, Password, Username, EmployeeID
FROM tbUserID
WHERE Username = ? AND Password = ?
```

Create two new parameters for the query. The first parameter should be named @Username, of the WChar type, and draw the form variable tfUsername with no default value. The second should be named @Password, of the WChar type, and draw the form variable tfPassword with no default value. When your dataset is complete, the dialog box should look like Figure 8.4.

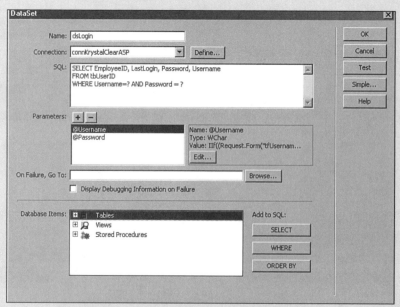

FIGURE 8.4   The completed dsLogin dataset.

9. Switch back to the Split Code and Design view and find the `</form>` tag. On a new line after the tag, add the following code block:

```
<%
if dsLogin.RecordCount > 0 then
Session("sessUserName") = Request.Form("tfUserName")
FormsAuthentication.RedirectFromLoginPage("tfUserName.value", true)
else if ((Request.Form("tfUserName"))) <> Nothing _
OR ((Request.Form("tfPassword"))) <> Nothing
response.Write("Login failed. Please try again.")
end if
%>
```

DOWNLOAD SNIPPETS

If you don't want to type in this code by hand, feel free to download the code blocks for the book in snippet form from http://www.krystalclearcommunication.com/snippets.asp.

As you will see, this block of code checks to see if the dsLogin recordset is empty (meaning that no records in the database matched the username/password combination). If the recordset is not empty, the user entered a valid username and password and is authenticated and redirected to the default.aspx page.

If, however, the dataset is empty, an invalid combination was entered and the Login Failed text is displayed.

10. Save the page.

Now that we have logged the user in, we need to update the LastLogin field that corresponds to the user's record. In addition, we need to set the sessDepartment and sessEditPages session variables so that the individual modules can tell what department the user works for and whether he is allowed to edit departmental pages.

11. Create a new page using the Main template and detach it from the template. With the cursor in the Main area, click the Align Center button and type **Thank you. Please click the button below to continue.** Press Enter.

12. Save this page as default.aspx.

13. Create a new dataset named dsUser. Using the Advanced mode, choose the connKrystalClearASP connection and create a SQL Query that looks like this:

```
SELECT tbUserID.Username, tbUserID.EmployeeID, tbHR.Department,
tbHR.EditPages, tbHR.FirstName, tbUserID.LastLogin
FROM tbUserID, tbHR
WHERE tbUserID.Username = ?  AND tbUserID.EmployeeID = tbHR.EmployeeID
```

This SQL query uses syntax in the SELECT and FROM statements called a join. A join is used to draw data from two tables rather than just one. In addition, the WHERE statement looks to see if the Username field in the tbUserID table matches a parameter and, if it does, checks to see if any of those records have the same EmployeeID.

This allows us to access an employee's HR file and UserID file when we only know his Username.

14. Create a new parameter named @Username. This parameter should be of the VarChar type and should draw from the sessUsername session variable. When completed, your dataset should look like Figure 8.5.

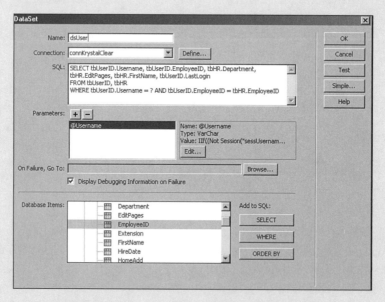

FIGURE 8.5   The completed dsUser dataset.

15. Now that we know who the user is, we can update his record. Place your cursor on the line below the Thank You text and choose Insert, Application Objects, Update Record, Record Update Form Wizard.

16. As shown in Figure 8.6, choose the connKrystalClear connection and the tbUserID table. Choose the record from the dsUser dataset, with the unique key column being EmployeeID. In the On Success, Go To field, type **intranet.aspx**. In the Form Fields panel, use the minus sign to remove all fields except the LastLogin field and change the LastLogin field to a Hidden Field. Finally, in the Default Value field, type **<%# Now()%>**. This updates the record with the current time and date.

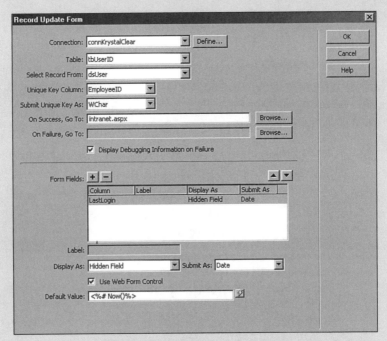

FIGURE 8.6   The Record Update Form updates the users last login.

17. Click OK to close the Record Update Form dialog box. Select the Update Record button and type **Continue** in the Label field of the Property inspector.

18. Place your cursor next to the yellow hidden field placeholders and select Insert, Form, Hidden Field from the menu bar. Name the hidden field hfDepartment. Click the lightning bolt icon next to the Value field in the Property inspector and choose the Department value from the dsUser dataset.

19. Insert an additional hidden field named hfEditPages and set it equal to the EditPages value in the dsUser dataset.

20. The last code we need to add to our page sets our sessDepartment and sessEditPages session variables when the form is submitted. Switch to the Split Code and Design view and add the following code at the top of your page on line 2 of your code:

```
<script runat="server" language="VB">
Sub Page_Load()
Session("sessDepartment")=Request("hfDepartment")
Session("sessEditPages")=Request("hfEditPages")
End Sub
</script>
```

When the page loads after the form is submitted, the session variables are updated prior to the record in the database being updated.

21. Save this page.

There is one more step we have to take to lock down our application and require a username and password to access the pages. ASP.NET uses a specific type of validation called *form validation* that must be enabled manually.

22. In Dreamweaver, open the web.config file located in the KrystalClear-ASP folder.

23. Add the following code between the `</appSettings>` tag and the `</configuration>` tag:

```
<system.web>
<customErrors mode="Off" />
<authentication mode="Forms">
<forms name="SECAUTH" loginUrl="login.aspx">
<credentials />
</forms>
</authentication>
<authorization>
<deny users="?" />
</authorization>
</system.web>
```

With this code in place, your page should look like Figure 8.7, and the KrystalClear-ASP folder will now require username and password authentication before allowing access to any page except the login.aspx page.

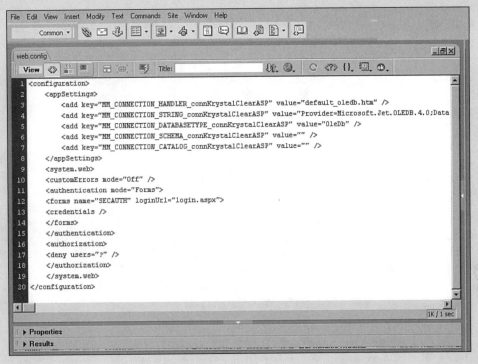

File   Edit   View   Insert   Modify   Text   Commands   Site   Window   Help

Common ▾

```
 1  <configuration>
 2      <appSettings>
 3          <add key="MM_CONNECTION_HANDLER_connKrystalClearASP" value="default_oledb.htm" />
 4          <add key="MM_CONNECTION_STRING_connKrystalClearASP" value="Provider=Microsoft.Jet.OLEDB.4.0;Data
 5          <add key="MM_CONNECTION_DATABASETYPE_connKrystalClearASP" value="OleDb" />
 6          <add key="MM_CONNECTION_SCHEMA_connKrystalClearASP" value="" />
 7          <add key="MM_CONNECTION_CATALOG_connKrystalClearASP" value="" />
 8      </appSettings>
 9      <system.web>
10      <customErrors mode="Off" />
11      <authentication mode="Forms">
12      <forms name="SECAUTH" loginUrl="login.aspx">
13      <credentials />
14      </forms>
15      </authentication>
16      <authorization>
17      <deny users="?" />
18      </authorization>
19      </system.web>
20  </configuration>
```

1K / 1 sec

▶ Properties
▶ Results

FIGURE 8.7   Your web.config with the new code that implements forms security.

24. Save the web.config page.

Exercise 8.3(b)   Creating Login Pages in ColdFusion

1. Create a new page using the Main template. Because we don't want the user to have access to any of the functionality that we will add to the template later, detach this page from the template by choosing Modify, Templates, Detach from Template from the menu bar.

2. Save the page as login.cfm.

3. Place your cursor in the main region, type **Login Page**, and press Enter. On the new line, add a new form.

4. With your cursor inside the form, add a table to your page with 3 rows, 2 columns, and a width of 300 pixels. Set the cell padding, cell spacing, and border to 1. In the top-left cell, type **Username:**. In the middle-left cell, type **Password:**.

5. Select the left column and reformat it using the BodyText style. Set the column width to 50% and click the Align Right button.

6. Place your cursor in the top-right cell and choose Insert, Form, Text Field. In the Properties inspector, set the name of the text field to tfUsername. Add a second textbox in the next cell down and name it tfPassword. In the Property inspector, set the Type field of the text field to Password.

7. In the lower-right cell, insert a button named btLogin. Set the label of this button to Login. With the form elements in place, your page should look like Figure 8.8.

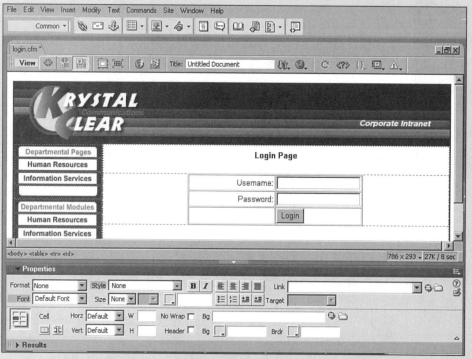

FIGURE 8.8   The login form with the necessary form elements.

8. Save the page.

The next step is to apply a server behavior that compares the data submitted in the form with that stored in the database. If the information matches, the user is logged in and redirected to a page where she receives a login validation. If, however, the data does not match, she receives a page that displays an error message.

9. In the login.cfm page, select the form and click the plus sign on the Server Behaviors panel. From the menu, choose User Authentication, Log In User.

10. In the Log In User dialog box, choose to get the input from form1 and set the Username field to tfUsername and the Password field to tfPassword.

11. Choose the connKrystalClearCF data source and the tbUserID table. Choose Username as the Username column and Password as the Password column.

12. As shown in Figure 8.9, type **validation.cfm** in the If Login Succeeds, Go to field and type **failure.cfm** in the If Login Fails, Go to field.

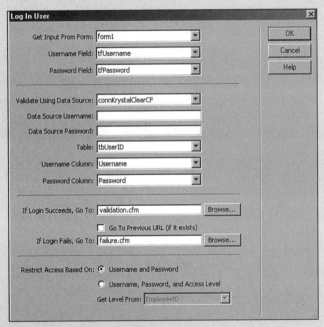

FIGURE 8.9   Complete the Log in User dialog box.

13. Click OK and save the page.

14. Create a new page based on the Main template and type **Login Failed. Please click the back button and try again.** in the editable region. Save this page as failure.cfm.

15. Create a new page based on the Main template and save the page as validation.cfm.

16. Click the plus sign on the Server Behaviors panel and choose Recordset(Query).

17. In the Recordset dialog box, name the recordset rsLogin, and choose the connKrystaClearCF connection and the tbUserID table. Switch to the Advanced view and modify the SQL Query so it looks like this:

```
SELECT tbUserID.Username, tbUserID.LastLogin,
tbUserID.UserID, tbHR.Department, tbHR.EditPages
FROM tbUserID, tbHR
WHERE tbUserID.Username = "#SESSION.MM_Username#"    AND
tbUserID.EmployeeID = tbHR.EmployeeID
```

Note   **THE MM_USERNAME SESSION VARIABLE**

When a user is successfully logged in using the Log in User server behavior, a new session variable is created that stores the person's username. This session variable, named MM_Username, travels with the user through the site and is used by Dreamweaver's authentication server behaviors to apply security to pages.

18. Create a new page parameter named SESSION.MM_Username with no default value. When your dataset is complete, the dialog box should look like Figure 8.10.

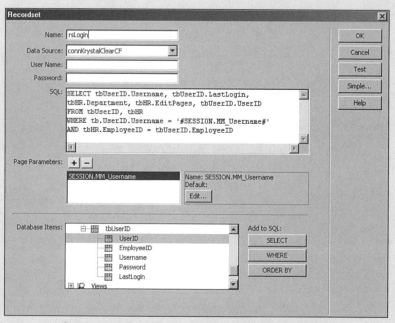

FIGURE 8.10   The completed rsLogin recordset.

19. Click OK to close the Recordset dialog box.

20. Place your cursor in the erMainData editable region and click the Align Center button. Type **Thank you. Please click the button below to continue.** Press Enter.

    Because we want to update the LastLogin field when a user logs in successfully, we need to add a form and elements that perform this action.

21. With your cursor on the bottom line, choose Insert, Application Objects, Update Record, Record Update Form Wizard. In the Record Update Form dialog box, choose the connKrystalClearCF connection and the tbUserID table. Choose to select the record from the rsLogin recordset and choose UserID as the unique key column. Redirect the user to intranet.cfm after updating the record.

22. As shown in Figure 8.11, remove all fields from the Form Fields panel except the UserID and LastLogin fields. Choose to display both these fields as hidden fields and set the Default Value of the LastLogin field to **<cfoutput>#DateFormat(Now(),"mm/dd/yyyy")#</cfoutput>**. Change the Submit As value for the LastLogin field to Date and click OK.

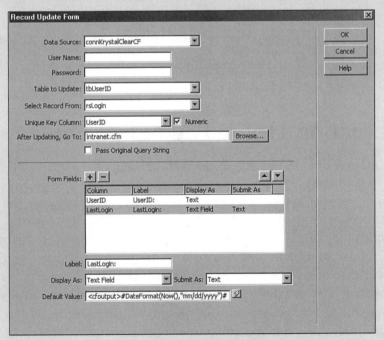

FIGURE 8.11   The Record Update Form that updates the LastLogin field.

23. Select the Submit button and change the Label to Continue in the Property inspector.

Now that the user has a way to update her record combination, the next thing we need to do is set our sessDepartment and sessEditPages session variables.

24. Switch to the Split Code and Design view and click the Thank You text. In the Code view, find the line of code that reads </cfquery> (around line 7) and add the following two lines of code directly below it:

```
<cfset Session.sessDepartment = #rsLogin.Department#>
<cfset Session.sessEditPages = #rsLogin.EditPages#>
```

25. Save the page.

    Only one more thing remains to complete the login section of the intranet. To use session variables in ColdFusion, you must first create a page within your site root that lets the ColdFusion server know that session variables are permitted.

26. Create a new blank ColdFusion page that is not based on any template. In the Code view of the page, remove any code and type the following code block:

```
CFAPPLICATION NAME="KrystalClear-CF" SESSIONMANAGEMENT="Yes" >
```

27. Save this page as Application.cfm.

Creating Home Page Links and Departmental Home Pages

After the user is logged in, he can access the home page for the KrystalClear intranet. This page provides access to the various departmental home pages, which, in turn, allow the user to view the pages stored in the page manager. The links to each department pass a variable in the querystring that identifies which departmental pages are being requested. The departmental home page captures that variable and builds a list of links to the various pages that are stored in the tbPageMgmt table that match the value passed in the department variable. Upon clicking any of those links, the user can access any page stored in the page manager.

To accomplish this, we need to create three pages. The first of these pages is the home page for the entire intranet application. This page contains a basic welcome message and text links to each of the departmental home pages. The second is the home page for each department, which uses a dataset/recordset to filter the records stored in the tbPageMgmt table and displays a list of links to each page. The third page is the departmental data page that displays the information stored in the page manager.

As you will see, by creating the two pages for each department, we provide each department with the ability to serve an infinite number of pages with the page manager.

Exercise 8.4(a)   Creating the Home Page and Departmental Pages in ASP.NET

1. Open the intranet_template_main.dwt.aspx page.

2. Because these elements should be present on the main pages of the intranet, we can make the changes there. Then, any pages that are spawned from the template (and still attached to it) will include the elements.

3. Place your cursor in the top row of the table that is located to the left of the erMainData editable region. Insert a new image by choosing Insert, Image from the toolbar. In the images subfolder of the site, choose the departmental.gif image.

4. Press Tab and insert the departmental_hr.gif image in the next cell down. Press Tab again and insert the departmental_is.gif image in the third cell. Press Tab one more time and insert the departmental_footer.gif in the bottom cell. With these images in place, your page should look like Figure 8.12.

5. Select the Human Resources image and type **department_home.aspx?Department=HR** in the Link field of the Property inspector.

6. Select the Information Services image and type **department_home.aspx?Department=IS** in the Link field of the Property inspector.

7. Save the template and close it.

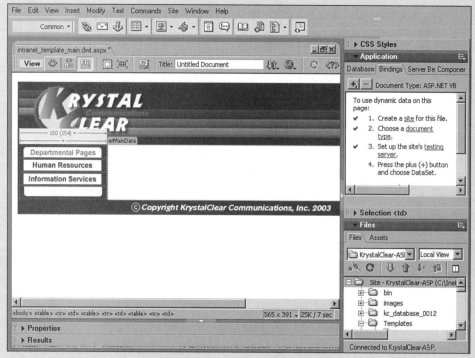

FIGURE 8.12   The Main template with departmental images placed.

8. Create a new page from the Main template and type **KrystalClear Communications Intranet** in the Title field.

9. Place your cursor in the erMainData field, click the Align Center field, and type **Welcome to the KrystalClear Communications Intranet!** and press Enter. Select this text and reformat it using the HeaderText style.

10. On the next line, type **Use the Departmental Pages links to the left to access the home pages for the various organizations within KrystalClear. In addition, click the Departmental Modules links to access Intranet applications that are specific to your department.**

11. Press Enter. Select the text and format it using the BodyText style.

12. Save the page as intranet.aspx.

Next, we need to create the page that displays links to the pages that are available for each department.

13. Create a new page from the Main template and type **KrystalClear Communications Intranet – Departmental Home Page** in the Title field.

14. Save the page as department_home.aspx.

15. Place your cursor in the erMainData editable region, type **Welcome to the placeholder home page!,** and press Enter. Reformat the welcome text using the HeaderText style.

16. Create a new dataset in the Simple view. As shown in Figure 8.13, name the dataset dsPages and use the connKrystalClear connection and the tbPageMgmt table. Select only the Department, PageID, and PageTitle text and set a filter that returns records where Department is equal to the URL Parameter Department.

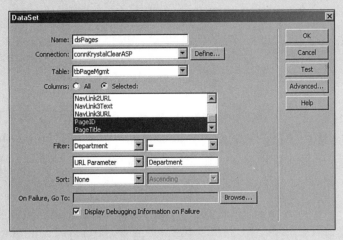

FIGURE 8.13   The dsPages dataset.

17. On the line below the welcome text, add a new datagrid. Name the datagrid dgPages and select records from the dsPages dataset. Choose to show all records.

18. Using the minus sign, remove the Department and PageID fields. Click the PageTitle field and change the column type to a Hyperlink field.

19. In the Hyperlink Column dialog box, change the Hyperlink Text Data field to PageTitle and the Linked Page Data field to PageID. Click the Browse button next to the Format String field and type **departmental_pages.aspx.** Click OK to close the Select File dialog box and click OK again to close the Hyperlink Column dialog box.

20. Click OK one last time to place the datagrid on the page.

21. In the welcome text, delete the word *placeholder*. Open the Bindings tab and click the plus sign next to the dsPages dataset. Drag the Department binding onto the page where the placeholder text used to be.

22. Save the page.

The last page we need to create displays the full contents of the record that was clicked in the department_home page.

23. Create a new page from the template and title the page KrystalClear Communications Intranet – Departmental Pages.

24. Save the page as departmental_pages.aspx.

25. Place your cursor in the erMainData editable region and click the Align Center button.

26. Insert a new table with 5 rows, 1 column, and a width of 85%. Set the border, cell padding, and cell spacing to 0.

27. Create a new dataset in the Simple view with the name dsPageData. Choose the connKrystalClear connection and the tbPageMgmt table. Choose all columns and set a filter that returns records where PageID equals the URL Parameter PageID.

28. Switch to the Bindings panel and drag the PageTitle binding into the top row of the table. Drag the MainPageData binding into the second row.

29. Drag the NavLink1Text binding into the third row. With the NavLink1Text data placeholder selected, click the folder icon next to the Link field in the Property inspector. In the Select File dialog box, choose to select the filename from the Data Sources and select the NavLink1URL. Click OK to close the Select File dialog box. Using the same procedure, place the other NavLink text on the page and link them to the appropriate URLs.

30. Highlight all of the fields in the table and choose Center from the Horiz menu in the Property inspector. As shown in Figure 8.14, all of the data placeholders are in position.

31. Save the page.

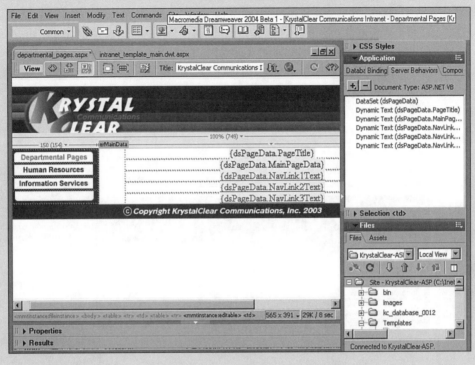

FIGURE 8.14   The page now has all the data placeholders in position.

Exercise 8.4(b)   Creating the Home Page and Departmental Pages in ColdFusion

1. Open the intranet_template_main.dwt.cfm page.

2. Because these elements should be present on the main pages of the intranet, we can make the changes there. Then, any pages that are spawned from the template (and still attached to it) will include the elements.

3. Place your cursor in the top row of the table that is located to the left of the erMainData editable region. Insert a new image by choosing Insert, Image from the toolbar. In the images subfolder of the site, choose the departmental.gif image.

4. Press Tab and insert the departmental_hr.gif image in the next cell down. Press Tab again and insert the departmental_is.gif image in the third cell. Press Tab one more time and insert the departmental_footer.gif in the bottom cell. With these images in place, your page should look like Figure 8.15.

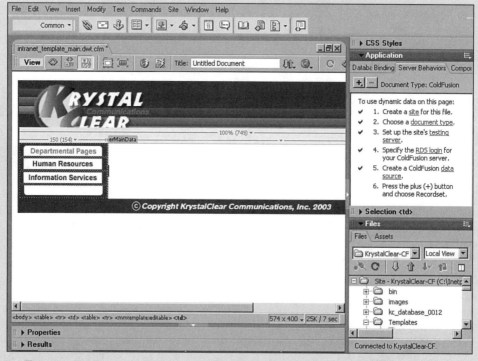

FIGURE 8.15   Your main template with the departmental page images in place.

5. Select the Human Resources image and type **department_home.cfm?Department=HR** in the Link field of the Property inspector.

6. Select the Information Services image and type **department_home.cfm?Department=IS** in the Link field of the Property inspector.

7. Save the template and close it.

8. Create a new page from the Main template and type **KrystalClear Communications Intranet** in the Title field.

9. Save the page as intranet.cfm.

10. Place your cursor in the erMainData field, click the Align Center field, type **Welcome to the KrystalClear Communications Intranet!,** and press Enter. Select this text and reformat it using the HeaderText style.

11. On the next line, type **Use the Departmental Pages links to the left to access the home pages for the various organizations within KrystalClear. In addition, click the Departmental Modules links to access intranet applications that are specific to your department.**

12. Press Enter. Select the text and format it using the BodyText style.

13. Click the plus sign on the Server Behaviors panel and choose User Authentication, Restrict Access To Page from the menu. In the If Access Denied, Go To field, **type login.cfm.**

14. Save the page.

Next, we need to create the page that displays links to the pages that are available for each department.

15. Create a new page from the Main template and type **KrystalClear Communications Intranet – Departmental Home Page** in the Title field.

16. Save the page as department_home.cfm.

17. Place your cursor in the erMainData editable region, type **Welcome to the placeholder home page!,** and press Enter. Reformat the welcome text using the HeaderText style.

18. Create a new recordset in the Simple view. As shown in Figure 8.16, name the recordset rsPages and use the connKrystalClearCF connection and the tbPageMgmt table. Select only the Department, PageID, and PageTitle text and set a filter that returns records where PageID is equal to URL Parameter PageID.

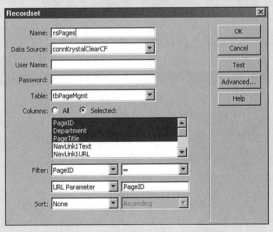

FIGURE 8.16   The rsPages recordset with filter.

19. On the line below the welcome text, add a new table that has 2 rows, 1 column, and a width of 350 pixels. Set the border, cell padding, and cell spacing to 1.

20. In the top row of the table, type **Page Title** and reformat the text using the HeaderText style.

21. Drag the PageTitle data binding from the Bindings panel into the bottom row of the table. With the data placeholder selected, type **departmental_pages.cfm** in the Link field of the Property inspector and click the folder icon next to that field. Click the Parameters button and create a parameter that has a name of PageID and a value of the PageID field stored in the rsPages recordset. Click OK to close the Select File dialog box.

22. Highlight both cells and click the Align Center button.

23. Select the bottom row of the table and click the plus sign on the Server Behaviors panel. From the menu, choose Repeat Region. In the Repeat Region dialog box, choose the rsPages recordset and repeat all records.

24. In the welcome text, delete the word *placeholder*. Open the Bindings tab and click the plus sign next to the rsPages dataset. Drag the Department binding onto the page where the placeholder text used to be. With all the elements in place, your page should look like Figure 8.17.

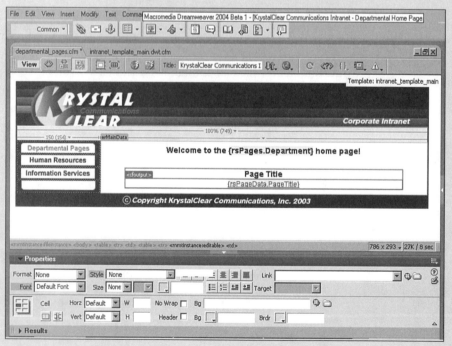

FIGURE 8.17   The departmental home page.

25. Click the plus sign on the Server Behaviors panel and choose User Authentication, Restrict Access to Page from the menu. In the If Access Denied, Go To field, type **login.cfm**.

26. Save the page.

The last page we need to create displays the full contents of the record that was clicked in the department_home page.

27. Create a new page from the template and title the page KrystalClear Communications Intranet – Departmental Pages.

28. Save the page as departmental_pages.cfm.

29. Place your cursor in the erMainData editable region and click the Align Center button.

30. Insert a new table with 5 rows, 1 column, and a width of 85%. Set the border, cell padding, and cell spacing to 0.

31. Create a new recordset in the Simple view with a name rsPageData. Choose the connKrystalClearCF connection and the tbPageMgmt table. Choose all columns and set a filter that returns records where PageID equals the URL Parameter PageID.

32. Switch to the Bindings panel and drag the PageTitle binding into the top row of the table. Drag the MainPageData binding into the second row.

33. Drag the NavLink1Text binding into the third row. With the NavLink1Text data placeholder selected, click the file icon next to the Link field in the Property inspector. In the Select File dialog box, choose to select the filename from the Data Sources and select the NavLink1URL. Click OK to close the Select File dialog box. Using the same procedure, place the other NavLink text on the page and link them to the appropriate URLs.

34. Highlight all of the fields in the table and click the Align Center button. As shown in Figure 8.18, all of the data placeholders are in position.

35. Click the plus sign on the Server Behaviors panel and choose User Authentication, Restrict Access to Page from the menu.

36. Save the page.

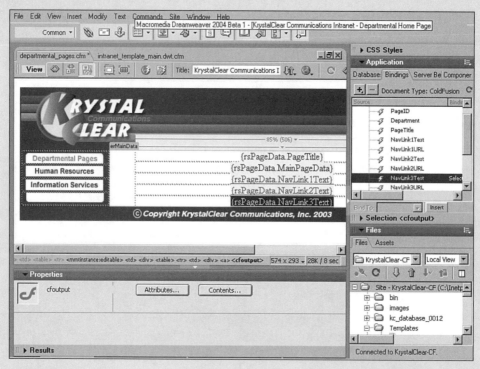

FIGURE 8.18   The Departmental Pages page with all the data placeholders in position.

Customizing Content

Although our intranet home page is functional, it still leaves a bit to be desired when it comes to providing the user with individualized information. To rectify this, we can add several pieces of dynamic data that make the intranet experience a bit more personal. In addition, because we created the session variable that contains the department that the user works for, we can display a link to the intranet module that corresponds to her department. Finally, if she is allowed to edit pages for her department, we can display a link to the page manager as well.

Building Links to Departmental Tools

The first step in customizing our welcome page for the user is to display a link to the departmental module that matches the value stored in the user's departmental session variable. For instance, if a staff member of Human Resources logs in, we want him to be able to see a link to the HR employee manager but not to the IS asset manager.

To accomplish this, we can use a combination of HTML hyperlinks with the Show Region server behavior to display only the sections of the page that are appropriate.

Exercise 8.5(a)   Building Links to Departmental Tools in ASP.NET

1. Open the intranet_template_main.dwt.aspx.

2. Select the departmental_footer.gif and press the right-arrow key to move the cursor to the right of the image. Press Tab to create a new row. Press Tab three more times to create new rows.

3. In the first empty row, insert the modules.gif image. In the next row down, insert the departmental_hr.gif image. In the next row down, insert the departmental_is.gif image. In the last row, insert the departmental_footer.gif. Your page should now look like Figure 8.19.

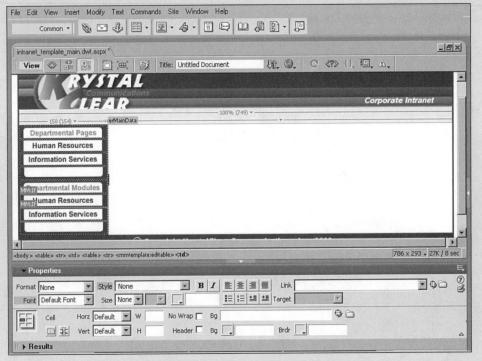

FIGURE 8.19   The updated Main template with the departmental tools images.

4. Set the Link field for the new HR button to search_employee.aspx (the search page we created in Chapter 5). Set the Link field in the new IS button to search_asset.aspx (the search page we created in Chapter 6, "Creating the Information Services Asset Management System").

5. Because we only want the HR image to be visible to the members of the HR staff, we are going to create a region that is visible only if the sessDepartment session variable is equal to HR. To do this, switch to the Split Code and Design view and highlight the cell that contains the new HR button. Insert a new line above the <tr> tag and type the following code:

```
<MM:If runat="server" Expression='<%#
➥(session("sessDepartment") = "HR") %>'>
<ContentsTemplate>
```

6. On a new line after the </tr> tag, add this code:

```
</ContentsTemplate>
</MM:If>
```

 CODE HINTS ENABLED

If you have Code Hints enabled in Dreamweaver, the </ContentsTemplate> and </MM:If> tags will be automatically generated. If they are generated, there is no need to retype them, simply move them to the correct position after the </tr> tag.

7. Select the row with the new IS button, insert a new line above its <tr> tag, and add this code:<MM:If runat="server" Expression='<%# (session("sessDepartment") = "IS") %>'> <ContentsTemplate>

8. On a new line after the </tr> tag, add this code:

```
</ContentsTemplate>
</MM:If>
```

9. Save the page and have the template update all pages that are linked to the template. Save all pages that are open in Dreamweaver.

10. Because the intranet.aspx page does not have any dynamic elements included in it, we have to add a dynamic element before it can process the MM:If statements we just added. To do this, simply copy the dsPages dataset from the departmental_home.aspx page by right-clicking the dataset in the Server Behaviors panel and pasting it into the Server Behaviors panel on the intranet.aspx page.

11. Save all the pages.

Exercise 8.5(b)   Building Links to Departmental Tools in ColdFusion

1. Open the intranet_template_main.dwt.cfm.

2. Select the departmental_footer.gif and press the right-arrow key to move the cursor to the right of the image. Press Tab to create a new row. Press Tab three more times to create new rows.

3. In the first empty row, insert the modules.gif image. In the next row down, insert the departmental_hr.gif image. In the next row down, insert the departmental_is.gif image. In the last row, insert the departmental_footer.gif.

4. Set the Link field for the new HR button to search_employee.cfm (the search page we created in Chapter 5). Set the Link field in the new IS button to search_asset.cfm (the search page we created in Chapter 6). With the images in place, your template should look like Figure 8.20.

5. Because we only want the HR image to be visible to the members of the HR staff, we are going to create a region that is visible only if the sessDepartment session variable is equal to HR. To do this, switch to the Split Code and Design view and highlight the cell that contains the new HR button. Insert a new line above the <tr> tag and type the following code:

```
<cfif session.sessDeparment EQ "HR">
```

6. On a new line after the </tr> tag, add this code:

```
</cfif>
```

7. Next, select the row with the new IS button, insert a new line above its <tr> tag, and add this code:

```
<cfif session.sessDeparment EQ "IS">
```

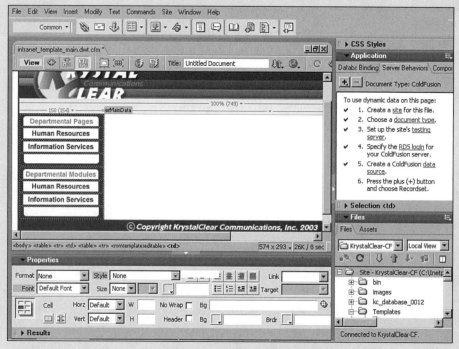

FIGURE 8.20   The template now contains links to the departmental modules.

8. On a new line after the `</tr>` tag, add this code:

   ```
   </cfif>
   ```

9. Save the page and have the template update all pages that are linked to the template. Save all pages that are open in Dreamweaver.

Displaying the Edit Pages Link

Some of the staff members at KrystalClear have been authorized to make updates to their departmental intranet pages and we need to provide these users with the ability to access the page manager. Because we stored that value (True or False) in a session variable when they logged on, we can use that session variable to determine whether the link should be displayed.

Exercise 8.6(a)   Displaying the Page Editor Link in ASP.NET

1. Open the intranet_template_main.dwt.aspx page.

2. Add one more row to the navigation table at the left of the page and insert the page_manager.gif image in the cell. Link the new image to page_manager.aspx.

3. Using the same method as before, we will create a region that only displays if the sessEditPages session variable is set to "True". Highlight the new cell and in the Code view, place the following code on a new line before the `<tr>` tag:

```
<MM:If runat="server" Expression='<%#
➥(session("sessEditPages") = "True") %>'>
<ContentsTemplate>
```

4. On a new line after the `</tr>` tag, add this code:

```
</ContentsTemplate>
</MM:If>
```

5. Save the page and allow the template to update all pages. Save all pages that are open in Dreamweaver.

Exercise 8.6(b)   Displaying the Page Editor Link in ColdFusion

1. Open the intranet_template_main.dwt.cfm page.

2. Add one more row to the navigation table at the left of the page and insert the page_manager.gif image in the cell. Link the new image to page_manager.cfm.

3. Using the same method as before, we will create a region that only displays if the sessEditPages session variable is set to "True." Highlight the new cell and in the Code view, place the following code on a new line before the `<tr>` tag:

```
<cfif session.sessDeparment EQ "HR">
```

4. On a new line after the `</tr>` tag, add this code:

```
</cfif>
```

5. Save the page and allow the template to update all pages. Save all pages that are open in Dreamweaver.

Logging Out Users

The final change that we need to make to the intranet pages is the ability to log out. Although closing the browser window will destroy the session variables and essentially log out the user, providing the user with the ability to log out manually allows him to keep his browser open and available for other uses. Using a simple server behavior, Dreamweaver makes the development of this process relatively easy.

Exercise 8.7(a)   Creating a Logout Page in ASP.NET

1. Create a new page from the internet_template_main.dwt.aspx template.

2. Place your cursor in the erMainData editable region and click the Align Center button. Type **Click here to logout.** and press Enter.

3. Save the page as logout.aspx.

4. Switch to the Split Code and Design view. On the new line, insert a form and add the `runat="server"` code to the form tag.

5. Inside the form, add an asp:button and name it btLogout. Set the text for the button to Logout.

6. With the button selected, add the following code to the button tag just before the />:

```
onClick="Logout_Click"
```

7. Create a new line at line 2 of your document and add the following code block:

```
<script language="VB" runat="server">
Sub Logout_Click(ByVal s As Object, ByVal e As EventArgs)
FormsAuthentication.Signout()
Session("sessDepartment") = ""
Session("sessEditPages") = ""
Response.Redirect("login.aspx")
End Sub
</script>
```

With your code in place, the page should look like Figure 8.21.

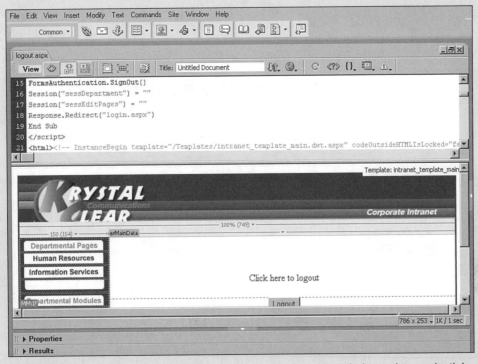

FIGURE 8.21   The code that logs out users out and destroys their session credentials.

8. As we did earlier, copy the dsPages dataset from the departmental_home.aspx page by right-clicking the dataset in the Server Behaviors panel and pasting it into the Server Behaviors panel on the this page.

9. Save the page.

10. Open the internet_template_main.dwt.aspx template and create a new cell in the navigation table on the left. Insert the logout.gif image and link it to logout.aspx.

11. Save the page and allow it to update all dependant pages.

Exercise 8.7(b)   Creating a Logout Page in ColdFusion

1. Open the internet_template_main.dwt.cfm page and create a new cell in the navigation table on the left. Insert the logout.gif image and link it to logout.cfm.

2. On the Server Behaviors panel, click the plus sign and choose User Authentication, Log Out User.

3. In the Log Out User dialog box, shown in Figure 8.22, in the Link Clicked drop-down box, choose Create New Link: "Log Out" and type **login.cfm** in the When Done, Go To field.

FIGURE 8.22   The Log Out User dialog box creates code that closes the user's session.

4. Click OK and save the page as logout.cfm.
5. Save the page and allow it to update all dependant pages.

Testing the Application

Now that we have all the pieces in place, the intranet application is ready for a trial run. After we log in to the intranet, we need to make sure our departmental links function properly and the departmental modules and edit pages links are customized. Before you begin the testing process, it is a good idea for you to create four users in the HR table and four entries in the tbUserId table that correspond to the new entries in the HR table. One of these entries should be a member of the HR department and should be allowed to edit pages. Another should be a member of the HR department, but should not be allowed to edit pages. The other two entries should be members of the IS staff, with one being allowed to make change to pages.

After you have the user accounts in place, it's time to give the application a whirl!

Exercise 8.8   Testing the Application in ASP.NET and ColdFusion

1. Open Internet Explorer and type **login.aspx** or **login.cfm** in the address bar and press Enter.

2. Type the username of one of your accounts in the Username field but leave the Password field blank. When you click the Login button, you should receive the error that you were not logged in.

3. Type the correct username and password combination in the login form and click Submit. As shown in Figure 8.23, you should receive a page that confirms you were logged in. Click the Continue button.

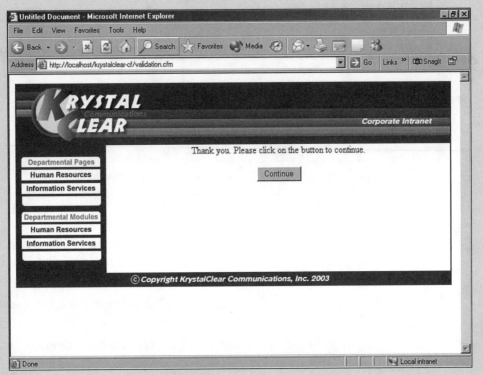

FIGURE 8.23   Your have been logged on.

4. In the intranet main page, you should see the Departmental links, the Module link that corresponds to the user's department, and the Logout link. If the user does not have the permission to edit pages, the page editor link is hidden, as shown in Figure 8.24.

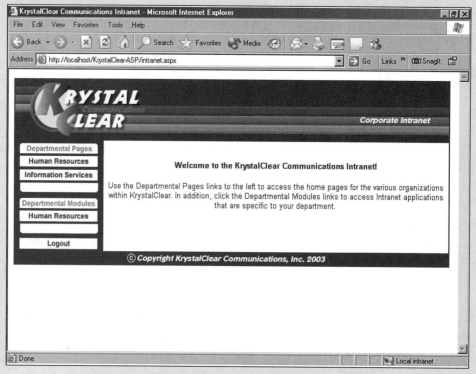

FIGURE 8.24   This user is a member of the Human
Resources staff, so the HR departmental link is visible.

5. Click the link to the Human Resources Departmental Page. As shown in
   Figure 8.25, the page titles that were entered into the page manager are
   visible.

6. Click any of the page titles and you should receive the full details of the
   page.

7. Depending on the user's department, click the departmental module that
   is visible. You should have complete access to add and update employees or assets.

8. Finally, click the Logout link to end your session.

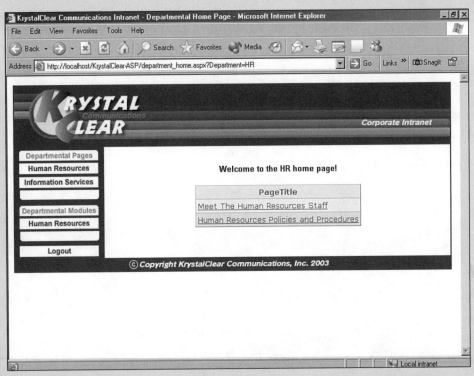

FIGURE 8.25 The page titles entered into the page manager are available.

Summary

This chapter brought the intranet modules we created earlier together into a functional application. Using login and logout procedures, we were able to determine information about our users and customize the content to only show appropriate elements. Although there are many areas in which you could improve the intranet application, it serves as a basic framework that demonstrates many of the features available in Dreamweaver that can assist you in the development of an intranet application.

As we move on to the next section of the book, we turn our focus to applications that are intended for the Web. In addition to topics such as creating searchable pages, administering Web pages, and basic eCommerce, we will also look at SQL Server and its application as a database back end.

Part III

Building Web-Strength Applications with SQL Server, ASP.NET/ColdFusion, and Dreamweaver MX 2004

CHAPTER 9

BUILDING A DATABASE FOR WEB APPLICATIONS

Now that the groundwork for the intranet application is completed, it's time to look at KrystalClear's request for a Web application. KrystalClear wants us to build a Web site for them that provides its customers with access to services beyond the basic corporate information that is often presented on static Web sites. Instead, KrystalClear wants to add functionality that allows its customers to view timely corporate events, product availability, and even basic online shopping. To accomplish this, we will again look to a database to store information such as media information, page content, search keywords, product information, and customer orders.

Because KrystalClear expects its Web site to draw substantially higher traffic than its intranet site, we are going to use Microsoft SQL Server (referred to simply as SQL Server throughout the rest of the exercises) as our database back end. SQL Server provides applications with a more robust database environment that is not subject to the limitations that restrict the use of Access to small- and medium-sized projects.

By the end of this chapter, you will understand the following:

- The pros and cons of choosing SQL Server for your database back end
- The process of installing and configuring SQL Server on your workstation
- How to use the Enterprise Manager to manage database content
- The process of building a SQL Server database
- What is involved in upsizing an existing Access database
- The steps involved in transferring data between SQL Server databases

Introducing SQL Server

Like Microsoft Access, SQL Server is a relational database management system that can be used to store and filter data using objects such as tables and queries. Unlike Access, however, SQL Server is not limited by a maximum file size or concurrent connections and boasts performance numbers that far exceed Access during heavy usage.

 WHICH EDITION OF SQL SERVER IS RIGHT FOR YOU?

There are seven different versions of SQL Server 2000 and choosing the one that is right for your organization can be a little nerve-racking. Microsoft has produced a white paper, however, that clearly explains the differences between the editions. You can find the white paper at `http://www.microsoft.com/sql/techinfo/planning/ChoosEd.doc`.

In addition to being more robust than Access, SQL Server also provides an easy-to-use interface, called the Enterprise Manager, that allows the user to manage multiple databases at the same time. In addition, using the Enterprise Manager, shown in Figure 9.1, the user can perform tasks such as adding, editing, and deleting fields in the database, querying records stored in the database, and even migrating data between the database containers.

SQL Server is not, however, without its cons. The most problematic issue for organizations is often cost. With a price tag ranging from $1,500 to $20,000 depending on the edition and licensing model chosen, small- to medium-sized organizations are often willing to put up with the limitations on Access to avoid the license cost of SQL Server.

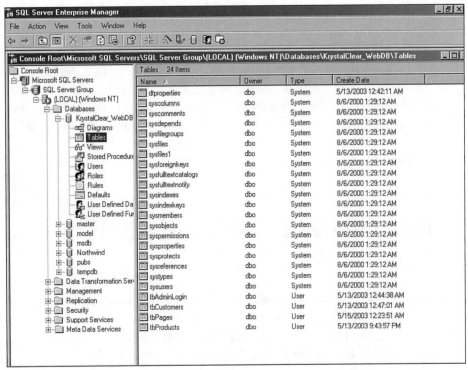

FIGURE 9.1   The Enterprise Manager provides an easy-to-use interface for managing databases.

Note **PER SEAT LICENSING VERSUS PROCESSOR LICENSING**

Prior to purchasing SQL Server, it is very important to understand the distinction between Per Seat/Client Access licensing and Per Processor Licensing.

With Per Seat/Client licensing, you purchase a single license for the server that stores the database and a Client Access License (CAL) for each workstation that will access the server. If your organization has 25 workstations, the Enterprise Edition with 25 CALs would cost you around $11,000.

Per Processor licensing, however, allows you to purchase a single license with unlimited CALs based on the number of processors that are contained within the server. For instance, if you were using your database as a back end for your corporate Web site and need to allow unlimited access to visitors to interact with the database, you could purchase a single processor license of the standard edition for around $5,000.

If your organization isn't ready to foot the bill for a dedicated SQL Server license, another option is to outsource your SQL Server needs to a remote host. Many hosts are adding SQL Server containers to their list of services that can be purchased as part of a plan or a la carte. Monthly cost of the service usually depends on the maximum size of the database container.

Before you choose between purchasing a server license or seeking a remote host, you can test SQL Server to be sure that it meets your organizational needs. Microsoft offers a 120-day, fully functional trial of the software that can be installed on any workstation running Windows NT, Windows 2000, or Windows XP. In addition, at the end of the trial period, the Evaluation Edition simply reverts to the Developer's Edition and leaves you with the ability to manage databases that are located on a server running the Standard Edition or Enterprise Edition. To demonstrate SQL Server's abilities, we'll be using this trial version for the remainder of the book.

Installing and Configuring SQL Server on Your Workstation

In the same way that IIS turns your workstation into a limited Web server, the trial version of SQL Server 2000 can convert your workstation into a database server. The only difference is that there is no limitation on the functionality of the software during the evaluation period.

Installing and configuring SQL Server, however, does require an understanding of the methods used to secure the application and the data contained within the databases. Failing to configure the security features within SQL Server can leave your workstation wide-open to hackers who want to tamper with your data or disrupt your workstation.

Exercise 9.1   Installing SQL Server

1. If you are not logged on already, log on to your workstation with Administrator privileges.

2. Download the latest version of the SQL Server trial edition by visiting `http://www.microsoft.com/sql/evaluation/trial/` and following the links to download the trial.

 INSTALLATION OF SERVICE PACK 3A

At the time of this writing, Microsoft also recommends that Service Pack 3A be installed after completing the SQL Server installation. Be sure to read all of the installation instructions and follow the recommendations carefully to fully protect your computer from outside attacks.

3. When the download is complete, disable any anti-virus software that is running and shut down any applications.

4. Double-click the setup executable to begin the installation process. As shown in Figure 9.2, when prompted to specify an installation folder, leave the default C:\SQLEVAL and click Finish.

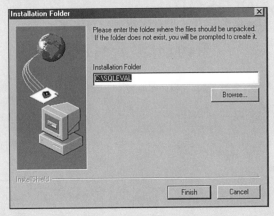

FIGURE 9.2   Choose to use the default installation folder.

5. After the installation package has been delivered, click OK to close the notification.

6. Browse to the C:\SQLEVAL folder and double-click the autorun.exe file. You are presented with the SQL Server Evaluation Edition menu shown in Figure 9.3.

7. Click the SQL Server 2000 Components and choose Install Database Server on the following menu to begin the installation process.

8. Click Next to install a new instance of SQL Server and choose to perform the installation on the local computer.

9. In the following dialog box, shown in Figure 9.4, choose to create a new instance SQL Server and click Next.

10. In the User Information dialog box, type your name and click Next. Read the license agreement and choose Yes to accept the terms.

11. Because we want to create database containers as well as manage them, choose to install both the server and client tools and click Next.

12. Choose to use the default installation and click Next.

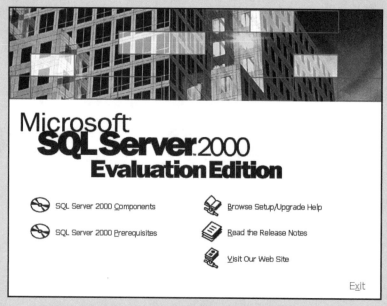

FIGURE 9.3   Install SQL Server via the main menu.

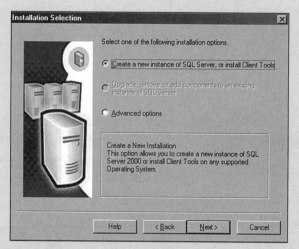

FIGURE 9.4   Create a new instance of SQL Server.

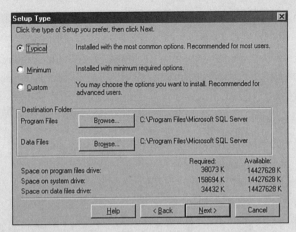

FIGURE 9.5 Choose a typical installation.

At this point, you need to choose how the SQL Server will be allowed to run. If you plan to allow your workstation to interact with other servers on your organization's network, you should create a user account in your domain for the server. Using this account, each server could then have access to the other servers on the network.

14. For our purposes, however, choose to use the same account for each service. In addition, choose to use the local system account to run the service. Click Next.

    If you are on a network that supports a variety of operating systems, and users on machines with operating systems other than Windows will be accessing the SQL Server, the Mixed Mode authentication would be appropriate. However, we will only be using the Windows Authentication Mode to confirm that the users accessing our machine are authenticated.

15. Choose the Mixed Mode as the authentication mode and type a unique password for the sa login.

 Warning USING A STRONG PASSWORD FOR THE SA ACCOUNT

Because your workstation is now running SQL Server, hackers may target it and attempt to gain access to your workstation and the data stored on it by attempting to crack the SA user account. For this reason, be sure to assign a strong password to the account that uses a combination of letters, numbers, and characters.

16. Click Next. After Setup has all the appropriate information, click Next to begin the process of copying the SQL Server files.

17. After the installation is finished, shown in Figure 9.6, click the Finish button to complete the process.

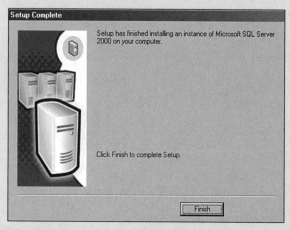

FIGURE 9.6   The installation of SQL Server is complete.

Understanding Security Issues Involved in Installing SQL Server

Now that you have SQL Server installed on your workstation, it's important to take a moment and talk a little bit about security. Recently, a vulnerability in the SQL Server application left many servers and workstations susceptible to the Slammer worm. Although this vulnerability has been removed in the newest versions of the SQL Server trial, you still should take steps to protect your workstation from any future attacks.

The first step in securing SQL Server is to ensure that you have installed the most recent version. If you downloaded the trial version awhile ago and are just getting around to installing it, check the SQL Server homepage to make certain that the version you are using is the most recent version. If not, uninstall your previous version and reinstall the most recent.

As we discussed earlier (but it's certainly worth repeating), making sure that your user accounts are secure goes a long way in locking down SQL Server. If you chose to authenticate SQL Server using the Windows Authentication Mode, be sure that all your user accounts are using strong passwords. If you chose to use the Mixed Mode, you have the added task of ensuring that the SQL Server account also uses a strong password.

The third step you can take to reduce the risk of having your workstation hacked is to disable the service when you aren't using it. As shown in Figure 9.7, after the service is started from the Start menu, you can then right-click the MSSQLServer icon in the system tray and start or stop the service using the SQL Server Service Manager.

FIGURE 9.7   You can stop the SQL Server service when you are not using it.

If you are working on a corporate LAN, it is especially important that you take the appropriate precautions to secure your workstation. Slammer can infect an entire enterprise simply by attacking one unsecured workstation. Don't let it be yours! In addition, it's a good idea to keep up-to-date with any potential security issues by visiting Microsoft's security site at `http://www.microsoft.com/technet/security/current.asp`.

Using the Enterprise Manager to Create the KrystalClear Database and Tables

With SQL Server installed, it's time to familiarize yourself with the Enterprise Manager and build the tables that will fuel our Web application. Before you can build the tables, however, you need to have an understanding of what it is KrystalClear wants.

The Web site that KrystalClear has asked us to build has five fundamental elements that work together to provide visitors with opportunities to learn about the company, search the site, browse the product catalog, and order products. In addition, KrystalClear would like an administrative section of the site that allows staff members to update product information and page content.

The first element that requires a database table is the front end for the site. Rather than creating dozens of static HTML pages to house our content, we can build a few dynamic pages and draw the content from our database. By storing the page content in the database, we also set up the ability for staff members to make updates to the site via their browser.

The second database-driven function that KrystalClear has requested allows visitors to search the site. Because our page content will be stored in the database, we can build an interface for users to search that content and the results page will return any database records that contain the search criteria.

The third element is one that has become very popular, as more and more companies are engaging in eCommerce. By storing the KrystalClear product catalog in a database that is accessible via the Web pages, we allow visitors to see what products KrystalClear offers 24 hours a day, 7 days a week. We can even build in the capability to display how many items are in stock.

Allowing visitors to view the catalog, however, is only one aspect of eCommerce. KrystalClear would like to make its site fully functional by allowing its visitors to order products at their leisure. To implement this, we must create a system that allows the visitor to create an account, log in, and then choose the items that she wishes to order. Upon completion of the order, we can then process the order by either emailing the order to a staff member for processing or by storing the order details in a database table for retrieval by a staff member.

To fulfill the requests of KrystalClear, we need to create four database tables. The first stores the page content for the Web front end, the second stores the login account information for the administrators, the third stores the customer information, and the final stores the product catalog.

Exercise 9.2   Creating the database tables with the Enterprise Manager

1. Open the Enterprise Manager by choosing Start, Programs, Microsoft SQL Server, Enterprise Manager.

2. In the Enterprise Manager, click the plus sign next to Microsoft SQL Servers. Next, click the plus sign next to the SQL Server Group and then click the plus sign next to your SQL Server machine. As shown in Figure 9.8, you can now see the various categories that can be managed from within the Enterprise Manager.

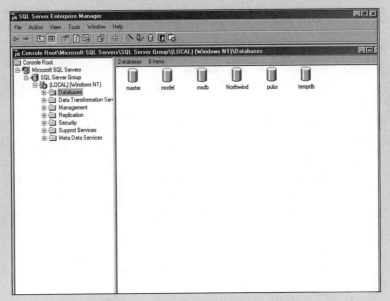

FIGURE 9.8   The SQL Server Enterprise Manager.

3. Right-click the Databases folder and choose New Database from the context menu. In the Database Properties dialog box, name the database KrystalClear_WebDB and click OK.

4. Click the plus sign next to the Databases folder, right-click the new KrystalClear_WebDB database, and choose New, Table from the context menu.

5. The first table we will create is the tbPages table that contains all of the page data for the KrystalClear Web site. In the New Table dialog box, add the eight fields shown in Table 9.1.

TABLE 9.1   Structure for the tbPages Table

COLUMN NAME	DATA TYPE	LENGTH	ALLOW NULLS	IDENTITY
PageID	int	4		Yes Identity Seed 1 and Identity Increment 1
PageName	varchar	25	Yes	
PageCategory	varchar	25	Yes	
ImageURL	varchar	50	Yes	
PageTitle	varchar	50	Yes	
PageContent	varchar	500	Yes	
LastUpdated	datetime	8	Yes	
PageActive	bit	1	Yes	

The PageID column is an Identity column, similar in nature to the AutoNumber column in an Access table. For each new record, a unique number is assigned in incremental order. In our case, the first number is 1 (Identity Seed) and the incremental value (Identity Increment) is 1 as well. The PageCategory field lets us know what section of the Web site the page should fall under. The ImageURL field allows us to display an image that is specific to the page. The PageTitle and PageContent fields contain the text that is displayed on the page. The LastUpdated field allows administrators to know when changes were made to the page and, finally, the PageActive field allows us to activate and deactivate pages without having to delete them from the database.

When your table is completed, the New Table dialog box should look like Figure 9.9.

6. Close the New Table dialog box and choose to save the changes to the table. Name the table tbPages.

7. In the Enterprise Manager, click the plus sign next to the KrystalClear_WebDB database to expand its contents. Next, select the Tables category and notice that along with the system tables, there is now a table named tbPages.

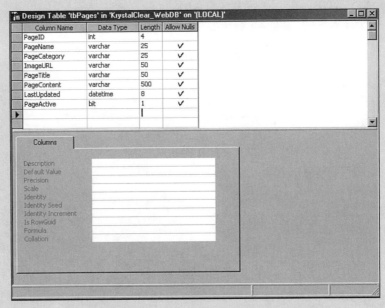

FIGURE 9.9 The structure of the new table.

8. With our first table in place, we now need to set up the remaining three. Following the same steps, create a new table with the structure shown in Table 9.2.

TABLE 9.2 Structure for the tbAdminLogin Table

COLUMN NAME	DATA TYPE	LENGTH	ALLOW NULLS	IDENTITY
UserID	int	4		Yes Identity Seed 1 and Identity Increment 1
Username	varchar	25	Yes	
Password	varchar	25	Yes	
LastLogin	datetime	8	Yes	

When completed, your table layout should look like Figure 9.10.

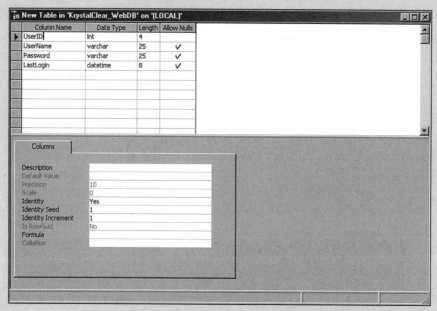

FIGURE 9.10   The tbAdminLogin table structure.

9. Save the table as tbAdminLogin. In the tbAdminLogin table, the UserID is an autoincrementing seed that is assigned by the database. As with most typical login tables, this one contains a field for username, password, and the last login of the user.

10. The third table we need to create will hold the customer information that allows the visitors to log in and order products from the KrystalClear catalog. Create a new table based on the information in Table 9.3.

TABLE 9.3   Structure for the tbCustomers Table

COLUMN NAME	DATA TYPE	LENGTH	ALLOW NULLS	IDENTITY
CustomerID	int	4		Yes Identity Seed 1 and Identity Increment 1
LastName	varchar	25	Yes	
FirstName	varchar	25	Yes	
Addr1	varchar	50	Yes	

Addr2	varchar	50	Yes
CustCity	varchar	50	Yes
CustState	varchar	4	Yes
CustZip	varchar	12	Yes
CustEmail	varchar	50	Yes
CCType	varchar	15	Yes
CCNumber	varchar	25	Yes
CCExp	varchar	10	Yes
LastLogin	datetime	8	Yes
Password	varchar	50	Yes
PasswordQuestion	varchar	50	Yes
PasswordAnswer	varchar	50	Yes

When completed, your table layout should look like Figure 9.11. This table stores the typical user information regarding the customers who wish to log in to the site and order products.

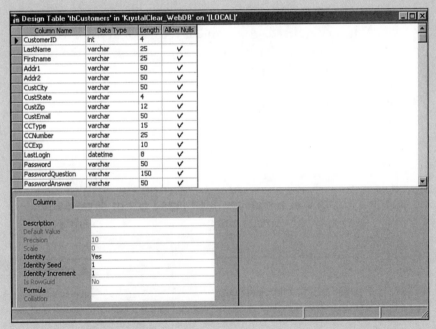

FIGURE 9.11   The tbAdminLogin table structure.

11. Save the table as tbCustomers.

12. The final table to be created is the tbProducts field that is the data warehouse for our product catalog. Create a new table using the structure in Table 9.4.

TABLE 9.4   Sample Data for tbProducts Table

Column Name	Data Type	Length	Allow Nulls	Identity
ProductID	int	4		Yes Identity Seed 1 and Identity Increment 1
ProductTitle	varchar	25	Yes	
ProductCost	float	8	Yes	
ProductCategory	varchar	25	Yes	
ProductDescription	varchar	500	Yes	
ProductPhoto	varchar	50	Yes	
InInventory	int	4	Yes	

When completed, your table layout should look like Figure 9.12. This table stores the basic product information and the number of items that are currently in inventory.

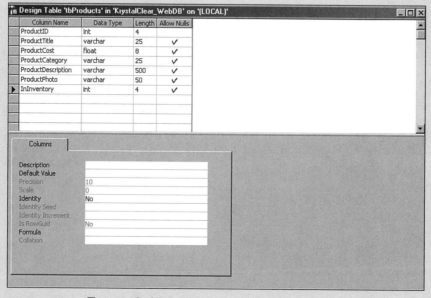

FIGURE 9.12   The tbProducts table structure.

13. In the Enterprise Manager, you should now see four additional tables in the KrystalClear_WebDB database. These tables are shown in Figure 9.13.

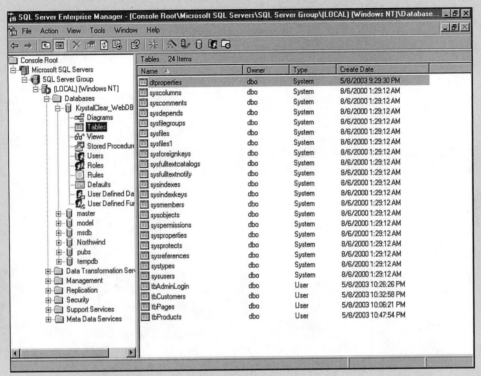

FIGURE 9.13 Four new tables have been added to the database.

Setting Database Permissions

Now that the database tables are in place, we need to ensure that the appropriate system accounts can access the database and, when appropriate, read from and write data to the tables. Unlike Microsoft Access, database permissions in SQL Server are not set at the file level but are set from within the Enterprise Manager.

Exercise 9.3   Using the Enterprise Manager to Set Permissions

1. Open the Enterprise Manager and expand the databases category.

2. Expand the KrystalClear_WebDB database container and right-click the Users icon. From the context menu, choose New Database User.

3. In the Database User Properties dialog box, choose <new> from the Login name drop-down box.

4. In the SQL Server Login Properties dialog box, shown in Figure 9.14, click the ellipses button and choose the IUSR account for your local machine.

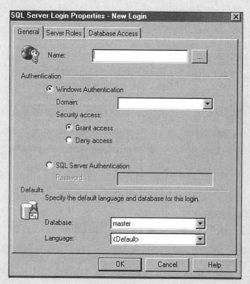

FIGURE 9.14   The SQL Server Login Properties dialog box.

5. Click the Add button and click OK.

6. As shown in Figure 9.15, set the default database to the KrystalClear_WebDB and the default language to English.

7. Click the Database Access tab and check the Permit check box next to the KrystalClear_WebDB database. In the bottom panel of the SQL Server Login Properties dialog box, set the database role for the IUSR account to public, db_datareader, and db_datawriter.

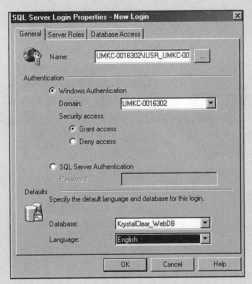

FIGURE 9.15   Set the default database and language for the IUSR account.

8. Click OK to close the dialog box.
9. If you are planning to build the KrystalClear database on the ASP.NET platform, follow the steps again to add the ASPNET account with the same permissions as the IUSR account.

 THE ASPNET ACCOUNT

The ASPNET account will only be available if you have the ASP.NET framework installed.

10. Click OK to close the Database User Properties dialog box.
11. Close the Enterprise Manager.

Summary

In this chapter, you learned the fundamentals of installing SQL Server, building a custom database, and creating tables. In addition, you learned how to add permissions for the user accounts that need to access the database for our Web application to function properly.

In the next chapter, we will create the file and folder structure necessary for the application. In addition, we will build a new Dreamweaver MX 2004 site for our project and create a connection to our new SQL Server database.

CHAPTER 10

CONFIGURING YOUR WORKSTATION TO BUILD THE WEB APPLICATION

With the SQL Server database in place and the tables created, the next step is to configure your local workstation to create and serve the dynamic pages. This process entails building the appropriate directory structure, creating a Dreamweaver site for the KrystalClear Web application, and building a connection between Dreamweaver MX 2004 and your SQL Server database.

Although some of the information in this chapter is repetitive of the information in Chapter 4, "Configuring Your Workstation for Application Development," the folders, Dreamweaver site, and database connection are different from those used for the intranet application. If you have already read Chapter 4 and followed the exercises, this chapter should be a breeze.

By the end of this chapter, you will have the following:

- A Web server application installed and configured on your local workstation
- The ASP.NET and/or ColdFusion application server installed and configured to serve dynamic pages
- A directory structure created for the Web application on your local workstation
- A functional connection to your SQL Server database

Installing and Configuring the Web Server Software and Application Server Software

As we did with the intranet application, we need to ensure that your local workstation is capable of serving both static HTML page and dynamic pages using the ColdFusion server and/or the ASP.NET framework. The first step is to use the IIS Management Console to ensure that your Web services are started and capable of serving static pages.

Exercise 10.1   Starting the Internet Information Services

1. Open Notepad by choosing Start, Program Files, Accessories, Notepad.

2. In the new Notepad document, type **Testing static pages** and save the document as c:\inetpub\wwwroot\test2.htm.

 NO WWWROOT FOLDER?

If you don't have a wwwroot folder, you probably skipped reading Chapter 4. Take a moment to go back over the exercises in that chapter to ensure that you have IIS installed and configured properly.

3. Open Internet Explorer and type **http://localhost/test2.htm** in the address bar. As shown in Figure 10.1, you should now see the test page.

4. If you could not view the page, right-click My Computer and choose Manage from the context menu.

5. In the Computer Management Console, shown in Figure 10.2, expand the Services and Applications section and then expand the Internet Information Services category.

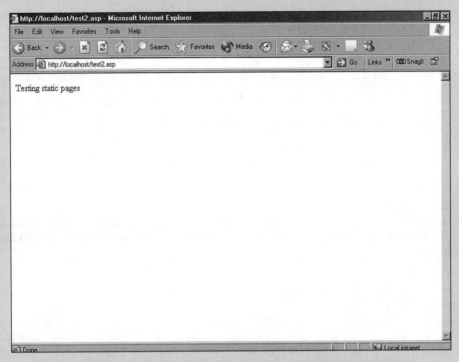

FIGURE 10.1 Your workstation is properly serving static HTML pages.

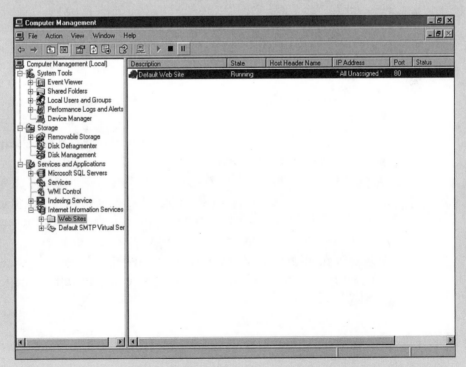

FIGURE 10.2 Use the Computer Management Console to start the Web services.

6. Expand the Web Sites folder and select the Default Web Site. On the menu bar, click the Start Service button that looks like a triangle pointing to the right.

7. With the Web services started, repeat step 3 in this exercise to test your workstation's capability to serve static pages.

After you have the Web services started and your workstation can serve HTML pages, the next step is to ensure that the ASP.NET framework and/or the ColdFusion Server are installed and configured properly.

Exercise 10.2(a)   Testing and Installing the ASP.NET Framework

1. Open Notepad, open a new document, and type the following code:

```
<script language="vb" runat="server">
Sub Page_Load()
time.text=Hour(Now) & ":" & Minute(Now)
End Sub
</script>
<html>
<body>
The ASP.NET framework reports the time to be  <asp:label id="time"
runat="server" />
</body>
</html>
```

2. Save the page to the c:\Inetpub\wwwroot folder and name it **testaspx2.aspx**.

3. Open Internet Explorer and type **http://localhost/testaspx2.aspx**. If your workstation is properly configured, you should see the page shown in Figure 10.3 that displays the dynamic time.

4. If you do not see the time or the page does not load, check that you have the .NET framework installed. You can download the installation file for the .NET Framework from `http://www.asp.net`.

5. If you need additional help installing ASP.NET, Exercise 4.2 contains the complete instructions for downloading and installing the framework.

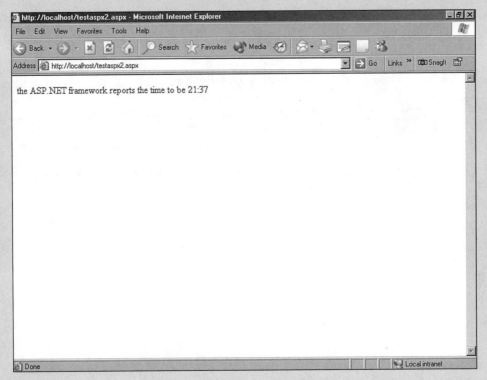

FIGURE 10.3 The ASP.NET page displays the time dynamically generated by the Web server.

Testing the installation of ColdFusion is very similar to the testing process for ASP.NET. By creating a test page, we can first check to see if the application server is running. If the test page loads successfully, your workstation is ready to serve ColdFusion pages. If, however, the page does not load or the dynamic element does not display, it's likely that the ColdFusion Server is not installed or is configured incorrectly.

Exercise 10.2(b)   Testing and Installing the ColdFusion Server

1. Open Notepad, open a new document, and type the following code:

```
<html>
<body>
The ColdFusion server reports the time to be
<cfoutput>
    #timeformat(now(),'hh:mm:ss')#
</cfoutput>
</body>
</html>
```

2. Save the page to the c:\Inetpub\wwwroot folder and name it **testcf2.cfm**.

3. Open Internet Explorer and type **http://localhost/testcf2.cfm**. If your workstation is properly configured, you should see the page shown in Figure 10.4 that displays the dynamic time.

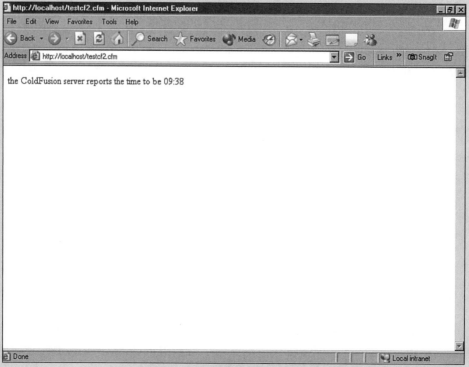

FIGURE 10.4   The ColdFusion page displays the time from the Web server.

4. If you do not see the time or the page does not load, check that you have the ColdFusion Server software installed. You can download a 30-day trial of the ColdFusion Server from Macromedia at `http://www.macromedia.com/cfusion/tdrc/index.cfm`.

5. If you need additional help installing and configuring the ColdFusion Server, Exercise 4.3 contains the complete instructions for downloading and installing the application.

Resource   GETTING STARTED WITH COLDFUSION

If you are just getting started with ColdFusion and have downloaded the 30-day trial, you might also check out the ColdFusion Get Started resource provided by Macromedia at `http://www.macromedia.com/software/coldfusion/resources/get_started/web_app_developers/`

Building the Directory Structure

The next step in configuring the workstation is to create the folders for the application files. When we built the intranet application, we placed the intranet files in one directory. In addition, the images for the site were placed in an images subfolder. We will follow this directory structure for the Web application as well, with one exception.

KrystalClear has asked for an administration feature that allows members of the KrystalClear staff to log in and update the Web pages and the product catalog. Because we need to restrict access to this section, we'll create a separate subfolder that contains the pages for the admin section.

KEEPING THE SEARCH ENGINE ROBOTS OUT OF YOUR ADMIN SECTION

Because we want access to the administrative section to be restricted to KrystalClear employees with the proper authorization, we also don't want the login page listed in the search engines. To avoid keeping the contents of the admin folder from being indexed by the search engines, you can create a simple text file named robots.txt that contains the following code:

```
User-agent: *
Disallow: /kcadmin0023/
```

This file should then be saved to the root directory of your Web server. When search engine robots first come to your site, they search for the robots.txt file and then know not to index any of the files stored in the kcadmin0023 folder. We're not going to worry about this step in building our folders because it is highly unlikely that a search engine robot will be attempting to index the files stored on your local workstation.

For complete details on using a robots.txt file, check out `http://www.robotstxt.org/wc/norobots.html`.

As we did with the intranet applications, we also need to create two separate directories for the different platforms. This allows us to keep the ColdFusion files separate from the ASP.NET files, which can aid in the troubleshooting process.

Exercise 10.3   Creating the Necessary Folders

1. Using Windows Explorer or My Computer, browse to the C:\Inetpub\wwwroot path and create a new folder by choosing File, New, Folder from the menu bar. Name the new folder KrystalClearWeb-ASP.

2. Open the new folder by double-clicking it. Create two new subfolders. Name the first **kcadmin0023** and the second **images**.

CREATIVE NAMING FOR THE ADMINISTRATIVE SECTION

When you build an administrative section for any Web application, it's a good idea to choose a creative name for the folder that contains those files. Hackers love to spend their free time trying to find weaknesses in your pages, but using a unique name for the administrative section keeps them from knowing where the pages are located. Using a generic name like admin, however, allows the hacker to easily guess where your files are located and makes it easier for him to get busy hacking your files.

In the case of our Web application, the kcadmin0023 name uses a numeric suffix that was randomly generated.

3. Return to the c:\Inetpub\wwwroot folder, right-click the KrystalClearWeb-ASP folder, and choose Copy from the context menu. Right-click in any white space on the page and choose Paste from the context menu.

4. Rename the second folder KrystalClearWeb-CF. These two new folders, shown in Figure 10.5, will serve as the locations for the KrystalClear Web application.

WHAT ABOUT FOLDER PERMISSIONS?

If you recall with the intranet application, we needed to set folder permissions so that the intranet pages could read and write to the Access database. Because we are using a SQL Server database to fuel our application, this step is no longer necessary. As long as the IUSR account has access to the pages, no additional permissions are required.

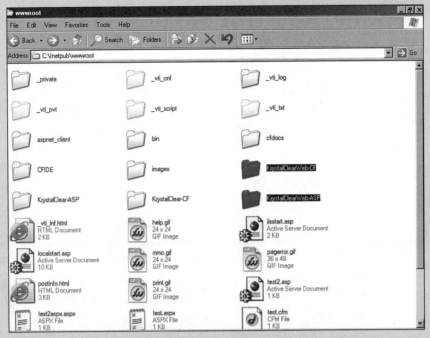

FIGURE 10.5   These folders will house the KrystalClear Web application.

5. Open the Computer Management Console by right-clicking the My Computer icon on your desktop and choosing Manage from the context menu.

6. In the Computer Management Console, expand the Services and Applications category, expand the Internet Information Services category, and then expand the Web Sites category.

7. Right-click the Default Web Site and choose New, Virtual Directory from the menu.

8. In the Virtual Directory Wizard, click Next.

9. In the Alias field, type **KrystalClearWeb-ASP** and click Next.

10. Browse to the c:\Inetpub\wwwroot\krystalclear-asp folder and click Next.

11. Set the permissions to Read, Run, and Write and click Next.

12. Click Finish.

13. Follow the same steps to create a virtual directory for the KrystalClearWeb-CF folder. Name the virtual directory KrystalClearWeb-CF.

14. Close the Computer Management Console.

Downloading the Support Files for the Internet Application

With the folders in place, the next step is to download the support files and place them in the proper locations. The support files for the site are simply the images that will be used when we start building the layout for our site. Rather than having you create the images from scratch (that's an entirely different book on Fireworks), you can just download them from the site used for this book and be ready to start developing your pages.

Exercise 10.4   Downloading and Extracting the Support Files

1. Open Internet Explorer and type **http://www.krystalclearcommunication.com/downloads** in the address bar.

2. Download the support files for the Web application to your local hard drive.

3. After the file is downloaded, double-click the executable and, as shown in Figure 10.6, choose to extract the contents to the c:\Inetpub\wwwroot\KrystalClearWeb-ASP\images folder.

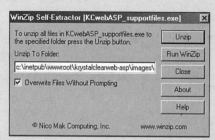

FIGURE 10.6   Extract the support files to the appropriate folder.

4. Double-click the executable again and extract the contents to the c:\Inetpub\wwwroot\KrystalClearWeb-CF\images folder.

5. Close Internet Explorer.

Creating a Dreamweaver Site for the Internet Application

As we did with the intranet site, the first step in building our application pages in Dreamweaver is to build a Dreamweaver site. By setting up an individual site for both the ASP.NET application and the ColdFusion application, we can develop the site on both platforms and Dreamweaver can track our changes and ensure that the pages with a site are linked properly.

Exercise 10.5(a)   Creating an ASP.NET Site in Dreamweaver

1. Open Dreamweaver.
2. Open the Site panel by choosing Window, Files from the menu bar.
3. In the Files panel, shown in Figure 10.7, click the menu button and choose Site, New Site. If you are in the Advanced view, switch to the Basic view of the Site Definition dialog box.

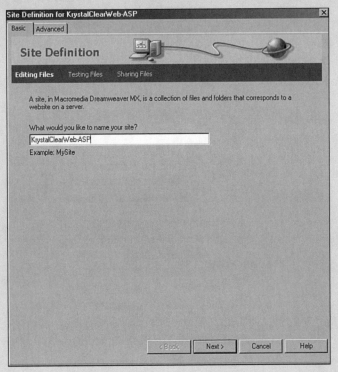

FIGURE 10.7   The Site panel allows you to manage your Dreamweaver sites.

4. Name the new site KrystalClearWeb-ASP and click the Next button.

5. Click the radio button that indicates that you want to use a server technology and choose ASP.NET VB from the drop-down list. Click Next.

6. Because you will be using your workstation to test your pages, choose to edit and test locally. If you are using an operating system other than Windows and would like to build your pages on your workstation and test them remotely, you can choose to edit locally and then upload to a remote testing server.

7. Browse to the KrystalClearWeb-ASP folder you created earlier and click Next.

8. Make sure that the URL to your site is `http://localhost/ krystalclearweb-asp/` and click the Test URL button. After Windows confirms that the root folder exists and IIS is running, it returns the confirmation message shown in Figure 10.8.

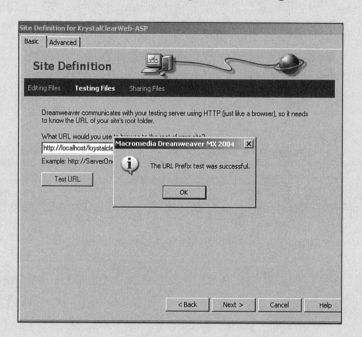

FIGURE 10.8   The Test URL functions as anticipated.

9. Click Next. Choose not to use a remote server.

10. Click Next and, as shown in Figure 10.9, Dreamweaver displays detailed information about your new site's settings.

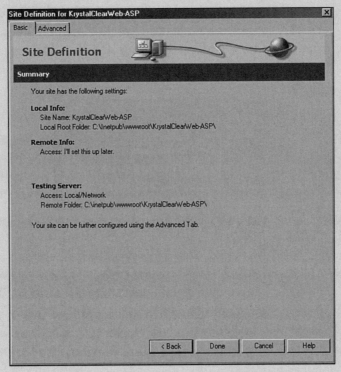

FIGURE 10.9   Your site's settings.

11. Click Done and your site is complete.

As we did earlier with the intranet project, KrystalClear's Web project is being built on both the ASP.NET and the ColdFusion platforms so you can gain exposure to the development process in both. Creating a ColdFusion site in Dreamweaver is very similar to the ASP.NET site, with just a few slight modifications.

Exercise 10.5(b)   Creating a ColdFusion Site in Dreamweaver

1. Open Dreamweaver.

2. Open the Site panel by choosing Window, Files from the menu bar.

3. In the Files panel, click the menu button and choose Site, New Site. If you are in the Advanced view, switch to the Basic view of the Site Definition dialog box.

4. Name the new site KrystalClearWeb-CF and click the Next button.

5. Click the radio button that indicates that you want to use a server technology and choose ColdFusion from the drop-down list. Click Next.

6. Because you will be using your workstation to test your pages, choose to edit and test locally. If you are using an operating system other than Windows and would like to build your pages on your workstation and test them remotely, you can choose to edit locally and then upload to a remote testing server.

7. Browse to the KrystalClearWeb-CF folder you created earlier and click Next.

8. Make sure that the URL to your site is `http://localhost/krystalclearweb-cf/` and click the Test URL button. After Windows confirms that the root folder exists and IIS is running, it returns the confirmation message.

9. Click Next. Choose not to use a remote server.

10. Click Next and Dreamweaver displays detailed information about your new site's settings.

11. Click Done and your site is complete.

Building the Database Connection

The final step in configuring your workstation for the Web application is to build a connection to the database. Creating this connection is very similar to the process we followed for the intranet application. Because we are using a SQL Server database, however, there are a few minor differences.

Exercise 10.6(a)   Building a Database Connection for the ASP.NET Site

1. If it is not already open, open Dreamweaver.

2. Open the Site panel by choosing Window, Site.

3. In the Site panel, choose the KrystalClearWeb-ASP site from the drop-down list.

4. Choose File, New from the menu bar. In the New Document dialog box, choose a Dynamic Page that uses the ASP.NET VB technology. Click Create.

5. Open the Databases panel by choosing Window, Databases from the menu bar.

6. In the Databases panel, shown in Figure 10.10, you should now see ASP.NET VB, indicating that the pages you are currently developing use the ASP.NET VB server technology.

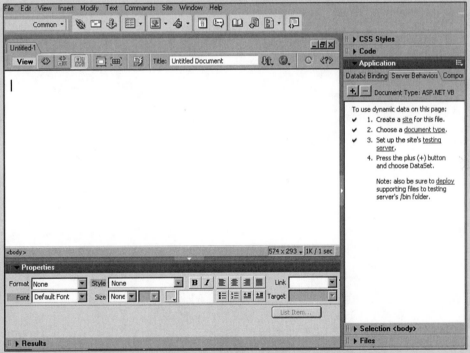

FIGURE 10.10   The pages in your site will be developed using the ASP.NET VB language.

7. Click the plus symbol on the Databases tab and choose SQL Server Connection from the menu.

8. In the SQL Server Connection dialog box, type **connKrystalClearWebASP** as the Connection Name.

9. In the Connection String panel, modify the information so that it looks like the following code block:

```
Persist Security=False;
Data Source=(local)
Initial Catalog=KrystalClear_WebDB;
UserID=;
Password=;
Trusted_Connection=Yes;
```

The SQL Server Connection dialog box should now look like Figure 10.11.

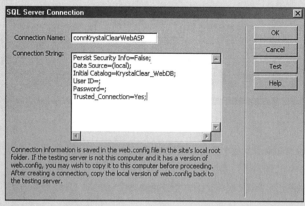

FIGURE 10.11   Configure your connection to the SQL Server database.

10. Click the Test button to ensure that your syntax is correct. If you typed everything correctly, Dreamweaver displays the confirmation message shown in Figure 10.12.

11. Click OK to close the connection confirmation and click OK to close the SQL Server Connection dialog box.

12. Click the plus sign next to the connKrystalClearWebASP connection and click the plus sign next to the Tables category. As shown in Figure 10.13, the tables we created earlier are now accessible to Dreamweaver.

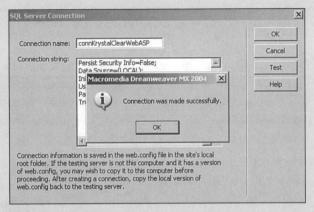

FIGURE 10.12   The connection test was successful.

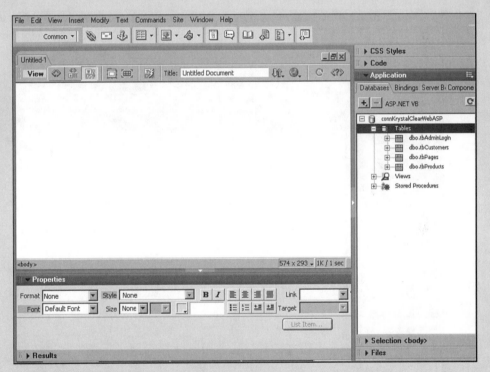

FIGURE 10.13   The connection is completed and the tables are now accessible.

To create the database connection for the ColdFusion platform, we have to turn to the ColdFusion manager.

Exercise 10.6(b)   Creating a Database Connection for the ColdFusion Site

1. Open the ColdFusion Administrator. In Windows 9x or 2000, you can access the Administrator by clicking Start, Programs, Macromedia ColdFusion, Administrator. In Windows XP, you can access the Administrator by clicking Start, All Programs, Macromedia ColdFusion, Administrator.

2. When prompted, enter the Administrator password that you chose when you installed ColdFusion.

3. In the Administrator, shown in Figure 10.14, click the Data Sources link in the left navigation menu.

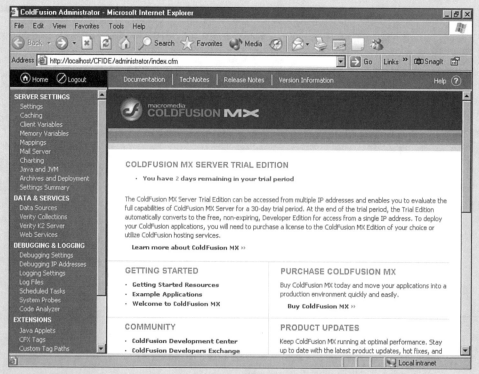

FIGURE 10.14   The ColdFusion Administrator allows you to create database connections.

4. In the Data Sources window, shown in Figure 10.15, type **connCrystalClearWebCF** for the name and choose Microsoft SQL Server as the driver type. Click the Add button.

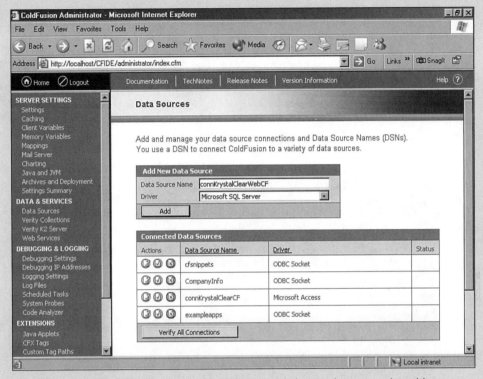

FIGURE 10.15 Name the data source and choose the appropriate driver.

5. In the Microsoft SQL Server Data Source window, type **KrystalClear_WebDB** as the database name. Next, type **localhost** as the Server.

6. Click the Submit button to create this new data source.

7. In the Microsoft SQL Server Data Source dialog box, shown in Figure 10.16, set the Database name as the KrystalClear_WebDB and the Server as localhost. Type **SA** as the username and then type the strong password you assigned to the SA account when setting up SQL Server.

8. Click Submit to create the data source.

9. Close the ColdFusion Administrator.

10. Open Dreamweaver and switch to the KrystalClearWeb-CF site.

11. Create a new dynamic document using the ColdFusion platform.

12. In the Databases panel, click the link to specify the RDS login for your ColdFusion server. In the Login dialog box, shown in Figure 10.17, type the password that you used to access the ColdFusion Administrator.

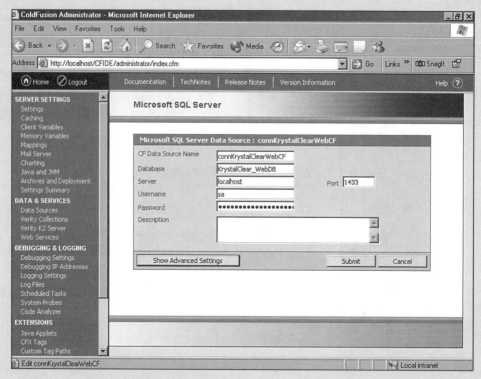

FIGURE 10.16   Assign the properties of the new connection.

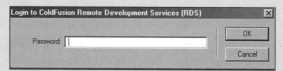

FIGURE 10.17   Type the password to establish the RDS login.

13. In the Databases panel, you should now see the connKrystalClearWebCF database. Click the plus sign next to the database and then click the plus sign next to the Tables category. You should now be able to see the tables you created earlier in the database.

Summary

In this chapter, we set up the Web server and application server software so that your workstation can act as a limited Web server. If you already had the applications installed, this chapter helped you ensure that both static and dynamic pages are being served properly. In addition, we created the directory structure for the site and downloaded the support files that are used in the next chapter to create the framework for the site. Finally, we created a Dreamweaver site for the Web application and built a connection to the SQL Server database.

In the next chapter, we will begin developing the layout for our Web pages. In addition, the next chapter walks you through the process of adding rollover images and dynamic images to the pages. Finally, we'll look at the process of building custom hyperlinks that allow data to be drawn from the database and displayed on the page.

CHAPTER 11

CREATING THE FRONT END FOR THE WEB APPLICATION

Now that the database has been built, the directory structure is in place, and a connection to the database has been built, we can start building the Web pages that make up the KrystalClear Web site. One of the biggest benefits of database-driven sites is the fact that we don't have to create a separate page for each piece of content that we want our visitors to access. Instead, we can build a few pages that change based on the information that is drawn from the database.

In this chapter, we will focus on the mix of both static and dynamic elements. We'll begin by building a page template that contains the necessary tables and then we will add the static graphics to the page template. With the tables and images in place, we'll examine the process of creating dynamic images such as database-driven images and rollover images. Finally, we'll look at the process of developing dynamic hyperlinks that signal the page to draw data from our database.

By the end of this chapter, you will have completed the following:

- Created the table structure for the Web application page template
- Added static and dynamic images to the pages
- Built a series of dynamic links that will be used to draw content from the database
- Created the necessary pages to build the rest of the application

Building the Basic Page Layout

The first step in laying out the pages for the Web application is create a template that contains objects that will be common to all pages in the application. To start, we need to build the table structure that places the objects in the proper locations and provides an attractive, well-organized, visual representation of the information.

The basic layout of the Web pages is made up of a table with three rows. The top row of the table will contain the header image, the bottom will contain the footer image, and the middle row will contain a series of additional tables used to display links, images, and content.

Exercise 11.1   Adding the Proper Tables to the Page

1. Open Dreamweaver MX 2004 and create a new page based on the ASP.NET or ColdFusion platform, depending on what platform you are developing on.

2. Place your cursor in the page and click the Align Center button on the toolbar.

3. From the menu bar, choose Insert, Table and add a table that has 4 rows, 1 column, and a width of 745 pixels. Set the border thickness to 0 and the cell padding and cell spacing to 2.

4. Set the background color of the table to #000099 by typing the value in the Bg Color field of the Property inspector.

5. Place your cursor in the second row from the top and insert a new table. The table should have 1 row, 6 columns, and a width of 730 pixels. Set the border at 1 and the cell padding and cell spacing at 0.

6. With the embedded table selected, type **#D1EBFA** in the Bg Color field of the Property inspector. Next, type **#0099FF** in the Brdr Color field of the Property inspector. With the table in place, your page should look like Figure 11.1. For reference purposes throughout the chapter, we'll refer to this table as the navbar table.

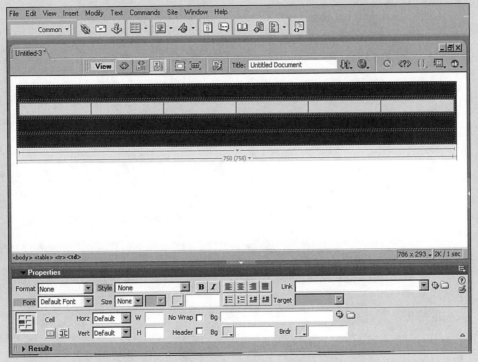

FIGURE 11.1   The page contains several of the necessary tables.

7. Place your cursor in the third row down and insert a new table. This table should have 1 row, 2 columns, and a width of 750 pixels. Set the border, cell padding, and cell spacing to 0.

8. Place your cursor in the left cell and type **150** in the W field of the Property inspector to set the width of the column to 150 pixels. Click the Align Center button.

9. Place your cursor in the right cell and set the width of the column to 550 pixels. Click the Align Center button.

10. Place the cursor back in the left cell. Insert another table that has 4 rows, 1 column, and a width of 150. Set the border, cell padding, and cell spacing to 0. For references throughout the chapter, we'll refer to this section of the page as the module table.

11. In the new table, place your cursor in the second row down and insert a new table. The table should have 2 rows, 1 column, and a width of 148 pixels. Set the border to 1 and the cell padding and cell spacing to 0.

12. Set the background color for the new table to #D1EBFA and the border color to #0099FF.

13. Place your cursor in the bottom cell of the new table and insert another table. This table should have 4 rows, 1 column, and a width of 145 pixels. Set the border, cell padding, and cell spacing to 0.

14. Select the table with the light blue border and choose Edit, Copy from the menu bar. Place your cursor in the bottom cell of the table in the left column and choose Edit, Paste from the menu bar. With the completed table structure in place, your page should look like Figure 11.2.

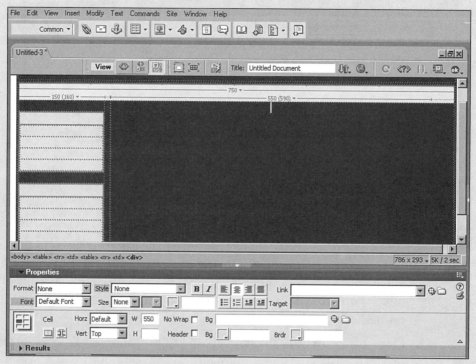

FIGURE 11.2   The basic table structure has been created.

15. Save the page as kcweb_template.aspx or kcweb_template.cfm.

DREAMWEAVER TEMPLATES VERSUS HTML TEMPLATES

As you develop both static and dynamic applications with Dreamweaver, it's likely that you'll build applications (as we did in the intranet chapters) that make use of the template feature included with Dreamweaver. Dreamweaver's capability to generate pages from a template is extremely useful in many cases—especially when you need to create a large number of pages that rely on the same structure.

That is not to say, however, that *all* your applications will use the Dreamweaver template feature. In the case of the Web application, we are going to build a template but not use the Dreamweaver template feature to update it. Keep in mind that just because a feature exists in Dreamweaver, it doesn't mean you *have* to use it. The Template feature of Dreamweaver is usually suitable for sites that contain 50 pages or fewer. When a site has more than 50 pages, modifications to the template become time consuming because each time a minor change is made to the template, all of the dependent pages have to then be updated and uploaded to the server.

If you choose to build templates that are not managed by Dreamweaver, you should be aware of some things. First, non-Dreamweaver templates are not automatically updated. Therefore, they are useful as a boilerplate for pages that will have a lot of similarity but need to be unique in certain aspects. Second, avoid saving your non-Dreamweaver templates in the Templates folder within your site. Saving them in this folder can only lead to confusion later down the road. Finally, remember that saving your own non-Dreamweaver templates requires that do not use the File, Save As Template command. If you use this command, you'll end up either saving your template as a Dreamweaver template or getting a bunch of errors if you don't have any editable regions defined.

With the tables in place, the next step is to add images such as the corporate logo and navigation buttons. Although some of the images are static, others use JavaScript behaviors to act as rollover buttons. Some of the images for the pages are going to be hard-coded into the page layout, whereas the source code for others is drawn dynamically from the database. For those images that are dynamically generated, we also need to ensure that the page only attempts to display them when there is a record available that contains a valid link to an image. Attempting to display an image from an empty dataset/recordset can result in an error message that keeps the entire page from displaying properly.

Exercise 11.2   Adding Static and Rollover Images

1. In the new page, place your cursor in the top row of the first table we inserted into the page. Choose Insert, Image from the menu bar and navigate to the images subfolder. Select the kcweb_logo.jpb image and click OK.

2. In the bottom row of the first table we inserted, insert the kcweb_footer.jpg, With the header and footer in place, your page should look like Figure 11.3.

FIGURE 11.3   The header and footer images have been placed.

3. In the module table section of the page (the tables on the left side of the page), place your cursor in the top-most cell that has a light-blue background.

USING THE TAG SELECTOR

As you can see, the art of nesting tables can get very complicated. For this reason, it's a good idea for you to get comfortable using the tag selector located just below the Page Layout view of Dreamweaver. The tag selector allows you to place your cursor anywhere on the page and see what tags affect that location.

4. Click the Align Center button and insert the kcweb_productstab.gif image.

5. Place your cursor in the top cell of the bottom module table and click the Align Center button. Insert the kcweb_searchtab.gif image in this cell. Your page should now look like Figure 11.4.

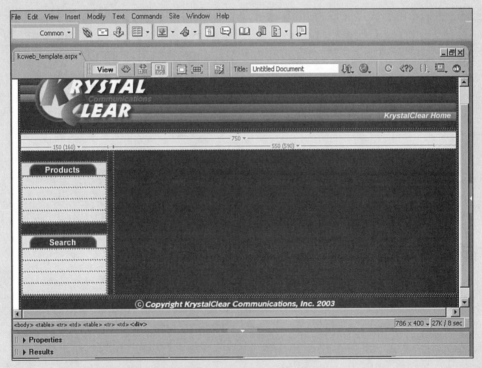

FIGURE 11.4   The module header tabs are in place.

6. Our next step is to place rollover images in the navbar table. Highlight all the cells in the navbar table and click the Align Center button. Set the width of each field to 125 pixels.

7. Place your cursor in the left-most column of the navbar table and choose Insert, Image Objects, Rollover Image from the menu bar.

8. In the Insert Rollover Image dialog box, shown in Figure 11.5, name the image imgProductsButton. Click the Browse button next to the Original Image field and choose the kcweb_productsbutton_up.gif. Next, click the Browse button next to the Rollover Image field and choose kcweb_productsbutton_over.gif. In the URL field, type **default.aspx?PageID=ProductsHome** or **default.cfm?PageID=ProductsHome**, depending on your platform.

ADDING ALT TEXT TO YOUR IMAGES

When building pages for the Web, it's a good idea to keep in mind that your pages should be accessible to visitors with disabilities. One of the best ways to accomplish this is to fill in alternative text for each of your graphics using the ALT field in the Property inspector.

For a great resource on this topic, check out *Building Accessible Websites* (New Riders, 2002) by Joe Clark.

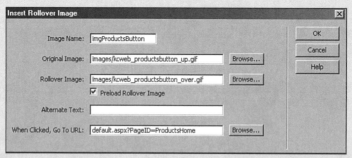

FIGURE 11.5   The Insert Rollover Image dialog box allows you to easily create interactive images.

9. Click OK to close the dialog box.
10. Follow this procedure again to insert four more rollover images into the next cells. Use the information in Table 11.1 to insert the appropriate images and create the correct links. Build the images from left to right in the navbar table.

EASY ROLLOVER

You can also easily add a rollover image to your page by placing your cursor in the page, clicking the Image button on the Insert Bar, and choosing Rollover Image.

TABLE 11.1 Settings for the Rollover Images

IMAGE NAME	ORIGINAL IMAGE	ROLLOVER IMAGE	URL
imgProducts Button	kcweb_products button_up.gif	kcweb_products button_up.gif	default.aspx? PageName= ProductsHome
			Or
			Default.cfm? PageName= ProductsHome
imgCoverage Button	kcweb_coverage button_up.gif	kcweb_coverage button_up.gif	default.aspx? PageName= CoverageHome
			Or
			Default.cfm? PageName= CoverageHome
imgAbout Button	kcweb_about button_up.gif	kcweb_about button_up.gif	default.aspx? PageName= AboutHome
			Or
			default.cfm? PageName= AboutHome
imgNews Button	kcweb_news button_up.gif	kcweb_news button_up.gif	default.aspx? PageName= NewsHome
			Or
			Default.cfm? PageName= NewsHome

continues

TABLE 11.1   Settings for the Rollover Images (Continued)

IMAGE NAME	ORIGINAL IMAGE	ROLLOVER IMAGE	URL
imgCareers Button	kcweb_careers button_up.gif	kcweb_careers button_up.gif	default.aspx? PageName= CareersHome Or Default.cfm? PageName= CareersHome

11. Leave the last cell in the navbar table empty as we will use this for our login/logout button functionality in Chapter 14, "Allowing Visitors to Create User Accounts." With the rollover images in place, your page should now look like Figure 11.6.

FIGURE 11.6   The rollover images have been placed.

12. Save the page.

Creating Static and Dynamic Hyperlinks

Now that the images are in place, the next step is to create a series of hyperlinks that allow the visitor to navigate the site. For this application, we'll start by creating a single hyperlink that is part of an image map. The image map allows us to create different hyperlinks for sections of a single image. As you will see in the exercise, creating the image map in Dreamweaver is as simple as drawing the region for the link and typing in the URL for the link.

With the image map in place, we need to create a few more links that allow our visitors to browse the available products by category. These links are typical hyperlinks with additional variables tagged on to the end. These variables can be used to draw content from the database, and that content can then be displayed on the page.

HOW MANY VARIABLES CAN YOU PASS?

When creating dynamic hyperlinks, there is no limit on the number of variables that can be passed. Some browsers and proxy servers, however, limit the number of characters that can be passed. For instance, Microsoft reports that Internet Explorer limits URL lengths to 2,083 characters, whereas some proxy servers may limit URL length to as few as 255 characters.

For this reason, it's wise to keep the name of your variables rather short and be cautious as to how many variables are being passed in the URL.

Exercise 11.3   Building Hyperlinks

1. In the template page, select the company logo. In the Property inspector, click the rectangle shape below the Map name field.

2. Using your mouse, draw a rectangle shape over the KrystalClear Home text in the corporate logo. In the Link field of the Property inspector, type **default.aspx** or **default.cfm**.

3. Draw another rectangle over the KrystalClear Communications logo on the far left of the image and set that link to default.aspx or default.cfm as well. As shown in Figure 11.7, the image map links are now displayed as shaded areas.

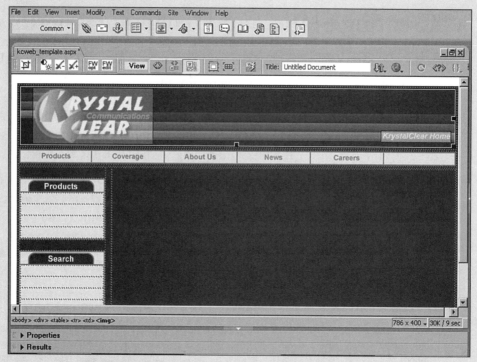

FIGURE 11.7   The image map links have been created.

4. The next step is to create our product category links. In the template page, select the four empty rows below the Products tab (not the Product rollover image) and click the Align Center button.

5. Create a new set of styles for the site by choosing New CSS Style from the Style field in the Property inspector.

6. In the New CSS Style dialog box, name the style .HeaderText and choose to make a custom style and define it in a new style sheet file. Click OK.

7. Save the style sheet to the KrystalClearWeb folder for your platform with the name krystalclearwebss.css.

8. In the CSS Style Definition dialog box, choose the Type category and set the font to Arial, the size to 14 pixels, and the Weight to Bold. Click OK.

9. Create an additional style called .BodyText and set the font to Arial, the size to 12, and the weight and style to Normal.

10. In the top empty row, type **Wireless Phones**. Select the text and reformat it using the BodyText style. With the text highlighted, type **default.aspx?PageName=Wireless** or **default.cfm?PageName=Wireless**, depending on your platform.

Tip

APPLY STYLES TO GROUPS

You can also apply styles to a groups of text by selecting the `<td>` tag in which the text is contained and applying the style to all text within the `<td>` region.

11. Place your cursor in the next row down and type **Pagers**. Reformat the text using the BodyText style and set the hyperlink to default.aspx?PageName=Pagers or default.cfm?PageName=Pagers.

12. Place your cursor in the next row down and type **PDAs**. Reformat the text using the BodyText style and set the hyperlink to default.aspx?PageName=PDAs or default.cfm?PageName=PDAs.

13. Place your cursor in the next row down and type Coverage **Plans**. Reformat the text using the BodyText style and set the hyperlink to default.aspx?PageName=Plans or default.cfm?PageName=Plans. With the links in place, your page should now look like Figure 11.8.

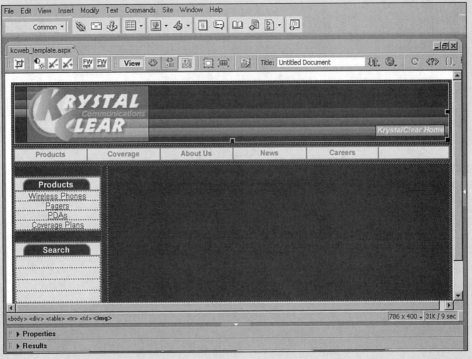

FIGURE 11.8   Dynamic links allow the visitor to view custom content stored in the database.

14. Highlight the four empty cells below the Search tab and choose Center from the Horz dropdown on the Property Inspector.

15. In the top empty row, type **Product Search**. Select the text and reformat it using the BodyText style. With the text highlighted, type **search.aspx?SearchName=Products** or **search.cfm?SearchName=Products**, depending on your platform.

16. Press Tab and type **Coverage Search**. Reformat the text using the BodyText style and set the hyperlink to search.aspx?SearchName=Coverage or search.cfm?SearchName=Coverage.

17. Press Tab and type **Careers Search**. Reformat the text using the BodyText style and set the hyperlink to search.aspx?SearchName=Careers or search.cfm?SearchName=Careers. With the links in place, your page should now look like Figure 11.9.

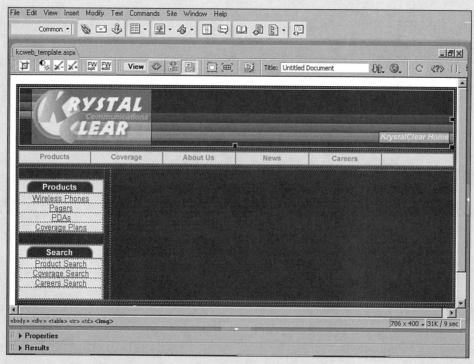

FIGURE 11.9   The new search links are in place.

18. Save the page.

Creating Pages Templates for the Various Sections of the Web Application

With the basic layout in place, we now need to customize our layout to accommodate the various sections of the site that have been requested. For instance, the informational pages such as the About Us page or the main welcome page need to have a slightly different layout than the Products pages or the Search page. By customizing each layout now, we can reuse the same page repeatedly to display all of the data stored in the database. We have already created a blank template that can be used as the foundation for the other required templates for elements such as the default page, the administrative pages, the Products pages, and the Search pages.

Creating the Default Page Template

The first custom page template that we need to build is for the default page that loads when the visitor types in the URL for the site. This page contains the traditional text welcoming the visitor to the site, but also serves to display dynamic content when the visitor clicks some of the links. For instance, when the visitor clicks the About Us button in the navigation bar, the default page is reloaded and the content stored in the database is displayed rather than the welcome text.

Because the buttons in the navigation bar contain dynamic variables, we can add a dataset/recordset to the page that draws records from the database based on the URL parameter. If the dataset/recordset is empty, we know that the visitor has arrived at the page by either clicking a link from another site or by typing in the URL directly. In this case, we display the welcome content. If, however, the recordset is not empty, we can deduce that the visitor arrived at the page by clicking a link within the site and, based on the URL variable, the page should display the appropriate content.

Although it sounds complicated, it's just a matter of an if-then statement that says, "If the URL does not contain a variable, treat this page as the welcome page. If it does contain a variable, don't display the welcome text, but display the content in the database."

Exercise 11.4   Adding Dynamic Content to Create the Default Page Template

1. Save the template page with a new name by choosing File, Save As from the menu bar. Name the file kcweb_default_template.aspx or kcweb_default_template.cfm.

2. Place your cursor in the main content area (to the right of the navigation buttons) and set the background color to #FFFFFF. In the Property inspector, set the Vert field to Top.

3. In the main content area, insert a table that contains 2 rows, 1 column, and has a width of 400 pixels. Set the border to 0 and the cell padding and cell spacing to 2.

4. On the line below the table, insert a second table with 2 rows, 2 columns, and a width of 500 pixels. Set the border to 0 and the cell padding and spacing to 2.

5. Highlight the left column of the bottom table and set the column width to 150 pixels. With the tables in place, your page should look like Figure 11.10.

6. Save the page.

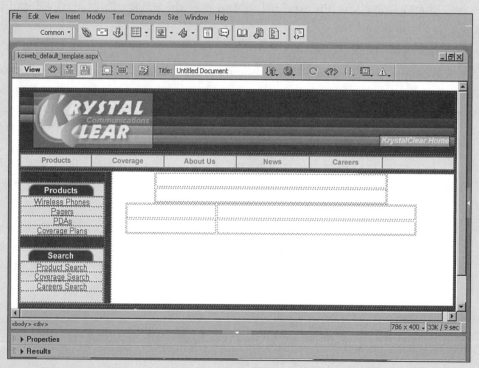

FIGURE 11.10   The default page template contains two additional tables.

Creating the Search Page Template

The search pages are a bit different from the main page layout. Rather than checking to see if there is a PageID in the URL, the search page checks to see if there are two variables containing a search type and a search term. If the variables do not exist, the search form is displayed. If, however, the variables do exist, the results are displayed in tabular form. To accomplish this, the search page requires a different dataset/recordset than the one that will be used in the default page layout. In addition, a separate set of tables is used to display the search results.

Exercise 11.5   Creating the Search Page Template

1. Open the kcweb_template page and save it as kcweb_search_template.aspx or kcweb_search_template.cfm.

2. Place your cursor in the main content area and set the background color to #FFFFFF. In the Property inspector, set the Vert field to Top.

3. In the main content area, insert a table that contains 3 rows, 1 column, and has a width of 400 pixels. Set the border to 0 and the cell padding and cell spacing to 2.

4. On the line below the new table, insert another table that contains 4 rows, 1 column, and has a width of 450 pixels. Set the border to 0 and the cell padding and cell spacing to 2. With the tables in place, your page should look like Figure 11.11.

5. Save the page.

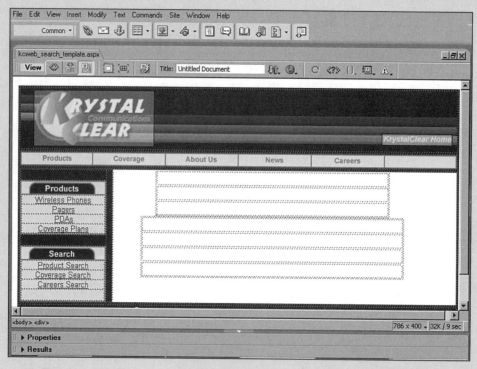

FIGURE 11.11   The search page template contains two additional tables.

Creating the Products Page Template

The final page template we need to create is for the pages that display the products in the catalog. Each product will have a photo, the product name, and the description of the product in a table in the main content region. In addition, we'll add a button that allows users to purchase the item online. Later, in Chapter 15, "Engaging in eCommerce," we'll see how to put that button into action.

Exercise 11.6   Building the Products Page Template

1. Open the kcweb_template page and save it as kcweb_products_template.aspx or kcweb_products_template.cfm.

2. Place your cursor in the main content area and set the background color to #FFFFFF. In the Property inspector, set the Vert field to Top.

3. In the main content area, insert a table that contains 1 row, 1 column, and has a width of 400 pixels. Set the border to 0 and the cell padding and cell spacing to 2.

4. On the line below the new table, insert another table that contains 1 row, 2 columns, and has a width of 450 pixels. Set the border to 0 and the cell padding and cell spacing to 2.

5. Place your cursor in the left column and set the width of the column to 150 pixels.

6. Place the cursor in the right column and insert a new table that has 3 rows, 2 columns, and a width of 300 pixels. Set the border to 0 and the cell padding and cell spacing to 2. With the tables in place, your page should look like Figure 11.12.

7. Save the page.

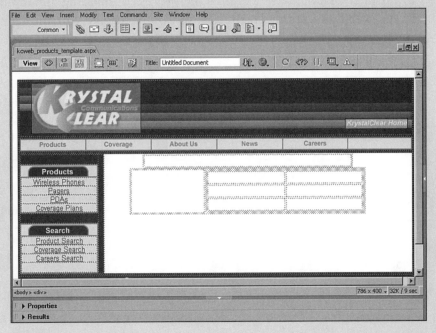

FIGURE 11.12   The products page template contains three additional tables.

Now that we have the three main template pages created, you might be wondering how we're going to sandwich all of our pages into those three "cookie-cutter" templates. The answer is we're not. These templates provide us a good place to start for the vast majority of our pages. However, we do not want to restrict the development and growth of the site to just these templates. That's why we originally saved the blank template with nothing in the main content region. For those pages that don't fit under one of the three main templates, we can use the blank template and build from scratch.

Summary

In this chapter, we built created the fundamental framework for the pages that will make up the KrystalClear Web application. In addition to the tables, we added both static and interactive images and developed a series of hyperlinks that will assist the visitors in navigating the site. In addition, by building the templates, we have created a set of pages that will be capable of serving up an almost limitless amount of data, effectively replacing hundreds of different pages that, in the past, had to be individually coded.

In the next chapter, we'll examine the process of building an administrative side to the Web application. This secure section of the site will allow KrystalClear staff members to add, edit, and deactivate page content, products, and customer accounts.

CHAPTER 12

BUILDING THE PAGE ADMINISTRATION MODULE

Even though Web applications are becoming increasingly complex in their use of various platforms, languages, and interactive capabilities, one thing has remained constant—content is king. Regardless of whether a site offers news, information, eCommerce, or any other type of service, if the content is not up-to-date, the visitor is not receiving the best possible service.

In the past, Web developers have not only been responsible for building the applications, but have been in charge of updates as well. The process of updating pages, however, can quickly become time consuming, which takes away from the time that the Web developer can use to come up with new ideas for the site. As a result, many Web developers have begun building content management systems (CMS) that allow other staff members to access the page content and make edits. By doing this, each department can assume responsibility for the accuracy of its section of the Web site. Inventory management can update the number and type of products that are in stock, public relations can add news releases at its convenience, and the Web developer can continue creating new and better ways to interact with Web site visitors.

In this chapter, we will build a simple content management system that allows authorized users to log in to a secured area of the site, view available pages, edit their content, and add new content when necessary.

In this chapter, you will do the following:

- Create a login and logout system for the secured pages
- Build a page that lists the pages that are part of the Web application
- Develop pages that allow the user to add new content
- Build pages that allow the user to edit existing content

Reviewing the Table Structure for the Administration Module

Before we start building pages, let's review the tbPages table that we created in Chapter 9, "Building a Database for Web Applications." The tbPages table, shown in Figure 12.1, contains eight different fields that contain data used to build each dynamic page.

The PageID field is an identity field meaning that it contains a unique numeric value that corresponds to the specific record. Because MSSQL Server increments this field by 1 for each new record, we can be assured that no two records will ever have the same value.

The PageName field contains a unique description that allows the user to quickly identify the record and its contents. Users should be careful to use this field as concisely as possible to clearly label each record.

The PageCategory field is also a user-defined field that allows us to group the pages into meaningful categories. For instance, some pages might fall into the AboutUs category, Catalog category, or ContactUs category, depending on their content.

The ImageURL, PageTitle, and PageContent fields all contain the data that is used to populate the content for each dynamic page. The ImageURL contains the location of a unique image for that specific page, the PageTitle contains the page header and content for the browser's title bar, and the PageContent contains all of the text that is displayed in the dynamic page.

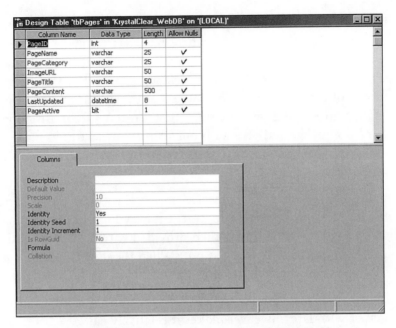

FIGURE 12.1   The structure of the tbPages table.

The LastUpdated and PageActive fields allow users to effectively administer the pages. By examining the contents of the LastUpdated field, the user can determine how old the content is and whether it needs to be updated. In addition, the PageActive field contains either a 1 or a 0 as its value. If the value is 1, the page is active and is accessible to visitors. If, however, the value is 0, the page will not be displayed on the KrystalClear site. By creating this field, we provide administrators with the ability to "turn on" and "turn off" pages without having to delete them.

Creating the Login/Logout Pages for the Module

With the appropriate database table in place, we now can turn our attention to the pages that are required to build this module of the Web application. For starters, we need to ensure that only authorized users are allowed to access the pages that make up the admin module.

After they are allowed to access the system, an authorized user will be taken to a page that lists the various database records that make up the content for the Web application. This page also contains links that allow the user to add a new record to the database (which in turn adds content to the Web application) or edit any of the existing records. Whether the user is adding a new record or updating an existing one, the user should receive a confirmation message upon completion of the activity. With our security measures in place, these pages should only be accessible to visitors who have provided a valid username and password.

Finally, after completing the necessary work with the database records, the user must also be able to terminate his session by logging out. To log out, the user clicks a logout button and is then provided with a message letting him know that he was successfully logged out. When the user is logged out, all session variables that contain information about that user are destroyed as well.

Although this may sound like a lot of work, using database-driven pages together with Dreamweaver makes it relatively easy.

Warning   LINKING TO THE ADMIN SECTION

When you create an administrative section for your Web application, it is unwise to place a link to the login page anywhere on your Web pages. This allows hackers to know the location of your administrative login pages and gives them a head start on hacking your site. Instead, require your users to type in the URL or place a shortcut on their desktop so that they can access the system. In addition, if there is no link to your admin section, the search engine spiders won't follow the link and try to list your administrative pages in their index.

Creating the Login Pages

Because we have our page template in place, building the login page is relatively simple. Using HTML or .NET elements, we can add a form to the page that asks the user for her username and password. After the information is submitted, the values are then compared with the records stored in the tbAdminLogin table. If the username and password combination match a record in the database, the user is presented with a welcome message and the module creates the necessary session variables that allows the user to move from page to page within the module without having to re-authenticate each time she changes pages.

Exercise 12.1(a)   Creating the Login Page in ASP.NET

1. Open Dreamweaver and open the kcweb_template.aspx page. From the menu bar, choose File, Save As and save the file in the kcadmin0023 folder as admin_login.aspx.

2. Place your cursor in the main content region at the right side of the page and set the Bg field on the Property inspector to #FFFFFF.

3. In the main content region, type **Admin Login** and press Enter. On the new line, add a new form and switch to the Split Code and Design view. Inside the form tag, type **runat="server"**. Switch back to the Design view.

4. With your cursor inside the form, add a table to your page with 3 rows, 2 columns, and a width of 300 pixels. In the upper-left cell, type **Username:**. In the middle-left cell, type **Password:**.

5. Place your cursor in the upper-right cell and choose Insert, ASP.NET Objects, asp:textbox. Set the ID of the textbox to tfUsername and click OK. Add a second textbox in the next cell down and name it tfPassword. In the Text Mode of the second textbox, choose Password.

6. In the lower-right cell, insert an asp:button named btLogin. Set the text of this button to Login. With the form elements in place, your page should look like Figure 12.2.

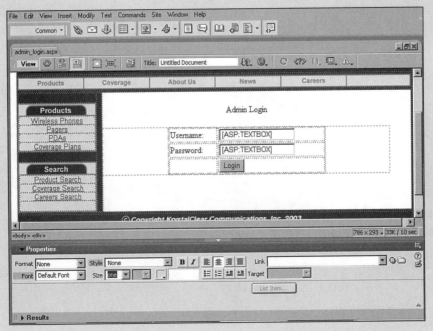

FIGURE 12.2   The login form with the necessary form elements.

7. The next step is to build a dataset that checks to see if the values submitted by the form match any records in the database. Click the plus sign on the Server Behaviors panel and choose DataSet.

8. In the DataSet dialog box, name the dataset dsAdminLogin, choose the connKrystalClearWebASP connection and the tbAdminLogin table. Switch to the Advanced view and modify the SQL Query so it looks like this:

```
SELECT *
FROM dbo.tbAdminLogin
WHERE Username = @Username AND Password = @Password
```

Create two new parameters for the query. The first is named @Username, is of the VarChar type, and draws the form variable tfUsername with no default value. The second is named @Password, is of the VarChar type, and draws the form variable tfPassword with no default value. When your dataset is complete, the dialog box should look like Figure 12.3.

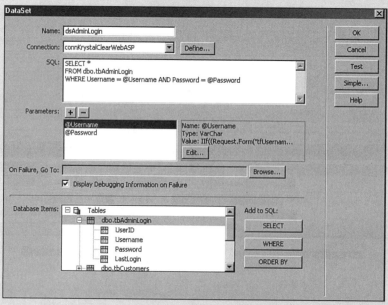

FIGURE 12.3   The completed dsAdminLogin dataset.

> **Note**
>
> **DIFFERENT PARAMETER PLACEHOLDERS**
>
> If you followed all the exercises in the intranet section of the book (Part II, "Creating Intranet-Strength Applications with MS Access, ASP/CF, and Dreamweaver MX 2004"), you probably remember that we used the ? placeholder when building our datasets. Because we are using MS SQL Server rather than Access, we need to use the @Username and @Password placeholders instead. If you use the ? placeholder with a SQL Server database, the application will fail and you will receive an incorrect syntax error when you load your page.

9. Click OK to close the recordset.
10. Switch back to the Split Code and Design view and find the `</form>` tag. On a new line after the tag, add this code block:

```
<%
if dsAdminLogin.RecordCount > 0 then
Session("sessAdminUserName") = Request.Form("tfUserName")
FormsAuthentication.RedirectFromLoginPage("admin", true)
else if ((Request.Form("tfUserName"))) <> Nothing _
OR ((Request.Form("tfPassword"))) <> Nothing
response.Write("Login failed. Please try again.")
end if
%>
```

As you will see, this block of code checks to see if the dsAdminLogin recordset is empty (meaning that no records in the database matched the username/password combination). If the recordset is not empty, the user entered a valid username and password, is authenticated as a member of the admin group, and is redirected to the page that he originally requested. If, however, the recordset is empty, an invalid combination was entered and the Login Failed text is displayed.

11. Save the page.

Now that we have logged the user in, we need to update the LastLogin field that corresponds to his record.

12. Open the kcweb_template.aspx page. From the menu bar, choose File, Save As and save the file in the kcadmin0023 folder as default.aspx.
13. Place your cursor in the main content area and set the background to #FFFFF. Type **Thank you. Please click the button below to continue.** Press Enter.
14. Create a new dataset named dsAdminUser. Using the Simple mode, choose the connKrystalClearWebASP connection and the tbAdminLogin table.

15. Choose to draw all columns from the table and set a filter where Username = Session Variable sessAdminUsername. When completed, your dataset should look like Figure 12.4.

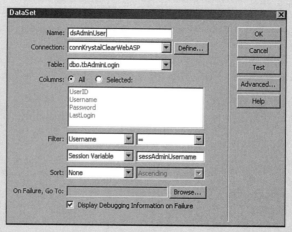

FIGURE 12.4   The completed dsAdminUser dataset.

16. Now that we know who the user is, we can update his record. Place your cursor on the line below the Thank You text and choose Insert, Application Objects, Update Record, Record Update Form Wizard.

17. As shown in Figure 12.5, choose the connKrystalClearWebASP connection and the tbAdminLogin table. Choose the record from the dsAdminUser dataset, with the unique key column being UserID. In the On Success, Go To field type **admin_page_manager.aspx**. In the Form Fields panel, use the minus sign to remove all fields except the LastLogin field and change the LastLogin field to a Hidden Field. Finally, in the Default Value field, type **<%# Now()%>**. This updates the record with the current time and date.

18. Click OK to close the Record Update Form Wizard dialog box.

19. Select the Update Record button and type **Continue** in the Label field of the Property inspector.

20. Save the page.

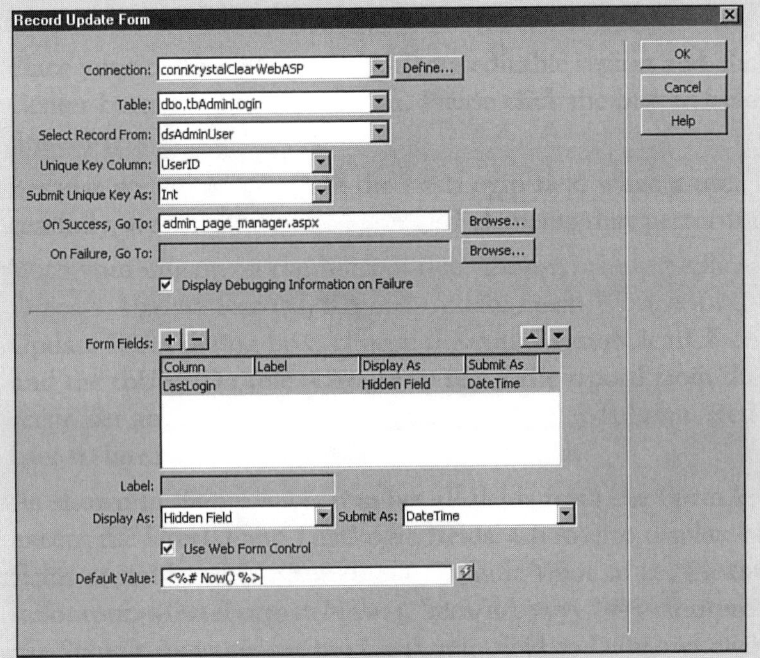

FIGURE 12.5 The Record Update Form updates the user's last login.

Exercise 12.1(b)   Building the Login Pages in ColdFusion

1. Open the kcweb_template.cfm page. From the menu bar, choose File, Save As and save the file in the kcadmin0023 folder as admin_login.cfm.

2. Place your cursor in the main content region at the right side of the page and set the Bg field on the Property inspector to #FFFFFF.

3. In the main content region, type **Admin Login** and press Enter. On the new line, add a new form.

4. With your cursor inside the form, add a table to your page with 3 rows, 2 columns, and a width of 300 pixels. Set the cell padding, cell spacing, and border thickness to 1. In the upper-left cell, type **Username:**. In the middle-left cell, type **Password:**.

5. Place your cursor in the upper-right cell and choose Insert, Form, Text Field. In the Properties inspector, set the name of the text field to tfUsername. Add a second textbox in the next cell down and name it tfPassword. In the Property inspector, set the Type field of the text field to Password.

6. In the lower-right cell, insert a button named btLogin. Set the label of this button to Login. With the form elements in place, your page should look like Figure 12.6.

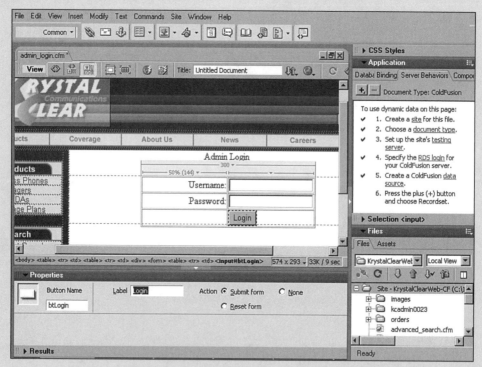

FIGURE 12.6   The login form with the necessary form elements.

7. Save the page.

The next step is to apply a server behavior that compares the data submitted in the form with that stored in the database. If the information matches, the user is logged in and redirected to a page where she receives a login validation. If, however, the data does not match, the user receives a page that displays an error message.

8. In the admin_login.cfm page, select the form and click the plus sign on the Server Behaviors panel. From the menu, choose User Authentication, Log In User. In the Log In User dialog box, choose the connKrystalClearWebCF data source and the tbAdminLogin table. Choose Username as the Username column and Password as the Password column.

9. As shown in Figure 12.7, type **admin_validation.cfm** in the If Login Succeeds field and type **admin_failure.cfm** in the If Login Fails field. Click OK.

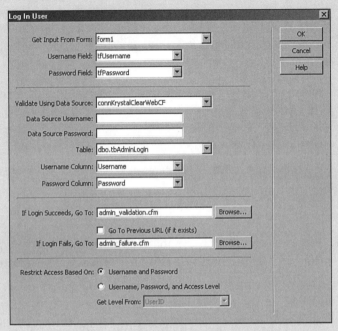

FIGURE 12.7   Complete the Log In User dialog box.

10. Save the page.

11. Create a new page based on the kcweb_template.cfm template and change the main content area background to #FFFFFF. Type **Login Failed. Please click the back button and try again** in the main content region. Save this page as admin_failure.cfm in the kcadmin0023 folder.

12. Create a new page based on the Main template and save the page as admin_validation.cfm. Click the plus sign on the Server Behaviors panel and choose Recordset(Query).

13. In the Recordset dialog box, name the recordset rsAdminLogin, choose the connKrystalClearWebCF connection and the tbAdminLogin table. Choose to select all fields where the Username field is equal to the session variable MM_Username. When your recordset is complete, the Recordset dialog box should look like Figure 12.8.

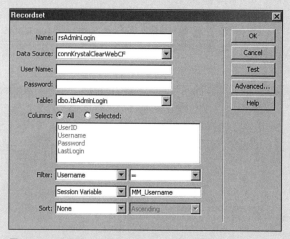

FIGURE 12.8   The completed rsAdminLogin recordset.

14. Click OK to close the Recordset dialog box.

15. Place your cursor in the main content region and type **Thank you. Please click the button below to continue.** Press Enter.

Because we want to update the LastLogin field when a user logs in successfully, we need to add a form and elements that perform this action.

16. With your cursor on the bottom line, choose Insert, Application Objects, Update Record, Record Update Form. In the Record Update Form dialog box, choose the connKrystalClearWebCF connection and the tbAdminLogin table. Choose to select the record from the rsAdminLogin recordset and choose UserID as the unique key column. Redirect the user to admin_pagemanager.cfm after updating the record.

17. As shown in Figure 12.9, remove all fields from the Form Fields panel except the UserID and LastLogin fields. Choose to display both these fields as hidden fields and set the Default Value of the LastLogin field to **<cfoutput>#DateFormat(Now(),"mm/dd/yyyy")#</cfoutput>**. Change the Submit As value for the LastLogin field to Date and click OK.

18. Select the button and change the Label to **Continue** in the Property inspector.

19. Save the page.

    Only one more thing remains to be done to complete the login section of the intranet. To use session variables in ColdFusion, you must first create a page within your site root that lets the ColdFusion server know that session variables are permitted.

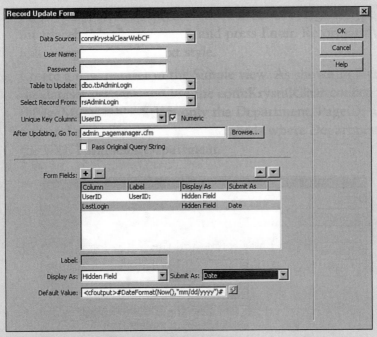

FIGURE 12.9 The Record Update Form dialog box that updates the LastLogin field.

20. Create a new blank ColdFusion page that is not based on any template. In the page, type the following code block:

```
<CFAPPLICATION NAME="KrystalClearWeb-CF"
SESSIONMANAGEMENT="Yes" >
```

21. Save this page as Application.cfm in the root site directory.

Creating the Logout Pages

After the user is finished using the module, we want her to be able to leave the application and know that another user cannot use the same machine to pick up where she left off. Luckily, Dreamweaver provides a server behavior that allows us to easily destroy the session variables that allow authorized users to access the module.

Exercise 12.2(a)   Creating the Logout Pages in ASP.NET

1. Open the kcweb_template.aspx page. From the menu bar, choose File, Save As and save the file in the kcadmin0023 folder as admin_logout.aspx.

2. Place your cursor in the main content region at the right side of the page and set the Bg field on the Property inspector to #FFFFFF. In the main content region, type **Click here to logout.** and press Enter.

3. Switch to the Split Code and Design view. On the new line, insert a form and add the `runat="server"` code to the form tag.

4. Inside the form, add an asp:button and name it btLogout. Set the text for the button to Logout.

5. With the button selected, add the following code to the button tag just before the `/>`:

```
onClick="Logout_Click"
```

6. Create a new line at line 2 of your document and add the following code block:

```
<script language="VB" runat="server">
Sub Logout_Click(ByVal s As Object, ByVal e As EventArgs)
FormsAuthentication.Signout()
Response.Redirect("admin_login.aspx")
End Sub
</script>
```

With your code in place, the page should look like Figure 12.10.

7. Save the page.

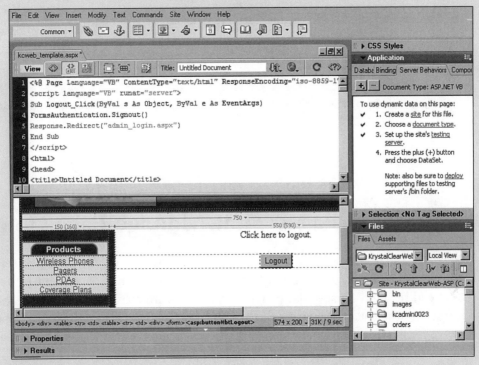

FIGURE 12.10   The code that logs users out and destroys their session credentials.

Exercise 12.2(b)   Creating the Logout Pages in ColdFusion

1. Open the kcweb_template.cfm page. From the menu bar, choose File, Save As and save the file in the kcadmin0023 folder as admin_logout.cfm.

2. Place your cursor in the main content region at the right side of the page and set the Bg field on the Property inspector to #FFFFFF. In the main content region, type **Click here to logout.** and press Enter.

3. On the Server Behaviors panel, click the plus sign and choose User Authentication, Log Out User.

4. In the Log User Out dialog box, shown in Figure 12.11, choose to create a new "Log Out" link and type **admin_login.cfm** in the When Done, Go To field.

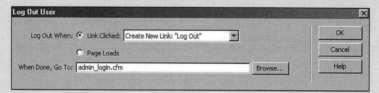

FIGURE 12.11   The Log Out User dialog box creates code that closes the user's session.

5. Click OK and save the page.

Building Pages That Manage Page Content

After the user is logged on to the system, we want him to be able to see the records that provide content to the Web application. To accomplish this, we need to build a page that provides the user with a listing of all the records. Just seeing the list of records isn't enough, however. We also need to give the user the ability to add a new record if the necessary content is not already contained in the database or edit records that currently contain content.

Displaying Editable Content

To display the records that are currently stored in the database, we can draw those records out of the appropriate table and store them in a dataset or recordset. After the dataset/recordset has been created, we can then list them on the page using Dreamweaver's data placeholders and server behaviors.

Because we also want the user to be able to add and edit content, the page that lists the content should also contain links to pages that allow the user to add new records to the database or edit existing content.

 Note **SEARCHING FOR PAGES**

As your Web application grows, you'll probably want to give your users the ability to search the records to easily find the page they want to edit. Because we covered the process of searching and editing records earlier in Chapter 5, "Creating the Human Resources Management System," and Chapter 6, "Creating the Information Services Asset Management System," we're not going to add that functionality to the module at this time. If you want to practice your new skills, however, finish this chapter, then go back, and try applying what you learned in those earlier chapters to add the search functionality.

Exercise 12.3(a)   Displaying Editable Pages in ASP.NET

1. Open the kcweb_template.aspx page. From the menu bar, choose File, Save As and save the file in the kcadmin0023 folder as admin_page_manager.aspx.

2. Place your cursor in the main content region at the right side of the page and set the Bg field on the Property inspector to #FFFFFF. In the main content region, type **Page Manager** and press Enter.

3. On the new line, type **Click here to add a new record** and press Enter. Highlight the Click Here text and link it to the admin_add_page.aspx page using the Property inspector.

4. Open the Server Behaviors panel and click the plus sign. From the menu, choose DataSet.

5. In the DataSet dialog box, shown in Figure 12.12, choose the Simple view and set the Dataset name as dsAdminPages and choose the connKrystalClearWebASP connection and the tbPages table.

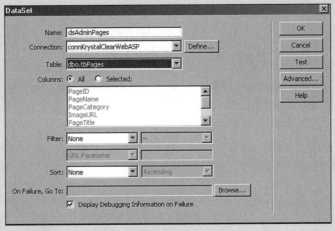

FIGURE 12.12   The DataSet dialog box allows you to build custom SQL queries that retrieve records from the database.

6. Choose the PageID, PageName, and LastUpdated fields and click OK to close the dialog box.

ALTERNATE SELECTION METHOD

Once you have selected one field in the Columns dialog box, holding the Ctrl key and click on the other field names to select them as well.

7. Now that the dataset is built, we have to display the editable pages in the page manager. Place your cursor on the new line underneath the Page Manager text. On the Server Behaviors panel, click the plus sign and choose DataGrid from the menu.

8. In the DataGrid dialog box, type **dgPages** as the ID and choose the dsPages dataset. Choose to display the first 10 records and include the navigation links to previous and next pages.

9. To allow authenticated users to edit existing pages, we need to add a column to the datagrid. Click any of the column titles, click the plus sign next to Columns:, and choose Hyperlink from the menu.

10. In the Hyperlink Column dialog box, type **Edit** as the Title and click the Static Text radio button. In the Static Text field, type **Edit**. Select the Data Field radio button and choose PageID from the drop-down list.

11. Click the Browse button next to the Format String field and type **admin_edit_page.aspx** in the File Name field. Click OK and you'll notice that Dreamweaver has reformatted the URL to include the PageID variable. When the link is clicked, not only will the user be directed to the edit page, but information about which page the user wants to edit is passed as well. Click OK.

12. Using the up and down arrows, reorganize the fields so they are in the following order:

```
PageID
PageName
LastUpdated
Edit
```

13. Click OK to close the DataGrid dialog box and, as shown in Figure 12.13, Dreamweaver adds a placeholder datagrid to the page.

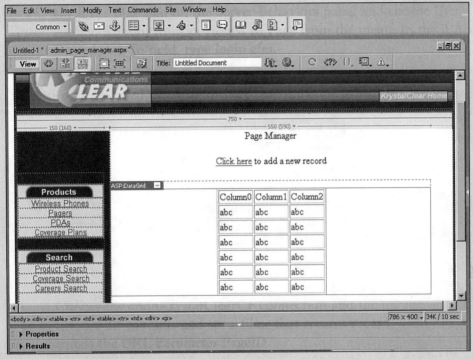

FIGURE 12.13   The datagrid placeholder has been added to your page.

14. On a new line below the datagrid placeholder, type **Click here to logout.** Highlight the Click Here text and link it to admin_logout.aspx.

15. Save this page.

Exercise 12.3(b)   Displaying Editable Pages in ColdFusion

1. Open the kcweb_template.cfm page. From the menu bar, choose File, Save As and save the file in the kcadmin0023 folder as admin_page_manager.cfm.

2. Place your cursor in the main content region at the right side of the page and set the Bg field on the Property inspector to #FFFFFF. In the main content region, type **Page Manager** and press Enter.

3. On the new line, type **Click here to add a new record.** Highlight the Click Here text and link it to the admin_add_page.cfm page using the Property inspector.

4. Open the Server Behaviors panel and click the plus sign. From the menu, choose RecordSet(Query).

5. In the RecordSet dialog box, shown in Figure 12.14, set the recordset name as rsPages and choose the connKrystalClearWebCF connection and the tbPages table.

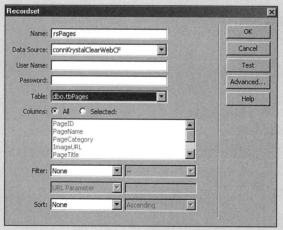

FIGURE 12.14   The Recordset dialog box allows you to retrieve records from your database.

6. Choose the PageID, PageName, and LastUpdated fields and click OK to close the Recordset dialog box.

7. Now that the recordset is built, we just have to display the search results on the page. Place your cursor on the line below the Page Manager text and insert a new table that has 2 rows, 4 columns, and a width of 425 pixels. Set the border, cell padding, and cell spacing to 1.

8. In the upper-left cell, type **PageID**. Press Tab and type **PageName**. Press Tab again and type **LastUpdated**. Leave the upper-right cell blank.

9. Select the top row of the table by placing your cursor over the left border of the upper-left cell and clicking. In the Property inspector, choose the HeaderText style and click the Align Center button. In the W field of the Property inspector, type **25%**.

10. Open the Bindings panel by choosing Window, Bindings from the menu bar. Click the plus sign next to the rsPages recordset to display the available fields. Drag the PageID and drop it in the lower-left cell under the PageID header cell. Drag the PageName field under the PageName header and the LastUpdated field under the LastUpdated header. Finally, in the lower-right cell, type **Edit**. Your page should now look like Figure 12.15.

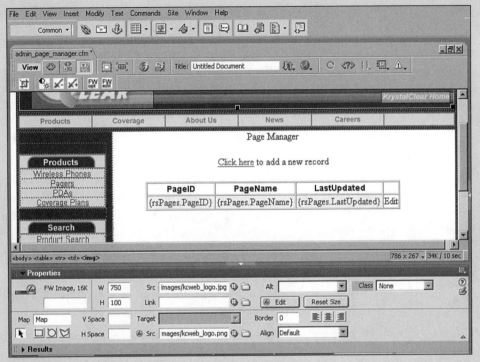

FIGURE 12.15   The column headers, data placeholders, and text are in place.

11. Select the bottom row of the table, reformat it using the BodyText style, and click the Align Center button.

12. The next step is to indicate that Dreamweaver should loop through all the fields in the recordset and display them all on the page. To do this, activate the Server Behaviors panel and click the plus sign. From the menu, choose Repeat Region.

13. In the Repeat Region dialog box, shown in Figure 12.16, choose the rsPages recordset and have the page display all records. Click OK to close the dialog box.

14. The last step is to modify the Edit text so that it is an active hyperlink that, when clicked, redirects the staff member to a page where he can edit the selected employee record. Highlight the Edit text and type **admin_edit_page.cfm** in the Link field of the Property inspector. Click the folder icon next to the Link field.

FIGURE 12.16   Using the Repeat Region dialog box, you can have your pages display all data in the recordset.

15. In the Select File dialog box, click the Parameters button. Enter **PageID** as the name of the parameter and click in the Value field. Click the lightning bolt icon in the far right of the Value field and choose PageID in the Dynamic Data dialog box. Click OK to close the Dynamic Data dialog box and click OK to close the Parameters dialog box. Finally, click OK again to close the Select File dialog box.

16. On a new line below the table, type **Click here to logout**. Highlight the Click Here text and link it to admin_logout.cfm.

17. To be sure that this page cannot be accessed without proper authentication, click the plus sign on the Server Behaviors panel and choose User Authentication, Restrict Access To Page from the menu.

18. In the Restrict Access To Page dialog box, restrict the access based on Username and Password. If access is denied, have the application redirect the user to admin_login.cfm.

19. Save this page.

Adding New Content

Adding content to our Web application is as easy as adding a new record to the database. Because the contents are drawn from the database table, users can fill out a form that contains the appropriate fields and submit the form contents to the database table. After the page is active, the content will be automatically available to the Web application.

To build the page that adds new records, we can use the Application objects contained within Dreamweaver.

Exercise 12.4   Adding New Pages to the Page Manager

1. Open the kcweb_template page for your platform. From the menu bar, choose File, Save As and save the file in the kcadmin0023 folder as admin_add_page.aspx or admin_add_page.cfm.

2. Place your cursor in the main content region at the right side of the page and set the Bg field on the Property inspector to #FFFFFF. In the main content region, type **Add New Page** and press Enter.

3. The next step is to add a form and table that allow an authenticated user to enter the appropriate page information and content. To do this, place your cursor on the line below the Add New Page text and choose Insert, Application Objects, Insert Record, Record Insertion Form Wizard from the menu bar.

4. In the Record Insertion Form dialog box, shown in Figure 12.17, choose the appropriate KrystalClearWeb connection and the tbPages table. In the On Success, Go To field, type **admin_page_added.aspx** or **admin_page_added.cfm**.

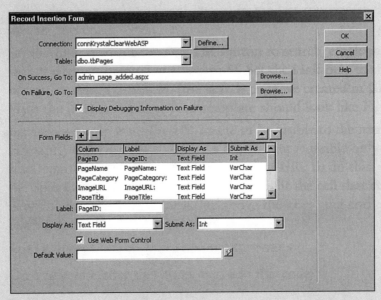

FIGURE 12.17   Choose a connection, table, and confirmation page.

5. In the Form Fields panel, remove the LastUpdated field from the list and use the up and down arrows to reorganize the fields into the following order:

```
PageID
PageName
PageCategory
PageTitle
PageContent
ImageURL
PageActive
```

6. Click the PageID column and click the minus sign to remove it from the list.

7. Click the PageActive form field and change the Display As value to Menu. We want this element to appear in the form as a drop-down menu that allows the visitor to choose either Yes or No.

8. Click the Menu Properties button and in the Menu Properties dialog box, enter the labels and values shown in Table 12.1.

TABLE 12.1   The Values for Your PageActive List

ITEM LABEL	ITEM VALUE
Yes	1
No	0

9. Click OK to close the Menu Properties dialog box and click OK on the Record Insertion Form dialog box. As shown in Figure 12.18, Dreamweaver inserts the appropriate form and form objects into your page.

10. If you are developing on the ColdFusion platform, restrict access to the page as we did in the previous exercise using the Restrict Access To Page server behavior.

11. Save the page.

12. The last step in the add page process is to create a confirmation page. Create a new page from the KCWeb_template and save the page as admin_page_added.aspx or admin_page_added.cfm.

13. Place your cursor in the main content region and type **Thank you. The new page has been added to the database. Please click here to return to the Page Manager.**

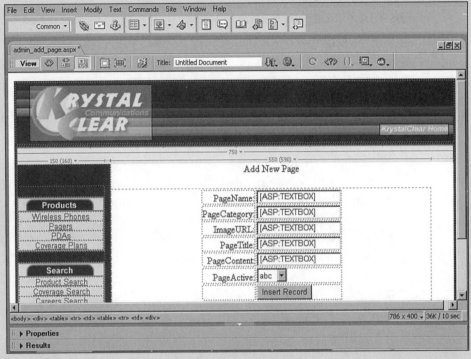

FIGURE 12.18   The data entry form has been added to the page.

14. Highlight the Click Here text and create a hyperlink by typing **admin_page_manager.aspx** or **admin_page_manager.cfm** in the Link field of the Property inspector.

15. If you are developing on the ColdFusion platform, restrict access to the page as well.

16. Save the page.

Editing Existing Content

Because we want the Web application page content to be as accurate and timely as possible, we need to give users the ability to edit records as content needs to be changed. By combining another of Dreamweaver MX 2004's application objects with a dataset/recordset and a querystring variable, we can easily create a page that allows the user to see what data is currently contained within the table and make any necessary adjustments.

Exercise 12.5   Editing Existing Pages

1. Open the kcweb_template page for your platform. From the menu bar, choose File, Save As and save the file in the kcadmin0023 folder as admin_edit_page.aspx or admin_edit_page.cfm.

2. Place your cursor in the main content region at the right side of the page and set the Bg field on the Property inspector to #FFFFFF. In the main content region, type **Edit Page** and press Enter.

3. Before we can edit the page content, we need to create a dataset or recordset that contains only the record we want to update. On the Server Behaviors panel, click the plus sign and choose DataSet if you are developing a page for ASP.NET or Recordset(Query) if you are developing a page for ColdFusion.

4. In the dialog box, be sure you are in the Simple view by clicking the Simple button.

5. If you are using ASP.NET, name the dataset dsUpdate and choose the connKrystalClearWebASP connection and the tbPages table. Choose to select all the fields.

    If you are using ColdFusion, name the recordset rsUpdate and choose the connKrystalClearWebCF connection and the tbPages table. Choose to select all fields.

6. Set a filter where PageID equals the URL Parameter PageID. When completed, your DataSet or Recordset dialog box should look similar to Figure 12.19. Click OK to close the dialog box.

7. Place your cursor on the line below the Edit Page text and choose Insert, Application Objects, Update Record, Record Update Form Wizard from the menu bar.

8. In the Record Update Form dialog box, choose the connKrystalClearWebASP connection if you are developing for ASP.NET or the connKrystalClearWebCF connection if you are developing for ColdFusion. Choose the tbPages table. (ColdFusion users should leave the Username and Password fields blank.) Choose to update the record from the dsUpdate dataset or the rsUpdate recordset with the unique key column being PageID.

9. For ASP.NET, in the On Success, Go To field, type **admin_page_updated.aspx**. For ColdFusion, in the After Updating, Go To field, type **admin_page_updated.cfm**.

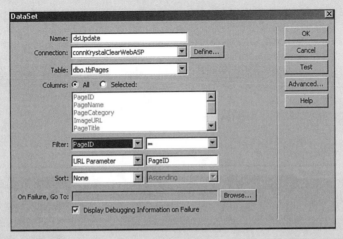

FIGURE 12.19   The proper elements for your new dataset or recordset.

10. In the Form Fields panel, select the PageID column and click the minus symbol. This prevents the user from modifying the unique PageID field, which helps maintain the integrity of the database.

11. Using the up and down arrows, reorganize the columns so they are in this order:

```
PageName
PageCategory
PageTitle
PageContent
ImageURL
PageActive
LastUpdated
```

12. Select the LastUpdated column and change it to a Hidden Field. Change the default value of this column to <cfoutput>#DateFormat(Now(),"mm/dd/yyyy")#</cfoutput>.

13. When completed, the dialog box should look similar to Figure 12.20. Click OK to create the form.

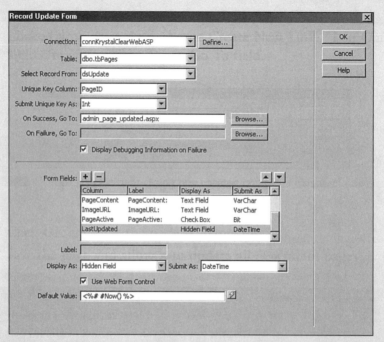

FIGURE 12.20   The completed Record Update Form dialog box.

14. If you are developing on the ColdFusion platform, restrict access to the page as we did in the previous exercise using the Restrict Access To Page server behavior.

15. ASP.NET users should save the page as admin_edit_page.aspx and ColdFusion users should save the page as admin_edit_page.cfm.

16. The last page we need to create is the confirmation page that indicates when a record has been successfully updated. Create a new page based on the KCWeb_template for your platform.

17. Place the cursor in the main content region and type **Thank You. The page has been successfully updated. Click here to return to the Page Manager.** Highlight the Click Here text and create a hyperlink to admin_page_manager.aspx or admin_page_manager.cfm by typing the value in the Property inspector.

18. Restrict access to this page as we did with previous pages.

19. Save the page as either admin_page_updated.aspx or admin_page_updated.cfm, depending on your platform.

Restricting Access to the Application

Because we want the Web application page content to be as accurate and timely as possible, we need to give users the ability to edit records as content needs to be changed. By combining another of Dreamweaver's application objects with a dataset/recordset and a querystring variable, we can easily create a page that allows the user to see what data is currently contained within the table and make any necessary adjustments.

Exercise 12.6(a)   Locking Down the kcadmin0023 Folder in ASP.NET

To lock down the admin folder, we need to activate the forms authentication that is available using ASP.NET. To activate this feature, we use a file named web.config to specify who is allowed to access pages in both the root folder and in the admin folder.

1. Open the web.config file located in the KrystalClearWeb-ASP folder.
2. Add the following code between the `</appSettings>` tag and the `</configuration>` tag:

```
<system.web>
<customErrors mode="Off" />
<authentication mode="Forms">
<forms name="SECAUTH" loginUrl="login.aspx">
<credentials />
</forms>
</authentication>
<authorization>
<allow users="*" />
</authorization>
</system.web>
```

With this code in place, your page should look like Figure 12.21 and the forms authentication is activated. Because we added the line **allow users="*"** we are basically telling the application that forms authentication is in use, but visitors should be allowed to access all the pages in the root directory without having a username and password.

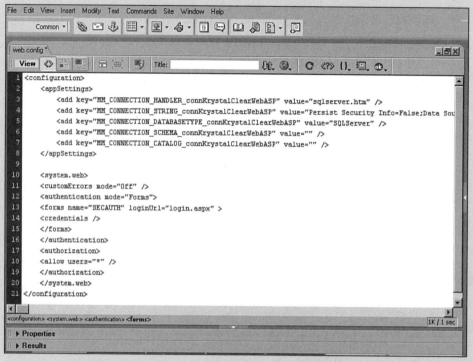

FIGURE 12.21   Your web.config with the new code that implements forms security.

3. Save the web.config page and close it.

Because we want to limit access to pages in the admin folder to those visitors who have a valid username and password, we need to create a second web.config file and place it in the admin folder.

4. Create a blank ASP.NET page in Dreamweaver.

5. Remove all Dreamweaver created code from the page and type the following code:

```
<configuration>
<system.web>
<authorization>
<allow users="admin" />
<deny users="*" />
</authorization>
</system.web>
</configuration>
```

With this code in place, the forms authentication is activated for the admin folder. Notice that this page allows users who have been authenticated as members of the admin group but denies access to any other users.

6. Save the page in the kcadmin0023 folder as web.config and close the page.

Exercise 12.6(b)   Locking Down the kcadmin0023 Folder in ColdFusion

1. Open the admin_validation.cfm page.
2. In the Server Behaviors panel, click the plus sign and choose User Authentication, Restrict Access To Page from the menu.
3. In the Restrict Access To Page dialog box, choose to restrict access based on username and password. In the If Access Denied field, type **admin_login.cfm**.
4. Click OK to close the dialog box.
5. Save the page.
6. Apply this server behavior to each of the pages in the Admin section, with the exception of the admin_login.cfm and admin_failure.cfm. Be sure to save each page after applying the server behavior.

Adding Pages to the Application

Now that the page administration module is complete, it's time to begin building the pages for our Web application. Before we can access the module, however, we need to create an administrator username and password so we can be authenticated. After we are logged in, we can then add pages and edit pages as we need.

Exercise 12.7   Logging on and adding pages

1. Open the SQL Server Enterprise Manager by choosing Start, Programs, Microsoft SQL Server, Enterprise Manager.

2. In the Enterprise Manager, expand the categories in the left pane so you can see the categories that make up the KrystalClearWebDB database.

3. Right-click the tbAdminLogin table in the right pane and choose Open Table, Return All Rows from the context menu.

4. In the Data in Table dialog box, add a new administrator account by typing **testadmin** in the Username field and **testpassword** in the Password field.

5. Close the Data in Table dialog box and close the Enterprise Manager. Now that we have an account, we need to log in to the page manager.

6. Open a browser window and type **http://localhost/KrystalClear Web-ASP/kcadmin0023/admin_page_manager.aspx** if you developed on the ASP.NET platform or **http://localhost/KrystalClearWeb-CF/ kcadmin0023/admin_page_manager.cfm** if you developed on the ColdFusion platform.

Because this page is protected and you are not yet authenticated, you should be automatically redirected to the admin login page. Enter the username and password combination that you created in the database table and log in.

NETWORK LOGIN PROBLEMS

If you are developing in ASP.NET and you receive a request for a network login when you try to submit a username/password via the form, give the Users group on your computer Read/Execute/Write privileges to the wwwroot folder or to the root folder of you Web application and it should get rid of the network login prompt.

7. After you reach the page manager, you'll notice that there are no records to be displayed. This is because there are currently no pages in the table.

8. Click the link to add a new page and add the nine pages shown in Table 12.2.

TABLE 12.2   Values for Page Records

Page Name	Page Category	Image URL	Page Title	Page Content	Page Active
Products Home	Products	images/ products home.jpg	Krystal Clear	KrystalClear offers a wide variety of products.	1
Coverage Home	Coverage	images/ coverage home.jpg	Krystal Clear	KrystalClear services cover a large portion of the continental United States and Canada.	1
About UsHome	AboutUs	images/ aboutus home.jpg	About Krystal Clear	KrystalClear Communications provides communication solutions to businesses and consumers.	1
NewsHome	News	images/ newshome.jpg	Krystal Clear News	News about KrystalClear keeps you up-to-date about our company.	1
Careers Home	Careers	images/ careers home.jpg	Krystal Clear Careers	KrystalClear is a great place to work.	1
Wireless	Products	images/ wireless home.jpg	Wireless Products	KrystalClear Wireless products include analog, digital, dual-band, and tri-band features.	1

TABLE 12.2   Continued

PAGE NAME	PAGE CATEGORY	IMAGE URL	PAGE TITLE	PAGE CONTENT	PAGE ACTIVE
Pagers	Products	images/ pagers.jpg	Pager Products	KrystalClear offers a broad range of pages from simple text pages to those with alpha-numeric capabilities.	1
PDAs	Products	images/ pdas.jpg	PDA Products	If you're looking for a quality PDA, KrystalClear has a broad range of solutions for you.	1
Plans	Products	images/ plans.jpg	Krystal Clear Plans	Staying in touch is important. KrystalClear has a wide variety of plans to meet your personal or corporate needs.	1

Notice that each time you return to the page manager, the page you have just added is added to the list of available pages.

9. With the pages added, click the link to log out and close your browser.

Summary

Managing a Web application after it has been implemented requires that users be able to add new content and update existing content. In this chapter, we looked at what it takes to build an administrative section of the Web application that allows authorized users to log in, view existing database records, add new content, and update information already stored in the database.

In the next chapter, we're going to build a search component that allows the user to match search criteria with information stored in the database tables. In addition, we will go beyond a simple search that uses a single term and afford the user a broad range of advanced search features.

CHAPTER 13

ADDING SEARCH CAPABILITIES TO THE WEB APPLICATIONS

One of the biggest benefits of building a database-driven Web application is the fact that visitors to your site can easily access a broad range of information. As the size of the application grows, however, it can become increasingly difficult for visitors to find the information they are seeking. To avoid this potential problem, Web developers often add functionality to the pages that allows the user to search the Web application for the appropriate content.

Because of the flexibility of the SQL language and the ease of creating search and results pages in Dreamweaver, we can add search functionality into the Web application that is as simple or as complex as necessary.

To provide visitors to the KrystalClear site with the ability to search, this chapter shows how to add a simple keyword search that allows visitors to submit a keyword or key phrase and view all Web pages that match the search criteria. In addition, we'll expand on that search functionality to develop a more advanced search module that allows the visitor to search either the page content and/or the page title and even search by page category.

By the end of this chapter, you will do the following:

- Understand the process that takes place when a visitor conducts a search
- Create a basic search page
- Develop a results page that displays the appropriate records
- Expand on the simple search feature to include advanced search features

Understanding the Fundamentals of Searches

Building a basic search feature for your Web site is actually easy. In fact, in previous chapters, we have engaged in searches for employees and assets; now we need to search for keywords. The principles are the same. The visitor submits her keyword or key phrase either by typing it into a text field and clicking the Submit button or by clicking a link that already contains the keyword in a variable. The results page (which is sometimes the same as the search page) then takes those terms and compares them with the appropriate field in the database. After the matching records are identified, they can be displayed on the page. If, however, no matches are located, the visitor can be notified and offered the opportunity to modify her search. Sound familiar?

After constructing the basic search functionality, we're going to extend it a bit to include some advanced features. Rather than just allowing users to search the page title by keyword or key phrase, we can also allow them to further narrow their searches by searching both the page title and the page content and by using delimiters such as page category. After you understand how to construct the basics and expand on them, the search functionality you can offer your visitors is only limited by the structure of your database.

Using Hyperlinks to Conduct Searches

The simplest type of search we can create for our visitors is one that provides them with data extracted from the database without any real effort on their part. Think back to Chapter 11, "Creating the Front End for the Web Application," and recall that we build several navigation links for the various sections of the site, products, and search options. All of these links contained not only a page name, but a dynamic variable as well. For instance, the About Us navigation hyperlink was `default.aspx?PageName=AboutHome` on the ASP.NET side and `default.cfm?PageName=AboutHome` on the ColdFusion side. Now look at the News navigation link, which uses the hyperlink `default.aspx?PageName=NewsHome` or `default.cfm?PageName=NewsHome`. Notice that, when clicked, both of these links open the exact same page, yet we expect different data to be displayed. When we click either of these links, we are asking the application to load the default page, then find and display the content for the page named AboutHome or NewsHome. Essentially, it's the same principle as a search, but with the search term hardcoded into the URL.

However, building the search term into the URL isn't enough. The default page has to know how to find the data as well. To accomplish this, we can add a dataset/recordset to the page and insert dynamic placeholders where the text will be when the page is loaded.

Exercise 13.1(a)   Adding the Dataset to the Default Page and Products Page in ASP.NET

1. Open Dreamweaver MX 2004 and open the kcweb_default_template.aspx page that we created earlier in Chapter 11.

2. Save the page as default.aspx. This will be the primary page that loads when the visitor visits the KrystalClear Web site.

3. Before we can display any dynamic content on the page, we need to first build a dataset that finds the correct information stored in the database. Open the Server Behaviors panel and click the plus sign. From the menu, choose DataSet.

4. In the DataSet dialog box, set the dataset Name as dsPageData and choose the connKrystalClearWebASP connection and the tbPages table.

5. As shown in Figure 13.1, choose to draw all columns where the PageName equals the URL Parameter PageName.

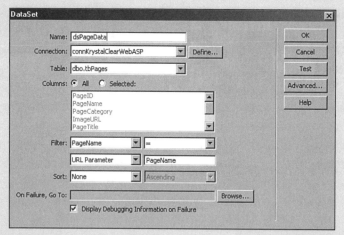

FIGURE 13.1   Building a dataset allows us to draw the page content from the database.

6. Click OK to create the dataset.

7. Save the page.

8. Open the kcweb_products_template.aspx page that we created earlier in Chapter 11.

9. Save the page as products.aspx. This page will display information about products being offered by KrystalClear.

10. Create a new dataset and name it dsProducts. In the Simple view, choose the connKrystalClearWebASP connection and the tbProducts table. Choose to draw all fields from the table and create a filter where ProductID equals the URL Parameter ProductID.

11. Click OK to create the dataset.

12. Save the page.

13. Click OK to create the dataset.

Exercise 13.1(b)   Adding the Recordset to the Default Page and Products Page in ColdFusion

1. Open the kcweb_default_template.cfm page that we created earlier in Chapter 11.

2. Save the page as default.cfm. This will be the primary page that loads when the visitor visits the KrystalClear Web site.

3. Before we can display any dynamic content on the page, we need to first build a recordset that finds the correct information stored in the database. Open the Server Behaviors panel and click the plus sign. From the menu, choose Recordset.

4. In the Recordset dialog box, set the recordset name as rsPageData and choose the connKrystalClearWebCF connection and the tbPages table.

5. Choose to draw all columns where the PageName equals the URL Parameter PageName.

6. Click OK to create the recordset.

7. Save the page.

8. Open Dreamweaver and open the kcweb_products_template.cfm page that we created earlier in Chapter 11.

9. Save the page as products.cfm. This page will display information about products being offered by KrystalClear.

10. Create a new recordset and name it rsProducts. In the Simple view, choose the connKrystalClearWebCF connection and the tbProducts table. Choose to draw all fields from the table and create a filter where ProductID equals the URL Parameter ProductID.

11. Click OK to create the recordset.

12. Save the page.

Building the Basic Search Page

Although hyperlink searches serve a purpose, they don't really allow the visitor to actively seek the content that he might like to view. To provide visitors with this ability, we need to create an actual search feature that lets them enter the search criteria and choose which of the results meets their needs.

To start, let's build a simple search feature that allows the user to enter one keyword or key phrase and compare it to the page titles that are stored in the tbPages table.

Exercise 13.2(a)   Building the Basic Search Page in ASP.NET

1. Open the kcweb_search_template.aspx page that we created earlier in Chapter 11.

2. Save the page as search.aspx.

3. Place your cursor in the top cell of the top table in the main content area, center the text, and type **Search KrystalClear Web Site**.

4. In the cell below the new text, insert a form by choosing Insert, Form, Form from the menu bar. In the Property inspector, name the form fmSearch. Switch to the Split Code and Design view and modify the form tag so it reads as follows:

```
<form name="fmSearch" method-"post" action="" runat="server">
```

5. Switch back to the Design view. Inside the form, center the text and type the phrase **Type your keyword or key phrase:**.

6. With your cursor to the right of the text, insert an ASP.NET text box by choosing Insert, ASP.NET Objects, asp:textbox from the menu bar. In the dialog box, set the ID to be tfSearch and click OK.

7. Press Enter to create a new line inside the form, and insert a Submit button by choosing Insert, ASP.NET Objects, asp:button from the menu bar. Set the button ID to btSubmit, type **Search** in the Text field, and click OK. With the button in place, your page should now look like Figure 13.2.

8. Save the page.

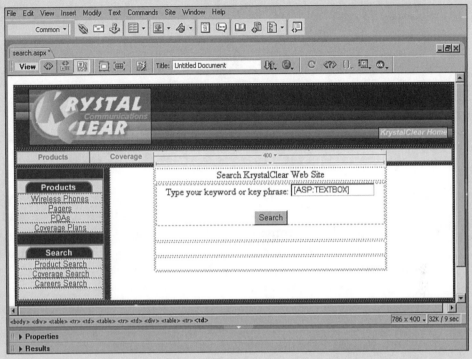

FIGURE 13.2   The search form has been created.

Exercise 13.2(b)   Building the Basic Search Page in ColdFusion

1. Open the kcweb_search_tempate.cfm page that we created earlier in Chapter 11 and save the page as search.cfm.

2. Place your cursor in the top cell of the top table in the main content area, center the text, and type **Search KrystalClear Web Site**.

3. In the cell below the new text, insert a form by choosing Insert, Form, Form from the menu bar. In the Property inspector, name the form fmSearch.

4. Inside the form, center the text and type the phrase **Type your keyword or key phrase:**.

5. With your cursor to the right of the text, insert an text field by choosing Insert, Form, Text Field from the menu bar. In the Property inspector, set the name of the text field to tfSearch.

6. Press Enter to create a new line inside the form and insert a Submit button by choosing Insert, Form, Button from the menu bar. Set the name of the button to btSubmit, type **Search** in the Label field of the Property inspector, and click OK.

7. Save the page.

Displaying the Basic Search Results

Now that the visitor can enter the search phrase, we need to build a way for the application to compare that phrase to the contents of the table and return only those records that contain matches. As we have done in the past, we can use a dataset/recordset in combination with a results table or datagrid to display records that might contain the data the visitor is looking for.

Exercise 13.3(a)   Displaying the Search Results in ASP.NET

1. In the search.aspx page, place your cursor after the Search button and press Enter.

2. Open the Server Behaviors panel and click the plus sign. From the menu, choose DataSet.

3. In the DataSet dialog box, choose the Simple view, set the Dataset name as dsResults, and choose the connKrystalClearWebASP connection and the tbPages table.

4. As shown in Figure 13.3, choose the PageID and PageTitle columns and create a filter that only finds records where PageTitle contains the Form Variable tfSearch.

USING THE CONTAINS FILTER

In previous chapters, we used % to build SQL queries that allowed users to only type in part of the search term. For instance, by using a % at the end of a variable, a user could type **cat** and return terms such as category or catalog. In addition, using the % at the beginning of the variable and entering the same search term would return results such as wildcat or tomcat. By using the contains filter in the Simple Recordset view, Dreamweaver places the % on both ends of the variable. Therefore typing in the search term **cat** would return catalog, category, wildcat, and tomcat.

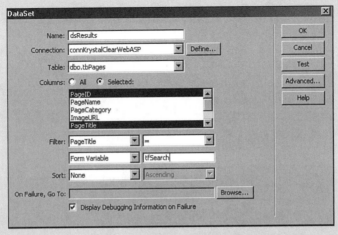

FIGURE 13.3   Set a filter for the dataset that only returns the requested fields.

5. If we leave the dataset as is, Dreamweaver will create it with no default value. This means whenever our page loads, the page will automatically generate a recordset that contains all the records. To avoid this, we can set a default value by clicking the Advanced button in the DataSet dialog box.

6. In the Parameters panel, click the Edit button and enter **123** as the default value so the code looks like this:

```
"%" + (IIF((Request.Form("tfSearch")<>Nothing),
Request.Form("tfSearch"),"123"))+"%"
```

7. Click OK to close the dialog box and click OK again to create the dataset.

8. Now that the dataset is built, we need to display the search results. Place your cursor on the line below the Search button and type **Search Results**. Press Enter.

9. Click the plus sign on the Server Behaviors panel and choose DataGrid from the menu.

10. In the DataGrid dialog box, type **dgResults** as the ID and choose the dsResults dataset. Choose to display the first 10 records and include the navigation links to previous and next pages.

11. Because we don't want the visitor to see the PageID, click the PageID column in the Columns panel and click the minus button.

12. After the search results are returned, we want the visitor to be able to click the Page Title to view the page in full. To do this, we need to change the PageTitle field into a hyperlink. Select the PageTitle field, click the Change Column Type button, and choose Hyperlink.

13. In the Hyperlink Column dialog box, shown in Figure 13.4, leave the title set to PageTitle. Set the Hyperlink Text to the Data Field: PageTitle. In the Linked Page section, click the radio button next to Data Field and choose PageID from the drop-down list.

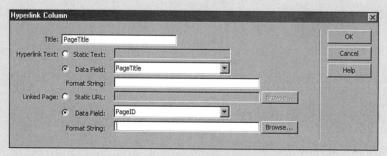

FIGURE 13.4   Change the PageTitle field to a hyperlink column.

14. Click the Browse button next to the Format String button. In the Select Field dialog box, type **default.aspx** in the File Name field and click OK. The Hyperlink Column dialog box should now look like Figure 13.5.

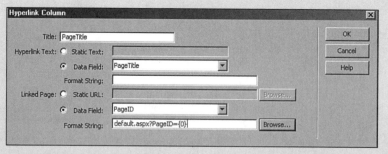

FIGURE 13.5   The format string for the hyperlink column has been created.

15. Click OK to close the Hyperlink Column dialog box and click OK to close the DataGrid dialog box. As shown in Figure 13.6, Dreamweaver adds a placeholder datagrid to the page.

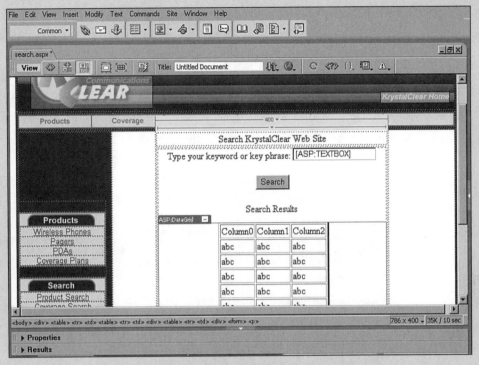

FIGURE 13.6 The datagrid placeholder is in place.

16. Because we only want the search results to show after the search has been submitted, highlight the Search Results text and the datagrid and click the plus sign on the Server Behaviors panel.

17. From the menu, choose Show Region, Show If Dataset Is Not Empty. In the dialog box, choose the dsResults dataset and click OK.

18. Save this page.

Exercise 13.3(b)   Displaying the Search Results in ColdFusion

1. In the search.cfm page, open the Server Behaviors panel and click the plus sign. From the menu, choose Recordset.

2. In the Recordset dialog box, choose the Simple view, set the recordset name as rsResults, and choose the connKrystalClearWebCF connection and the tbPages table.

3. In the Simple view, choose the PageID and PageTitle columns and create a filter that only finds records where PageTitle contains the Form Variable tfSearch. Click OK to close the dialog box.

4. Now that the recordset is complete, we need to display the search results. Place your cursor after the Search button and press Enter.

5. On the new line, type **Search Results** and press Enter again.

6. On the new line, insert a table that contains 2 rows, 1 column, and has a width of 100%. Set the cell padding, cell spacing, and border to 1.

7. In the top row of the new table, center the text and type **Page Title**. Reformat the text using the HeaderText style.

8. Place your cursor in the cell below the Page Title text and click the Align Center button on the Property inspector. Switch to the Bindings panel and drag the PageTitle data binding into the bottom row of the new table.

9. Select the bottom row of the table that now contains the PageTitle data placeholder.

10. Switch to the Server Behaviors panel and click the plus sign. From the context menu, choose Repeat Region.

11. In the Repeat Region dialog box, shown in Figure 13.7, choose the rsResults recordset and display 10 records at a time.

FIGURE 13.7   The Repeat Region server behavior loops through the recordset and displays all the results on the page.

12. Click OK to close the Repeat Region dialog box.

13. Because our table only contains one column, we have to fix a nasty little problem in Dreamweaver. When Dreamweaver applies the Repeat Region server behavior to a table with a single column, the structure of the code ends up repeating the region horizontally, rather than vertically. To fix this, we need to make a slight adjustment to the code.

14. Switch to the Split Code and Design view and find the line of code that reads as follows:

```
<tr><cfoutput query="rsResults"
➥startRow="#StartRow_rsResults#"
➥maxRows="#MaxRows_rsResults#">
```

Move the `<tr>` tag so it reads like this:

```
<cfoutput query="rsResults"
➥startRow="#StartRow_rsResults#"
➥maxRows="#MaxRows_rsRetults#"><tr>
```

15. Find the following line:

```
</cfoutput></tr>
```

Move the `<tr>` tag so it reads like this:

```
</tr></cfoutput>
```

16. Switch back to the Design view.

17. We need to link the page title to the details page that displays the entire contents of the record that has been returned. To do this, select the PageTitle data placeholder and click the folder next to the Link field in the Property inspector.

18. In the Select File dialog box, type **default.cfm** in the File Name field.

19. Click the Parameters button. In the Parameters dialog box, shown in Figure 13.8, type **PageID** as the parameter name. In the Value field, click the lightning bolt icon and choose the PageID column from the rsResults recordset.

FIGURE 13.8   Create a dynamic parameter for the link.

20. Click OK to close the Parameters dialog box and click OK again to close the Select File dialog box.

21. The final step we need to take is to ensure that the results table only displays after the search terms have been submitted. To do this, select the Search Results text and the results table.

22. On the Server Behaviors panel, click the plus sign and choose Show Region, Show If Recordset Is Not Empty.

23. In the Show If Recordset Is Not Empty dialog box, choose the rsResults recordset and click OK.

24. Save the page.

Expanding the Search Capabilities to Include Advanced Features

Although a simple search is great in many cases, it is possible that a simple search term may provide too many results for the visitor to sift through or may even return so many results that the Web server times out before the results are fully compiled. It is also possible that because the simple search is optimized for speed and only searches a specific field, it might actually return too few fields, which doesn't do the visitor any good if he cannot find the information. The best way to avoid these potential problems is to build an advanced search feature for those users who aren't finding what they need with the simple search.

Although the advanced search feature looks and works almost identical to the simple search, we can provide additional fields that allow the user to either expand or restrict his search based on the criteria he submits or the fields he chooses to search.

Exercise 13.4(a)   Adding Advanced Search Functionality in ASP.NET

1. In the search.aspx page, place your cursor in the bottom row of the table in the main content area.

2. Center the text and type **Click here for advanced search**.

3. Highlight the Click Here text and link it to advanced_search.aspx.

4. Save the page.

5. Save the page as advanced_search.aspx.

6. Modify the Click Here for Advanced Search text to read **Click here for basic search.**

7. Highlight the Click Here text and link it to search.aspx.

   To make this search more advanced, we want to give visitors the ability to search the PageTitle field, the PageContent field, or both. To do this, we need to first add a drop-down list that contains the values we want to pass.

8. Place your cursor just to the left of the asp:textbox and press Shift+Enter to create a line break. Next, place your cursor to the right of the asp:textbox and press Enter.

9. On the new line, type **Choose a search type:** and press Shift+Enter again.

10. On the new line, add an asp:dropdownlist by choosing Insert, ASP.NET Objects, asp:dropdownlist.

11. Name the drop-down list dlTable and click OK.

12. Select the new drop-down list and click the List Items button in the Property inspector. In the List Items dialog box, add two list items. The first should have a Label of **Search Page Title** and a value of **PageTitle** and the second should have a Label of Search **Page Content** and a value of **PageContent**. Click OK to close the dialog box.

13. Switch back to the Design view. The new drop-down list, shown in Figure 13.9, now allows the user to decide whether he wants to search the page content or the page title.

14. We need to modify the dataset so that it recognizes any values being passed by the new drop-down list.

15. In the Server Behaviors dialog box, double-click the dsResults dataset. Switch to the Advanced view and click the plus sign to create a new parameter.

16. In the Add Parameter dialog box, type **@Table** in the Name field and change the Type to VarChar.

17. Click the Build button and set the Name field to dlTable. Change the Source to Form Parameter and set the Default Value to PageTitle. Click OK to close the Build Value dialog box.

18. Click OK to close the Add Parameter dialog box.

19. Replace the PageTitle value in the WHERE statement with @Table LIKE @PageTitle. The dataset should now look like Figure 13.10.

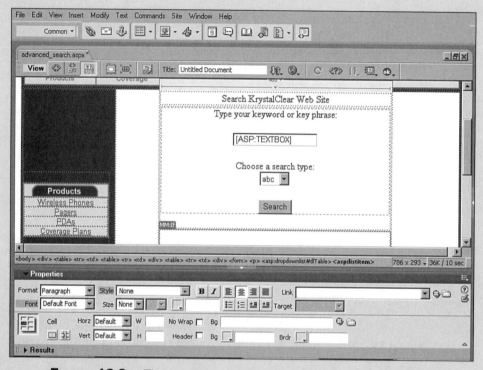

FIGURE 13.9   The new drop-down list allows for enhanced searching.

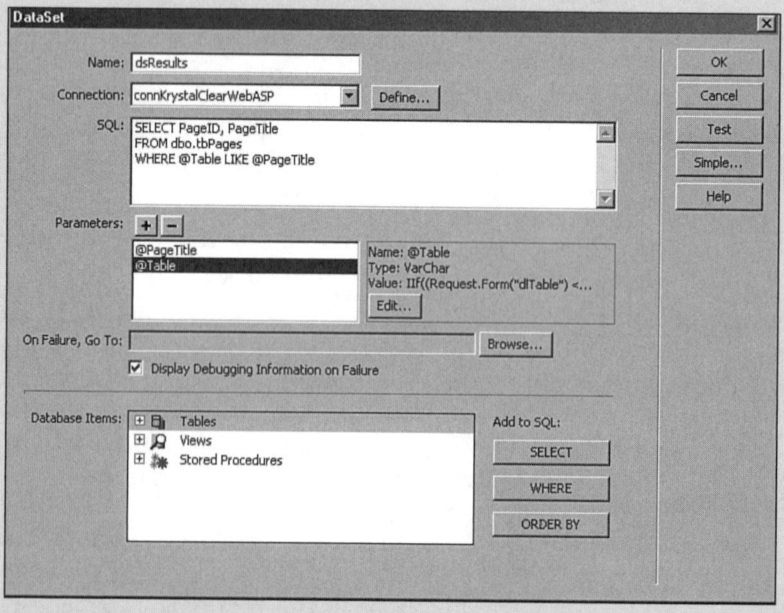

FIGURE 13.10   The dataset should now include features for advanced searching.

20. Click OK to apply the changes to the dataset.

21. Save the page.

Exercise 13.4(b)   Adding Advanced Search Functionality in ColdFusion

1. In the search.cfm page, place your cursor in the bottom row of the table and click the Align Center button on the Property inspector.

2. Type **Click here for advanced search.**

3. Highlight the Click Here text and link it to advanced_search.cfm.

4. Save the page.

5. Save the page as advanced_search.cfm.

6. Modify the Click here for advanced search text to read **Click here for basic search.**

7. Highlight the Click Here text and link it to search.cfm.

   To make this search more advanced, we want to give visitors the ability to search the PageTitle field, the PageContent field, or both. To do this, we need to first add a drop-down list that contains the values we want to pass.

8. Place your cursor just to the left of the tfSearch text field and press Shift+Enter to create a line break. Next, place your cursor to the right of the text field and press Enter.

9. On the new line, type **Choose a search type:** and press Shift+Enter again.

10. On the new line, add a new List/Menu object by choosing Insert, Form, List/Menu.

11. Name the drop-down list dlTable and click the List Values button on the Property inspector.

12. In the List Values dialog box, shown in Figure 13.11, add a new value with the label Search Page Title and the value PageTitle. Add a second value with the label Search Page Content and the value PageContent.

13. Click OK to close the List Values dialog box.

14. In the Initially Selected field of the Property inspector, choose Search Page Title.

FIGURE 13.11   The new drop-down list allows for enhanced searching.

15. With the new drop-down list in place, we now need to modify the recordset so that it recognizes any values being passed by the new drop-down list. In the Server Behaviors dialog box, double-click the rsResults recordset. Switch to the Advanced view and click the plus sign to create a new parameter.

16. In the Add Parameter dialog box, type **FORM.dlTable** in the Name field and set the default value to PageTitle.

17. Click OK to close the Add Parameter dialog box.

18. Replace the PageTitle value in the WHERE statement with #FORM.dlTable# LIKE '#FORM.tfSearch#'. The recordset should now look like Figure 13.12.

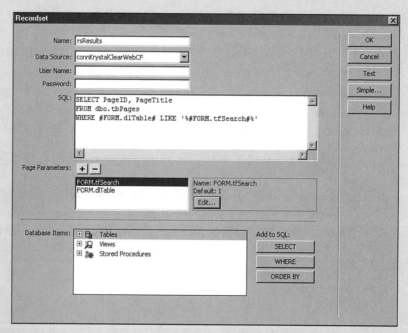

FIGURE 13.12   The dataset should now include features for advanced searching.

19. Click OK to apply the changes to the dataset.
20. Save the page.

Placing the Data Placeholders for the Detail Pages

Now that our visitors can conduct searches of the database by either clicking a link with an embedded search term or by submitting a simple or advanced search form, the last step is to allow them to see the full contents of the database record, rather than just the page title that is returned in the results page. Because we created a hyperlink in the results page that contains the page name, we can use the default page to display the full record.

Exercise 13.5(a) Placing the Data Placeholders in the Default Page in ASP.NET

1. Open the default.aspx page.
2. In the Data Bindings panel, drag the PageTitle data binding into the top table in the main content region and center the text.
3. Drag the PageContent data binding into the right cell of the bottom table.
4. Place your cursor in the upper-left cell of the bottom table and choose Insert, Image from the menu bar. In the Select Image Source dialog box, shown in Figure 13.13, click the Data Sources radio button at the top of the dialog box.
5. Choose the ImageURL field as the source and click OK.
6. Center the image in the cell. With the data placeholders in place, your page should now look like Figure 13.14.

   Because the default page is being used to display our search details, we need to be sure that the section of the page containing the details only shows when a search has been conducted (either via form or URL variable). To accomplish this, we need to hide the detail information when the dataset is empty and display welcome text instead. This welcome text is what should be displayed when a visitor first encounters the site and the default page loads.

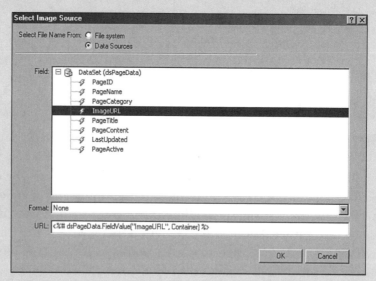

FIGURE 13.13   The Select Image Source dialog box allows you to insert an image into your page.

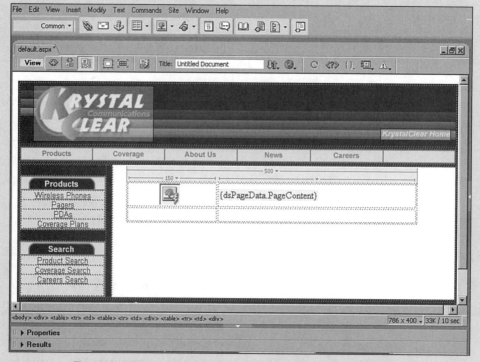

FIGURE 13.14   The default page with the data placeholders.

7. In the default.aspx page, create a new line below the tables that currently contain the data placeholders. On that new line, type **Welcome to the KrystalClear Web Site. Please use the navigation links to view the services and products that we offer.**

Note **CREATING BETTER INTRODUCTORY TEXT**

I know...the introductory text isn't that great, but it serves the purpose of demonstrating how to make some of our regions visible while others are not visible. When building your own Web applications, be sure that your introductory text is better than the text we use here. LOL!

8. Highlight this new text and click the plus sign on the Server Behaviors panel. From the context panel, choose Show Region, Show Region If Dataset Is Empty. In the Show Region dialog box, choose the dsPageData dataset and click OK.

9. Select everything above this text and click the plus sign on the Server Behaviors panel. From the context panel, choose Show Region, Show Region If Dataset Is Not Empty. In the Show Region dialog box, choose the dsPageData dataset and click OK.

10. Save the page.

Exercise 13.5(b)   Placing the Data Placeholders in the Default Page in ColdFusion

1. Open the default.cfm page.

2. In the Data Bindings panel, drag the PageTitle data binding into the top table in the main content region.

3. Drag the PageContent data binding into the right cell of the bottom table.

4. Place your cursor in the left cell of the bottom table and choose Insert, Image from the menu bar. In the Select Image Source dialog box, click the Data Sources radio button at the top of the dialog box.

5. Choose the ImageURL field as the source and click OK. Center the image in the cell.

Because the default page is being used to display our search details, we need to be sure that the section of the page containing the details only shows when a search has been conducted (either via form or URL variable). To accomplish this, we need to hide the detail information when the recordset is empty and display welcome text instead. This welcome text is what should be displayed when a visitor first encounters the site and the default page loads.

6. In the default.cfm page, create a new line below the tables that currently contain the data placeholders. On that new line, type **Welcome to the KrystalClear Web Site. Please use the navigation links to view the services and products that we offer.**

7. Highlight this new text and click the plus sign on the Server Behaviors panel. From the context panel, choose Show Region, Show Region If Dataset Is Empty. In the Show Region dialog box, choose the rsPageData dataset and click OK.

8. Select everything above this text and click the plus sign on the Server Behaviors panel. From the context panel, choose Show Region, Show Region If Dataset Is Not Empty. In the Show Region dialog box, choose the rsPageData dataset and click OK.

9. Save the page.

Summary

Adding search capability to your Web applications provides visitors with a way to find content that meets their specific needs. As your application grows, the search function often becomes increasingly useful to visitors. In addition, providing visitors with a variety of ways to search for content increases the chance that they will find what they are looking for and enjoy the experience of browsing your site.

The next chapter furthers the visitor's interaction with the KrystalClear site by demonstrating how to design and implement a system that allows users to create their own accounts to log in and out of the site. As you will see later on, allowing users to create individual accounts not only serves the site owner by providing information about the users, but also allows the visitor to interact with the site and engage in activities such as eCommerce.

CHAPTER 14

ALLOWING VISITORS TO CREATE USER ACCOUNTS

Now that the KrystalClear Web application has a structure, dynamic content, and the capability for visitors to easily locate the information they are looking for, the next step is to allow visitors to create their own individual accounts. By creating this capability, KrystalClear can offer visitors the ability to customize their experience with the site and interact with features such as ordering items from the product catalog.

To enable this feature, however, we need to take advantage of many of the skills we have covered in previous chapters. Not only will we add new records to the database, but also we will develop a login/logout system for the visitors and address security issues that will ensure that the account information is secure.

In this chapter, you will do the following:

- Build pages that allow visitors to create their own personal account
- Build a login/logout system for visitors to the site
- Develop a system that allows users to retrieve lost passwords

Reviewing the Database Tables

To allow visitors to create personal accounts, we need to have a table in the database where we can store their information such as username and password. If you recall, in Chapter 9, "Building a Database for Web Applications," we created a table called tbCustomers for exactly this purpose. Although the structure of the table, shown in Figure 14.1, contains far more fields than we will be using in this chapter (we'll use them in Chapter 15, "Engaging in eCommerce"), the table does contain a field that can contain a unique identifier and a password.

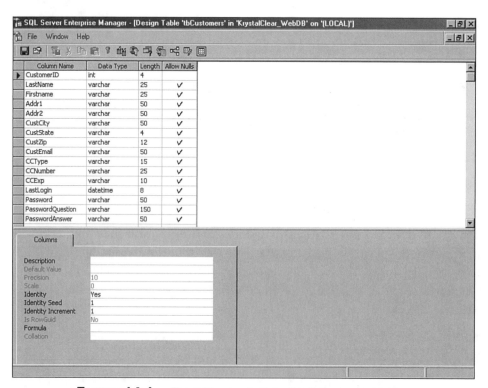

FIGURE 14.1   The table structure for the tbCustomers table.

For this application, we're going to ask visitors to use their email address as their username, rather than having them select a unique username. In addition, we'll provide users with the ability to retrieve their password if they should lose it by building a system that allows visitors to choose a unique question that will be asked when they want to retrieve their password. The password question and answer are stored in the tbCustomers table as well.

Building Pages That Allow Visitors to Create Custom Accounts

Adding new user accounts to the database is similar to adding any other type of record to the database. With the use of Dreamweaver MX 2004's Record Insertion Form Application Object, we can specify which information the users should supply and Dreamweaver will do the work for us.

Exercise 14.1(a)   Creating the New User Account Page in ASP.NET

1. Open the kcweb_template.aspx page for your platform. From the menu bar, choose File, Save As and save the file as create_customer_account.aspx.

2. Place your cursor in the main content region at the right side of the page and set the Bg field on the Property inspector to #FFFFFF. Next, type **Create new user account** and press Enter.

3. The next step is to add a form and table that allows an authenticated user to enter the appropriate page information and content. To do this, place your cursor on the line below the Create New User Account text and choose Insert, Application Objects, Insert Record, Record Insertion Form Wizard from the menu bar.

4. In the Record Insertion Form dialog box, shown in Figure 14.2, choose the connKrystalClearWebASP connection and the tbCustomers table. In the On Success, Go To field, type **account_created.aspx**.

5. In the Form Fields panel, use the minus sign to remove all fields except for CustEmail, Password, PasswordQuestion, and PasswordAnswer. Use the up and down arrows to arrange the fields in this order:

```
CustEmail
Password
PasswordQuestion
PasswordAnswer
```

6. Click the Password column and change the Display As field to Password Field. Change the Password Answer field to a Password Field as well. The dialog box should now look like Figure 14.3.

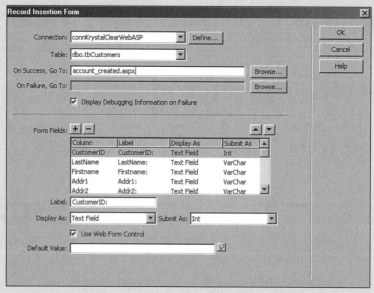

FIGURE 14.2 Use the Record Insertion Form application object to allow users to create new accounts.

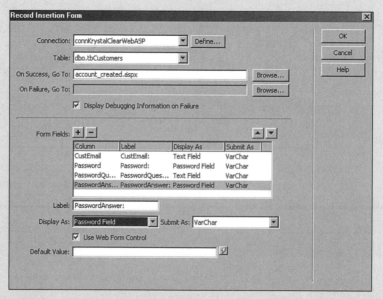

FIGURE 14.3 The Record Insertion Form dialog box with the appropriate values.

7. Select the CustEmail field and change the label to read **Please enter your email address:**.

8. Change the label for the Password field to **Please type a password:**.

9. Change the label for the PasswordQuestion field to **Please type a question that will allow you to retrieve a lost password:**.

10. Change the label for the PasswordAnswer field to **Please type the answer to your password question:**.

11. Click OK to create the form.

12. Place your cursor between the words "allow" and "you" in the third row and press Shift+Enter to create a line break. As shown in Figure 14.4, the page now allows users to create a new account.

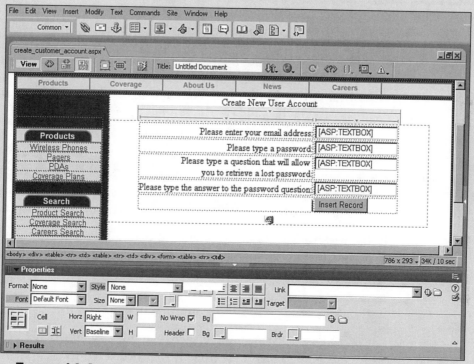

FIGURE 14.4   The Create New User Account form has been added to the page.

13. Save the page.

14. The last step in the new user account process is to create a confirmation page. Open the kcweb_template.aspx page for your platform. From the menu bar, choose File, Save As and save the file as account_ created.aspx.

15. Place your cursor in the main content region at the right side of the page and set the Bg field on the Property inspector to #FFFFFF. Next, type **Thank you. Your account was created. Click here to login to your account or click any navigation link to continue browsing the site.**

16. Select the Click Here text and link it to orders/customer_login.aspx.

17. Save the page.

Exercise 14.1(b)   Creating the New User Account Page in ColdFusion

1. Open the kcweb_template.cfm page for your platform. From the menu bar, choose File, Save As and save the file as create_customer_account.cfm.

2. Place your cursor in the main content region at the right side of the page and set the Bg field on the Property inspector to #FFFFFF. Next, type **Create new user account** and press Enter.

The next step is to add a form and table that allows an authenticated user to enter the appropriate page information and content. To do this, place your cursor on the line below the Create New User Account text and choose Insert, Application Objects, Insert Record, Record Insertion Form from the menu bar.

3. In the Record Insertion Form Wizard dialog box, choose the connKrystalClearWebCF connection and the tbCustomers table. In the On Success, Go To field, type **account_created.cfm.**

4. In the Form Fields panel, use the minus sign to remove all fields except for CustEmail, Password, PasswordQuestion, and PasswordAnswer.

5. Click the Password column and change the Display As field to Password Field. Click the Password Answer field to a Password Field as well. The dialog box should now look like Figure 14.5.

6. Select the CustEmail field and change the label to read **Please enter your email address:.**

7. Change the label for the Password field to **Please type a password:.**

8. Change the label for the PasswordQuestion field to **Please type a question that will allow you to retrieve a lost password:.** Place a break between the words "will" and "allow" by placing your cursor between the words and pressing <Shift>+<Enter>.

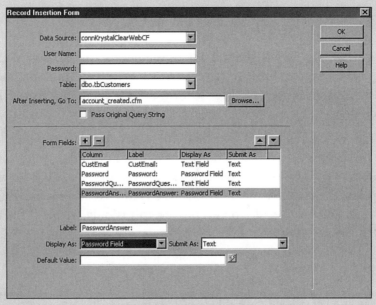

FIGURE 14.5   The Record Insertion Form dialog box with the appropriate values.

9. Change the label for the PasswordAnswer field to **Please type the answer to your password question:**.

10. Click OK to create the form.

11. Save the page.

12. The last step in the create new user account process is to create a confirmation page. Open the kcweb_template.cfm page for your platform. From the menu bar, choose File, Save As and save the file as account_created.cfm.

13. Place your cursor in the main content region at the right side of the page and set the Bg field on the Property inspector to #FFFFFF. Next, type **Thank you. Your account was created. Click here to login to your account or click any navigation link to continue browsing the site.**

14. Select the Click Here text and link it to orders/customer_login.cfm.

15. Save the page.

Providing a Way to Log In

With the new user account created, the next step is to give the user a way to log in. Using the skills we covered in Chapter 12, "Building the Page Administration Module," we can extend the login and logout process to include visitors who have created a user account.

When we created the admin login/logout system, we specifically did not want to link to the Login or Logout page so as to keep the search engines from indexing those pages. In the case of our visitors, however, we want to make it as easy as possible to login to their account. To accomplish this, we can create a login link that resides on each page and is only visible if the user is not logged in to the system.

Exercise 14.2(a)   Building the Login Page in ASP.NET

1. Open the kcweb_template.aspx page and use the Save As command to save the file in the orders folder as customer_login.aspx.

2. Place your cursor in the main content region at the right side of the page and set the Bg field on the Property inspector to #FFFFFF.

3. In the main content region, type **Customer Login** and press Enter twice.

4. On the bottom line, type **Click here if you have lost your password.** Highlight the Click Here text and link it to ../customer_lostpassword.aspx.

5. On the middle line (above the lost password text), add a new form and switch to the Split Code and Design view. Inside the form tag, type **runat="server"**. Switch back to the Design view.

6. With your cursor inside the form, add a table to your page with 3 rows, 2 columns, and a width of 300 pixels. Set the border, cell padding, and cell spacing to 1.

7. In the top-left cell, type **Username:**. In the middle-left cell, type **Password:**. Right-align the left column and set the column width to 50%.

8. Place your cursor in the upper-right cell and choose Insert, ASP.NET Objects, asp:textbox. Set the ID of the text box to tfEmail and click OK. Add a second text box in the next cell down and name it **tfPassword**. In the Text Mode of the second text box, choose Password.

9. In the lower-right cell, insert an asp:button named btLogin. Set the text of this button to Login. With the form elements in place, your page should look like Figure 14.6.

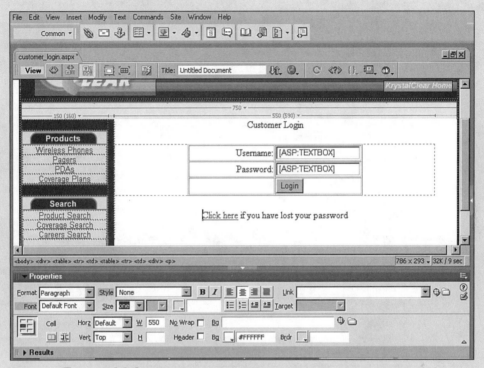

FIGURE 14.6   The Login page with the necessary form elements.

10. The next step is to build a dataset that checks to see if the values submitted by the form match any records in the database. Click the plus sign on the Server Behaviors panel and choose DataSet.

11. In the DataSet dialog box, name the dataset dsCustomerLogin and choose the connKrystalClearWebASP connection and the tbCustomers table. Switch to the Advanced view and modify the SQL Query so it looks like this:

```
SELECT custEmail, Password
FROM dbo.tbCustomers
WHERE custEmail = @Username AND Password = @Password
```

Create two new parameters for the query. The first is named @Username, is of the varchar type, and draws the form variable tfEmail with no default value. The second is named @Password, is of the varchar type, and draws the form variable tfPassword with no default value. When your dataset is complete, the dialog box should look like Figure 14.7.

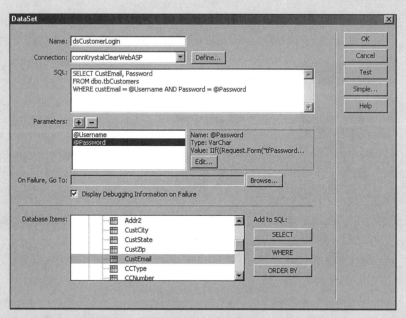

FIGURE 14.7   The completed dsCustomerLogin dataset.

12. Click OK to close the dataset.

13. Switch back to the Split Code and Design view and find the `</form>` tag. On a new line after the tag, add this code block:

```
<%
if dsCustomerLogin.RecordCount > 0 then
Session("sessCustomerUserName") = Request.Form("tfEmail")
FormsAuthentication.RedirectFromLoginPage("customer",
true)
else if ((Request.Form("tfEmail"))) <> Nothing _
OR ((Request.Form("tfPassword"))) <> Nothing
response.Write("Login failed. Please try again.")
end if
%>
```

As you will see, this block of code checks to see if the dsCustomerLogin record-set is empty (meaning that no records in the database matched the username/password combination). If the recordset is not empty, the user entered a valid username and password and he is authenticated as a member of the admin group and is redirected to the page that he originally requested. If, however, the recordset is empty, an invalid combination was entered and the Login Failed text is displayed.

14. Save the page.

Now that we have logged in the user, we need to update the LastLogin field that corresponds to his record.

15. Open the kcweb_template.aspx page. From the menu bar, choose File, Save As and save the file in the orders folder as default.aspx.

16. Place your cursor in the main content area and set the background to #FFFFF. Type **Thank you. Please click the button below to continue.** Press Enter.

17. Create a new dataset named dsCustomerUser. Using the Simple mode, choose the connKrystalClearWebASP connection and the tbCustomers table.

18. Choose to draw all columns from the table and set a filter where CustEmail is equal to the Session Variable sessCustomerUserName. When completed, your dataset should look like Figure 14.8.

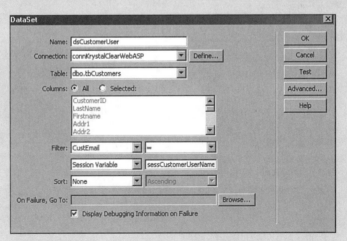

FIGURE 14.8 The completed dsCustomerUser dataset.

19. Now that we know who the user is, we can update his record. Place your cursor on the line below the Thank You text and choose Insert, Application Objects, Update Record, Record Update Form Wizard.

20. As shown in Figure 14.9, choose the connKrystalClearWebASP connection and the tbCustomers table. Choose the record from the dsCustomerUser dataset, with the unique key column being CustomerID. In the On Success, Go To field type **customer_checkout.aspx**. In the Form Fields panel, use the minus sign to remove all fields except the LastLogin field and change the LastLogin field to a Hidden Field. Finally, in the Default Value field, type **<%# Now()%#>**. This updates the record with the current time and date.

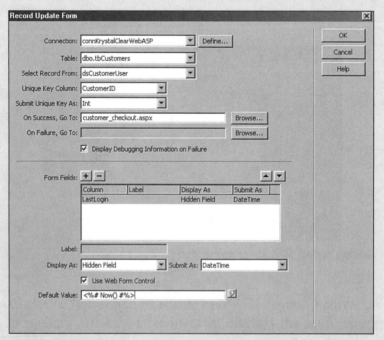

FIGURE 14.9   The Record Update Form updates the user's last login.

21. Click OK to close the Record Update Form dialog box.

22. Select the Update Record button and type **Continue** in the Label field of the Property inspector.

23. Save the page.

Exercise 14.2(b)   Building the Login Page in ColdFusion

1. Open the kcweb_template.cfm page. From the menu bar, choose File, Save As and save the file in the orders folder as customer_login.cfm.

2. Place your cursor in the main content region at the right side of the page and set the Bg field on the Property inspector to #FFFFFF.

3. In the main content region, type **Customer Login** and press Enter twice.

4. On the bottom line, type **Click here if you have lost your password.** Highlight the Click Here text and link it to ../customer_lostpassword.cfm.

5. On the middle line (just above the lost password text), add a new form.

6. With your cursor inside the form, add a table to your page with 3 rows, 2 columns, and a width of 300 pixels. In the upper-left cell, type **Username:**. In the middle-left cell, type **Password:**.

7. Place your cursor in the upper-right cell and choose Insert, Form, Text Field. In the Properties inspector, set the name of the text field to tfEmail. Add a second text box in the next cell down and name it **tfPassword**. In the Property inspector, set the Type field of the text field to Password.

8. In the lower-right cell, insert a button named btLogin. Set the label of this button to Login. With the form elements in place, your page should look like Figure 14.10.

9. Save the page.

The next step is to apply a server behavior that compares the data submitted in the form with that stored in the database. If the information matches, the user is logged in and redirected to a page where he receives a login validation. If, however, the data does not match, he receives a page that displays an error message.

10. In the customer_login.cfm page, select the form and click the plus sign on the Server Behaviors panel. From the menu, choose User Authentication, Log In User. In the Log In User dialog box, choose the connKrystalClearWebCF data source and the tbCustomers table. Choose CustEmail as the Username column and Password as the Password column.

11. As shown in Figure 14.11, type **customer_validation.cfm** in the If Login Succeeds, Go To field and type **customer_failure.cfm** in the If Login Fails, Go To field. Click OK.

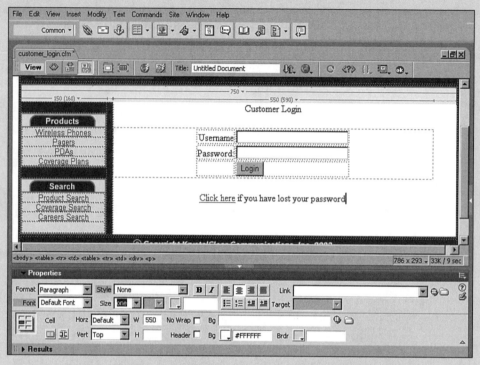

FIGURE 14.10   The login form with the necessary form elements.

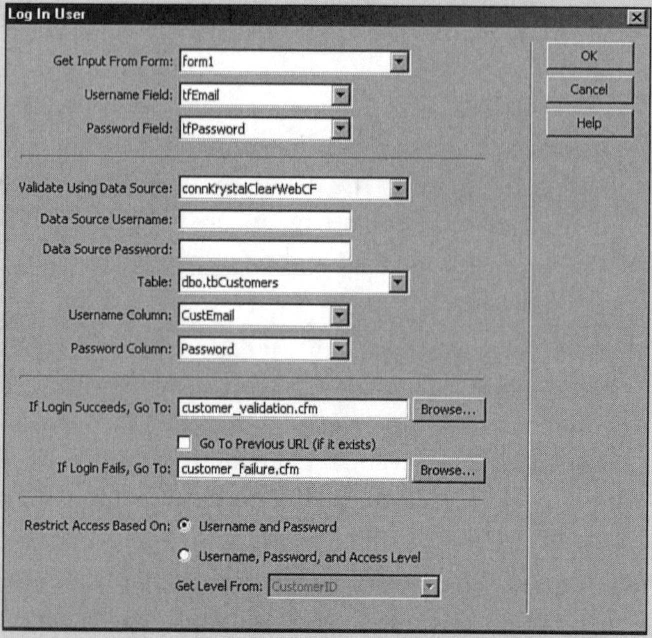

FIGURE 14.11   Complete the Log In User dialog box.

12. Save the page.

13. Create a new page based on the kcweb_template.cfm template and type **Login Failed. Please click the back button and try again** in the main content region. Save this page as customer_failure.cfm.

14. Create a new page based on the kcweb_template and save the page as customer_validation.cfm. Click the plus sign on the Server Behaviors panel, and choose Recordset(Query).

15. In the Recordset dialog box, name the recordset rsCustomerLogin, choose the connKrystalClearWebCF connection and the tbCustomers table. Choose to select all fields where the CustEmail field is equal to the Session Variable MM_Username. When your recordset is complete, the recordset dialog box should look like Figure 14.12.

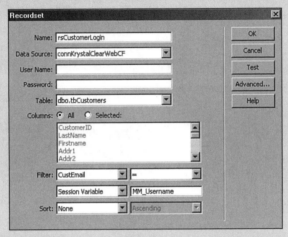

FIGURE 14.12   The completed rsCustomerLogin recordset.

16. Click OK to close the Recordset dialog box.

17. Place your cursor in the main content region and type **Thank you. Please click the button below to continue.** Press Enter.

   Because we want to update the LastLogin field when a user logs in successfully, we need to add a form and elements that perform this action.

18. With your cursor on the bottom line, choose Insert, Application Objects, Update Record, Record Update Form Wizard. In the Record Update Form dialog box, choose the connKrystalClearWebCF connection and the tbCustomers table. Choose to select the record from the rsCustomerLogin recordset and choose CustomerID as the unique key column. Redirect the user to customer_checkout.cfm after updating the record.

19. As shown in Figure 14.13, remove all fields from the Form Fields panel except the CustomerID and LastLogin fields. Choose to display both these fields as hidden fields and set the Default Value of the LastLogin field to **\<cfoutput\>#DateFormat(Now(),"mm/dd/yyyy")#\</cfoutput\>**. Change the Submit As value for the LastLogin field to Date and click OK.

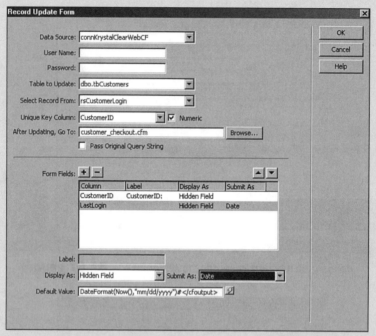

FIGURE 14.13   The Record Update Form that updates the LastLogin field.

20. Select the button and change the Label to Continue in the Property inspector.
21. Save the page.

Providing a Way to Log Out

Giving the user a way to log out is something we have done in the past, so adding it to our Web application should be a snap. Just as we did with the Login button, we also need to add a Logout button to the application that is only visible if the user is logged in.

Exercise 14.3(a) Creating the Logout Page in ASP.NET

1. Open the kcweb_template.aspx page. From the menu bar, choose File, Save As and save the file in the root folder as customer_logout.aspx.

2. Place your cursor in the main content region at the right side of the page and set the Bg field on the Property inspector to #FFFFFF. In the main content region, type **Click here to logout.** and press Enter.

3. Switch to the Split Code and Design view. On the new line, insert a form and add the **runat="server"** code to the form tag.

4. Inside the form, add an asp:button and name it btLogout. Set the text for the button to Logout.

5. With the button selected, add the following code to the button tag just before the />:

```
onClick="Logout_Click"
```

6. Create a new line at line 2 of your document and add the following code block:

```
<script language="VB" runat="server">
Sub Logout_Click(ByVal s As Object, ByVal e As
EventArgs)
FormsAuthentication.Signout()
Response.Redirect("../default.aspx")
End Sub
</script>
```

With your code in place, the page should look like Figure 14.14.

7. Save the page.

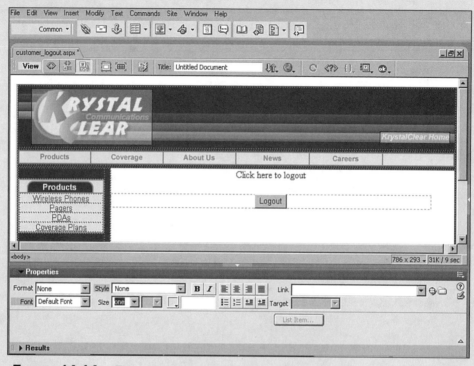

FIGURE 14.14   The code that logs users out and destroys their session credentials.

Exercise 14.3(b)   Creating the Logout Page in ColdFusion

1. Open the kcweb_template.cfm page. From the menu bar, choose File, Save As and save the file in the root folder as customer_logout.cfm.

2. Place your cursor in the main content region at the right side of the page and set the Bg field on the Property inspector to #FFFFFF. In the main content region, type **Click here to logout**. and press Enter.

3. On the Server Behaviors panel, click the plus sign and choose User Authentication, Log Out User.

4. In the Log User Out dialog box, shown in Figure 14.15, choose to Create a new "Log Out" link and type **default.cfm** in the When Done, Go To field.

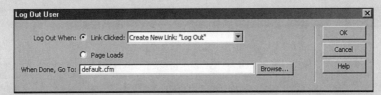

FIGURE 14.15   The Log Out User dialog box creates code that closes the user's session.

5. Click OK and save the page.

Helping Users Retrieve a Lost Password

One of the difficulties of building a Web application that uses visitor accounts is that users will occasionally lose their passwords. Rather than emailing back and forth with the user or conversing on the phone, some developers prefer to provide users with a method of retrieving the password themselves.

For the KrystalClear application, we asked users to enter a special question that allows us to confirm that the user is authorized to view the password. If the user answers that special question correctly, we can display the password on the screen for her.

THE BEST WAY TO HANDLE LOST PASSWORDS

Among Web developers, the topic of handling lost passwords is almost as touchy as the pronunciation of SQL. Some developers believe that the best way to handle a lost password is to reset the password to a new value and email that new value to the users. Others think that it's okay to simply display the password on the screen after some type of validation. So which way is the best?

The answer: it depends. The type of password retrieval you use depends entirely upon the level of sophistication you need for your application to maintain the security of your site.

If your site is a family photo album that is visited by your family and doesn't require a high level of security, you might consider displaying the password on the screen. If, however, your site engages in eCommerce and the visitor accounts contain credit card numbers, you might consider authenticating the visitor and then having him reset the password right then. If your site is somewhere between, you might just email the password to the visitor.

You will have to judge what level of security your Web application needs and what technology is available to you to meet those security needs.

Exercise 14.4(a)   Creating the Password Retrieval System in ASP.NET

1. Open the kcweb_template.aspx page and use the Save As command to save the file in the root folder as customer_lostpassword.aspx.

2. Place your cursor in the main content region at the right side of the page and set the Bg field on the Property inspector to #FFFFFF.

3. In the main content region, type **Retrieve lost password** and press Enter. On the new line, add a new form and switch to the Split Code and Design view. Inside the form tag, type **runat="server"**. Switch back to the Design view.

4. With your cursor inside the form, add a table to your page with 2 rows, 2 columns, and a width of 300 pixels. Set the border, cell padding, and cell spacing to 1.

5. In the upper-left cell, type **Email Address:** and right align the text.

6. Place your cursor in the upper-right cell and choose Insert, ASP.NET Objects, asp:textbox. Set the ID of the text box to tfEmail and click OK.

7. In the lower-right cell, insert an asp:button named btRetrieve. Set the text of this button to Retrieve Password. With the form elements in place, your page should look like Figure 14.16.

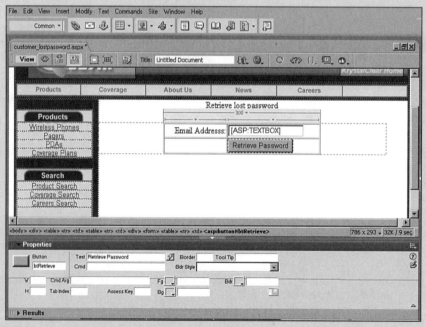

FIGURE 14.16   The password retrieval form with the necessary form elements.

8. The next step is to build a dataset that checks to see if the email address matches any records in the database. Click the plus sign on the Server Behaviors panel and choose DataSet.

In the DataSet dialog box, name the dataset dsCustomerPassword, choose the connKrystalClearWebASP connection and the tbCustomers table. In the Simple view, choose to only return the custEmail field and set a filter that returns only records where the custEmail equals the Form Variable tfEmail. When your dataset is complete, the dialog box should look like Figure 14.17.

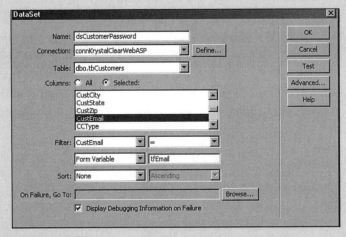

FIGURE 14.17   The completed dsCustomerPassword dataset.

9. Click OK to close the recordset.

10. Switch back to the Split Code and Design view and find the </form> tag. On a new line after the tag, add this code block:

```
<%
if dsCustomerPassword.RecordCount > 0 then
Session("sessCustomerPassword") = Request.Form("tfEmail")
Response.Redirect("customer_question.aspx")
else if ((Request.Form("tfEmail"))) <> Nothing
response.Write("The entered address does not match any in our system.
Please try again.")
end if
%>
```

If the email address exists in the database, this block of code automatically redirects the user to the page where she can view and answer her password question. If the email address does not match one in the system, the user is asked to try again.

11. Save the page.

The last step we need to take is to create the page that allows the user to view her question and provide an answer. If the answer is correct, the page will then display the user's password.

12. Open the kcweb_template.aspx page. From the menu bar, choose File, Save As and save the file in the root folder as customer_question.aspx.

13. Place your cursor in the main content area and set the background to #FFFFF. Type **Your password retrieval question is:** and press Enter twice.

14. Create a new dataset named dsCustomerQuestion. Using the Simple mode, choose the connKrystalClearWebASP connection and the tbCustomers table.

15. Choose to draw all columns from the table and set a filter where CustEmail is equal to the Session Variable sessCustomerPassword. When completed, your dataset should look like Figure 14.18.

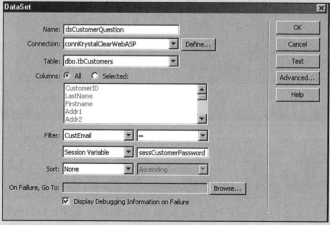

FIGURE 14.18   The completed dsCustomerPassword dataset.

16. Now that we have the user's email address, we can draw her password question from the database and display it. From the Data Bindings panel, drag the PasswordQuestion data binding onto the page on the line below the text you typed.

17. We need to provide the user with a way to submit the answer to the question. On the bottom blank line, insert a form and add the `<runat="server">` code that we have added for all our ASP.NET forms. Switch back to the Design view.

18. With your cursor inside the form, insert an ASP.NET text box on the top new line by choosing Insert, ASP.NET Objects, asp:textbox from the menu bar. In the dialog box, set the ID to tfAnswer and click OK.

19. To the right of the asp:textbox, insert a Submit button by choosing Insert, ASP.NET Objects, asp:button from the menu bar. Set the button ID to btSubmit, type **Submit** in the Text field, and click OK. With the button in place, your page should now look like Figure 14.19.

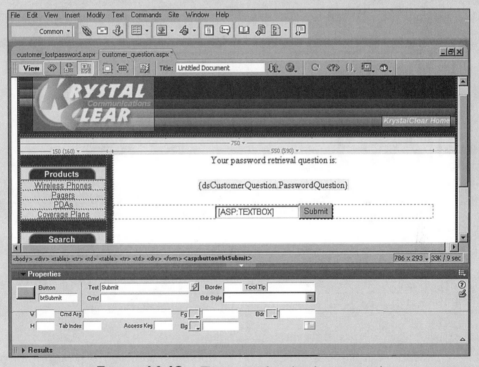

FIGURE 14.19   The answer form has been created.

The last step is to create an additional recordset that compares the answer submitted to the answer stored in the database. If the answer matches the answer in the table, we can display it on the screen.

20. Create a new dataset. In the Simple view, name the dataset dsPassword and choose the connKrystalClearWebASP connection and the tbCustomers table.

21. Select only the Password field and create a filter where Password equals the Form Variable tfAnswer. Click OK to create the recordset.

22. Place your cursor just to the right of the Submit button and press Enter.

23. On the new line, type **Your password is:**. Drag the Password data binding in the dsPassword dataset from the Data Bindings panel. Place it directly to the right of the Your Password Is text. With all the elements in place, your pages should look like Figure 14.20.

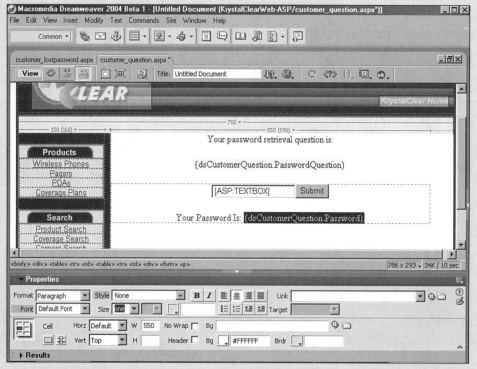

FIGURE 14.20   All the elements are in place for the password retrieval system.

Even though we have placed all the elements, we need to be sure that the Your Password Is text is only visible when the user submits the answer to the question. To do this, we can use Dreamweaver's Show Region server behavior.

24. Select the text that says, "Your password is," and the data placeholder for the Password field. Click the plus sign on the Server Behaviors panel and choose Show Region, Show If DataSet Is Not Empty.

25. In the Show If Dataset Is Not Empty dialog box, choose the dsPassword dataset and click OK.

26. Save the page.

Exercise 14.4(b)   Creating the Password Retrieval System in ColdFusion

1. Open the kcweb_template.cfm page and use the Save As command to save the file in the root folder as customer_lostpassword.cfm.

2. Place your cursor in the main content region at the right side of the page and set the Bg field on the Property inspector to #FFFFFF.

3. In the main content region, type **Retrieve lost password** and press Enter. On the new line, add a new form.

4. With your cursor inside the form, add a table to your page with 2 rows, 2 columns, and a width of 300 pixels. Set the cell padding, cell spacing, and border thickness to 1. In the upper-left cell, type **Email Address:**.

5. Place your cursor in the upper-right cell and choose Insert, Form, Text Field. Set the name of the text box to tfEmail in the Property inspector.

6. In the lower-right cell, insert a form button and name it btRetrieve. Set the text of this button to Retrieve.

7. The next step is to build a recordset that checks to see if the email address matches any records in the database. Click the plus sign on the Server Behaviors panel and choose RecordSet.

8. In the RecordSet dialog box, name the dataset rsCustomerPassword, choose the connKrystalClearWebCF connection and the tbCustomers table. In the Simple view, choose to only return the custEmail field and set a filter that returns only records where the custEmail equals the Form Variable tfEmail.

9. Click OK to close the recordset.

10. Switch back to the Split Code and Design view and find the `</form>` tag. On a new line after the tag, add this code block:

```
<cfif dsCustomerLogin.RecordCount GT 0>
Session("sessCustomerPassword") = Request.Form("tfEmail")
Response.Redirect("customer_question.cfm")
<cfelse>
The entered address does not match any in our system.
Please try again.
</cfif>
```

If the email address exists in the database, this block of code automatically redirects the user to the page where she can view and answer her password question. If the email address does not match one in the system, the user is asked to try again.

11. Save the page.

The next step we need to take is to create the page that allows the user to view her question and provide an answer. If the answer is correct, the page will then display the user's password.

12. Open the kcweb_template.cfm page. From the menu bar, choose File, Save As and save the file in the root folder as customer_question.cfm.

13. Place your cursor in the main content area and set the background to #FFFFF. Type **Your password retrieval question is:** and press Enter twice.

14. Create a new recordset named rsCustomerQuestion. Using the Simple mode, choose the connKrystalClearWebCF connection and the tbCustomers table.

15. Choose to draw all columns from the table and set a filter where CustEmail is equal to the Session Variable sessCustomerPassword. When completed, your recordset should look like Figure 14.21.

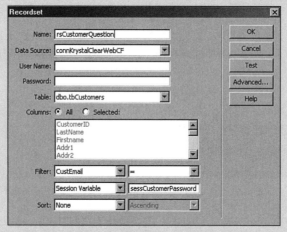

FIGURE 14.21   The completed rsCustomerPassword dataset.

16. Now that we have the user's email address, we can draw her password question from the database and display it. From the Data Bindings panel, drag the PasswordQuestion data binding onto the page on the line below the text you typed.

17. We need to provide the user with a way to submit the answer to the question. On the bottom blank line, insert a form.

18. With your cursor inside the form, insert a text field on the top new line by choosing Insert, Form, Text Field from the menu bar. In the Property inspector, name the text field tfAnswer.

19. To the right of the text field, insert a Submit button by choosing Insert, Form, Button from the menu bar. Name the button **btSubmitand** click OK.

We need to create an additional recordset that compares the answer submitted to the answer stored in the database. If the answer matches the answer in the table, we can display it on the screen.

20. Create a new recordset. In the Simple view, name the dataset rsPassword and choose the connKrystalClearWebCF connection and the tbCustomers table.

21. Select only the Password field and create a filter where Password equals the Form Variable tfAnswer. Click OK to create the recordset.

22. On a new line below the form, type **Your password is:**. Drag the Password data binding in the rsPassword dataset from the Data Bindings panel. Place it directly to the right of the Your Password Is text.

Even though we have placed all the elements, we need to be sure that the Your Password Is text is only visible after the user submits the answer to the question. To do this, we can use Dreamweaver's Show Region server behavior.

23. Select the text that says, "Your password is," and the data placeholder for the Password field. Click the plus sign on the Server Behaviors panel and choose Show Region, Show If Recordset Is Not Empty.

24. In the Show If Recordset Is Not Empty dialog box, choose the rsPassword recordset and click OK.

25. Save the page.

Building Links for Logging In, Logging Out, and Creating an Account

Now that we have the pages in place, the last thing we need to do to allow visitors to create custom user accounts is to build the links that allow them access the pages. For the KrystalClear application, we want three links. The first is the Login button, which should only be visible when the user is not logged in. The second is the Logout button, which should only be visible when the user is logged in. The final link is a text link that allows the visitor to create a new account. This link, like the Login button, should only be visible when the user is not logged in.

To hide the buttons during various states, we can check to see if the session variable for an authenticated user exists. If it does, we know that the user is logged in. If it doesn't exist, the user is currently logged out. Based on the state of the session variable, we can tell the application which links to display.

Note **MORE EFFICIENT WAYS OF ACCOMPLISHING THE SAME RESULT?**

After reading how we are going to approach the method of hiding and displaying the login, logout, and create account links, I'm sure there are several code gurus out there who are moaning right now. Although checking the value against the session variable and using the server behaviors to display or hide links is not necessarily the most efficient method of accomplishing the goal, it serves the purpose of showing just how you can accomplish a task in Dreamweaver without having to write a single line of code.

Exercise 14.5(a)   Creating the Login, Logout, and New Account Links in ASP.NET

1. Open the default.aspx page.

2. At the top of the page, we created a series of navigational links. To the right of the Careers button, we left an empty cell. Place your cursor in that cell and insert a new table with 3 rows and 1 column. Set the width to 125 pixels, the cell padding and cell spacing to 1, and the border to 0. Select all three rows and choose Center from the Horz field in the Property inspector.

3. In the top row, insert the image kcweb_logoutbutton.gif and link the button to the customer Login page by typing **customer_logout.aspx** in the Link field of the Property inspector.

4. In the middle row, insert the image kcweb_loginbutton.gif and link the button to the customer Login page by typing **customer_login.aspx** in the Link field of the Property inspector.

5. In the bottom row, type **Create Account** and link the text to create_customer_account.aspx. With the three links in place, your page should now look like Figure 14.22.

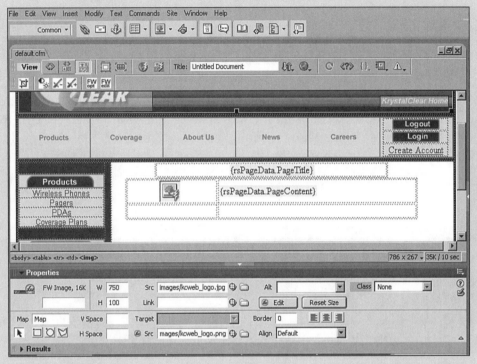

FIGURE 14.22   The page now contains the login, logout, and create account links.

We need to create a dataset that compares the value of the sessCustomerUsername session variable with the records in the database. If the recordset returns a matching record, we know that the sessCustomerUsername session variable has been set and we can display the Logout button. If, however, the dataset is empty, we know the sessCustomerUsername session variable has not been set and we can display the Login and Create Account links.

6. Create a new dataset named dsUser. Using the Simple mode, choose the connKrystalClearWebASP connection and the tbCustomers table.

7. Choose to draw only the CustEmail field from the table and set a filter where CustEmail is equal to the Session Variable sessCustomerUsername. Click OK to close the recordset.

8. Highlight the table row that contains the Logout button. On the Server Behaviors panel, click the plus sign and choose Show Region, Show Region If Dataset Is Not Empty. In the dialog box, choose the dsUser dataset and click OK.

HIGHLIGHTING A ROW IN THE TAG SELECTOR

If you're having trouble highlighting the row because it is so small, use the Tag selector and click the `<tr>` tag.

9. Highlight the two table rows that contain the Login button and the Create Account link. On the Server Behaviors panel, click the plus sign and choose Show Region, Show Region If Dataset Is Empty. In the dialog box, choose the dsUser dataset and click OK.

10. Save the page.

Exercise 14.5(b)   Creating the Login, Logout, and New Account Links in ColdFusion

1. Open the default.cfm page.

2. At the top of the page, we created a series of navigational links. To the right of the Careers button, we left an empty cell. Place your cursor in that cell and insert a new table with 3 rows and 1 column. Set the cell padding and cell spacing to 1 and the border to 0.

3. In the top row, insert the image kcweb_logoutbutton.gif and link the button to the customer Login page by typing **customer_logout.cfm** in the Link field of the Property inspector.

4. In the middle row, insert the image kcweb_loginbutton.gif and link the button to the customer Login page by typing **customer_login.cfm** in the Link field of the Property inspector.

5. In the bottom row, type **Create Account** and link the text to create_customer_account.cfm.

   We need to create a recordset that compares the value of the MM_Username session variable with the records in the database. If the recordset returns a matching record, we know that the MM_Username session variable has been set and we can display the Logout button. If, however, the recordset is empty, we know the MM_Username session variable has not been set and we can display the Login and Create Account links.

6. Create a new recordset named rsUser. Using the Simple mode, choose the connKrystalClearWebCF connection and the tbCustomers table.

7. Choose to draw only the CustEmail field from the table and set a filter where CustEmail is equal to the Session Variable MM_Username. Click OK to close the recordset.

8. Highlight the table row that contains the Logout button. On the Server Behaviors panel, click the plus sign and choose Show Region, Show Region If Dataset Is Not Empty. In the dialog box, choose the rsUser dataset and click OK.

9. Highlight the two table rows that contain the Login button and the Create Account link. On the Server Behaviors panel, click the plus sign and choose Show Region, Show Region If Recordset Is Empty. In the dialog box, choose the rsUser recordset and click OK.

10. Save the page.

 Note **APPLYING THE SAME BEHAVIOR ON OTHER PAGES**

Obviously, we would want the login, logout, and create account links to be visible on pages other than the default page. Luckily, you don't have to go through all of these steps just to make this happen. Instead, open the page you want to work with, copy and paste the recordset, and then copy and paste the table with the images. With a few clicks of your mouse, you can set this system up on as many pages as you need.

Summary

By allowing your visitors to create custom user accounts, you open up a completely new arena of interactivity with your visitors. After you know who your users are, you can engage in activities such as online discussions, the buying and selling of merchandise, and eLearning. This chapter showed you how to develop pages that allow users to create their new account and then log in and log out of the system using those credentials.

In the next chapter, we're going to finish up the framework of the site by allowing visitors with user accounts to order a product from the catalog. Using a combination of Dreamweaver server behaviors and session variables, we'll look at what goes into the process of engaging in eCommerce and discuss some of the issues that arise when selling products and services on the Web.

CHAPTER 15

ENGAGING IN ECOMMERCE

Now that you have your database in place, the pages are created, and visitors can create user accounts, you're ready to engage in eCommerce...right? Well, almost! Along with the technical issues involved in developing a sales processing system, there are a host of security issues that arise.

In this chapter, we'll look at the process of building a simple product catalog and a system of pages that allow an authenticated user to purchase an item from that catalog. In addition, we'll discuss a variety of ways to approach eCommerce and suggest some issues to be aware of.

By the end of this chapter, you will do the following:

- Understand the fundamentals of engaging in eCommerce
- Build a product catalog that allows user to select a product for purchase
- Create a sales processing system that allows the user to purchase a single item

Reviewing the Database Tables

As we have done with the other chapters, let's look at the tables that will fuel our product catalog and the sales processing system. In the last chapter, we worked with the tbCustomers table and allowed the user to create a user account. To accomplish that task, we only used six of the sixteen fields in the table shown in Figure 15.1.

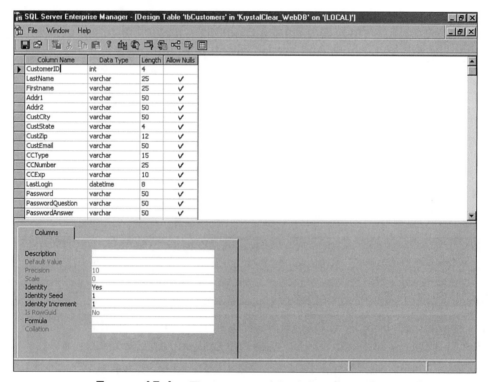

FIGURE 15.1   The structure of the tbCustomers table.

The other 10 fields will contain the data used for processing the customer's order. Information such as the customer's address and credit card number will aid us in building the processing system.

The tbProducts table is also fundamental to our eCommerce system. To engage in eCommerce, we need to be able to offer product information to visitors in hopes that they will want what KrystalClear is selling. The seven fields in the tbProducts table, shown in Figure 15.2, will store the information we want to present to potential customers, similar to the way the records in the tbPages store page content.

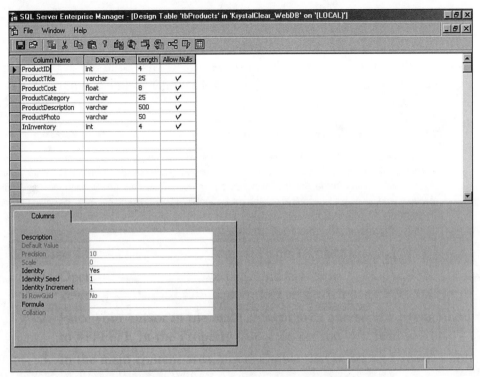

FIGURE 15.2   The structure of the tbProducts table.

Building an Online Catalog

Before we can engage in eCommerce, we need to have something to sell. Luckily, KrystalClear has provided us with several sample products, which we can use to populate the database table and construct our catalog. After the data is entered into the database, we can display the product information using datasets/recordsets just as we displayed custom page content in earlier chapters.

After we have the product information in place, however, we need to provide the user with a link to the specific product. To do this, we'll need to modify the pages currently stored in the tbPages table to include dynamic links to the Products page.

Adding Products to the Database

The first step in building the online catalog is to enter our product information into the tbProducts table. Because we already have the table structure in place, we can use the SQL Server Enterprise Manager to add the data.

CREATING A WAY TO ADD PRODUCTS TO THE DATABASE USING YOUR BROWSER

At this point, you have seen several examples of how to build pages that add records to a database table. In addition, you have seen how to build pages that allow you to edit existing records. If you want to put your skills to the test, expand on the Administrative section we built in Chapter 12, "Building the Page Administration Module," and develop a system that only allows authenticated users to add pages to the database and edit existing pages.

Exercise 15.1   Adding Records to the tbProducts Table

1. Open the SQL Server Enterprise Manager by choosing Start, Programs, Microsoft SQL Server, Enterprise Manager.

2. In the Enterprise Manager, expand the categories in the left pane so that you can see the categories contained in the KrystalClear_WebDB database.

3. Single-click the Tables category and right-click the tbProducts table in the right page. From the context menu, choose Open Table, Return All Rows.

4. Using the Data in Table tbProducts dialog box, add the records shown in Table 15.1.

TABLE 15.1   Values for the tbProducts Table

PRODUCT TITLE	PRODUCT COST	PRODUCT CATEGORY	PRODUCT DESCRIPTION	PRODUCT PHOTO	IN INVENTORY
Noykra 5511 Digital Phone	119.00	Wireless	The Noykra 5511 provides superior digital quality at an affordable price.	images/5511.jpg	35

TABLE 15.1   Values for the tbProducts Table

PRODUCT TITLE	PRODUCT COST	PRODUCT CATEGORY	PRODUCT DESCRIPTION	PRODUCT PHOTO	IN INVENTORY
SurePage A105	19.95	Pagers	The SurePage A105 allows users to receive digital and alphanumeric pages for an affordable price.	images/ A105.jpg	16
DigitalDivide PP106	349.95	PDA	The PP106 provides superior digital connectivity with outstanding functionality.	images/ PP106.jpg	75
KrystalClear Talk Anytime	39.00	Plans	The Talk Anytime plan offers 10,000 anytime minutes and a low rate beyond those minutes.	images/ talkanytime.jpg	9999

5. Close the Data in Table dialog box and close the Enterprise Manager.

Creating a Product Page and a Link to Purchase the Product

With the products in place in the table, we now have to create links on our products pages that allow the user to purchase the product. Although the Purchase button can be a static part of the overall page, the link that it uses needs to contain a link to the Checkout page and a dynamic variable that allows the dynamic pages to know what product is being ordered. To create this dynamic link, we'll use the fields in our table to provide the dynamic variable.

After we have the Product page created, we need to modify each of the product category home pages to include links to the specific products so that users can navigate the site and find the product that suits their needs.

Exercise 15.2(a)   Adding the Purchase Link to the Products Page in ASP.NET

1. Open the products.aspx page.

2. Open the Bindings panel and expand the dsProducts dataset. Drag the ProductTitle binding in to the top table inside the main content region. Center the data placeholder.

3. Place your cursor inside the leftmost cell in the second table in the main content region. With your cursor in the cell, choose Insert, Image from the menu bar. In the Select Image Source dialog box, choose to select the filename from Data Sources and choose the ProductPhoto field. Click OK. With the image placeholder in place, the page should look like Figure 15.3.

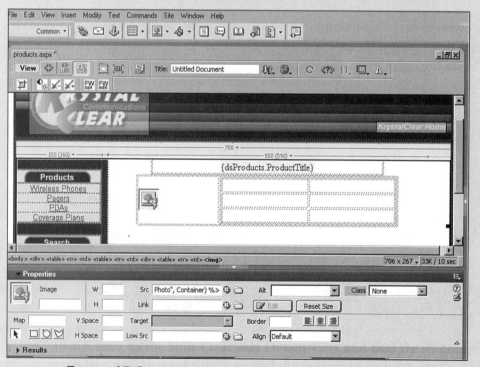

FIGURE 15.3   The page with the title and image placeholder.

4. Place your cursor just to the right of the image placeholder and press Enter.

5. From the menu bar, choose Insert, Image and select the purchase.gif button from the images subfolder.

6. With the purchase.gif button selected, click the folder icon next to the Link field in the Property inspector.

7. In the Select File dialog box, shown in Figure 15.4, navigate to the orders subfolder and type **customer_checkout.aspx** in the File Name field.

FIGURE 15.4   This link should go to the customer_checkout.aspx page.

8. Click the Parameters button and create a parameter with the name ProductID. In the Value field, click the lightning bolt icon and choose the ProductID field in the dsProducts dataset. Click OK to close the Dynamic Data dialog box and OK again to create the link.

9. To the right of the image placeholder is a table containing 3 rows and 2 columns. Place your cursor in the upper-left cell in the table and type **Product Cost:**.

10. In the middle-left cell, type **Product Description:**.

11. In the lower-left cell, type **# In Stock:**

12. From the Bindings panel, drag the ProductCost binding into the upper-right cell, the ProductDescription binding into the middle-right cell, and the Inventory binding into the lower-right cell. With the images and placeholders in place, your page should now look like Figure 15.5.

FIGURE 15.5   All the placeholders and images are in place.

13. Save the page.

Exercise 15.2(b)   Adding the Purchase Link to the Products Page in ColdFusion

1. Open the products.cfm page created in Chapter 13, "Adding Search Capabilities to the Web Applications."

2. Open the Bindings panel and expand the rsProducts recordset. Drag the ProductTitle binding in to the top table inside the main content region. Center the data placeholder.

3. Place your cursor inside the leftmost cell in the second table in the main content region. With your cursor in the cell, choose Insert, Image from the menu bar. In the Select Image Source dialog box, choose to select the filename from Data Sources and choose the ProductPhoto field. Click OK.

4. Place your cursor just to the right of the image placeholder and press Enter.

5. From the menu bar, choose Insert, Image and select the purchase.gif button from the images subfolder.

6. With the Purchase button selected, click the folder icon next to the Link field in the Property inspector.

7. In the Select File dialog box, navigate to the orders subfolder and type **customer_checkout.cfm** in the File Name field.

8. Click the Parameters button and create a parameter with the name ProductID. In the Value field, click the lightning bolt icon and choose the ProductID field in the rsProducts dataset. Click OK to close the Dynamic Data dialog box and OK again to create the link.

9. To the right of the image placeholder is a table containing 3 rows and 2 columns. Place your cursor in the upper-left cell in the table and type **Product Cost:**.

10. In the middle-left cell, type **Product Description:**.

11. In the lower-left cell, type **# In Stock:**

12. From the Bindings panel, drag the ProductCost binding into the upper-right cell, the ProductDescription binding into the middle-right cell, and the Inventory binding into the lower-right cell. With the images and placeholders in place, your page should now look like Figure 15.6.

13. Save the page.

FIGURE 15.6   All the placeholders and images are in place.

Building the Checkout Process

After the user indicates that he wants to purchase a product, we need him to provide us with the appropriate shipping and credit card information to complete the transaction. To accommodate this, we need to develop a system that first requires the user to log on to his account. After the user is logged on, we can display the information we have on file and ask the user to update the information so that it is current. We can also ask the user to confirm any credit card information we have on file and provide an alternate credit card if he so desires. Finally, with the user information updated, we can process the order and complete the transaction.

Confirming the User Information

Confirming the information on file for the user is relatively easy. We can create a form that contains the data currently stored in the user's customer record in the tbCustomers table. This form not only displays the information currently stored in the record, but also serves as an update form that allows the user to change any information and submit the new data.

By providing the customer with the ability to update his account prior to processing the order, we ensure that the shipping and payment information is as current as possible, which should help avoid incorrect transactions and shipping errors.

Exercise 15.3(a)   Building the Page That Confirms the User Information in ASP.NET customer_checkout.aspx

1. Open the kcweb_default_template.aspx page and choose File, Save As from the menu bar. Save the file to the orders folder with the name customer_checkout.aspx.

2. Before we can add data to the page, we need to build two datasets—one that contains the customer information and another that contains the product information.

3. Create a new dataset and name it **dsCustomers**. In the Simple view, choose the connKrystalClearWebASP connection and the tbCustomers table. Choose to draw all fields from the table and create a filter where CustEmail equals the Session Variable sessCustomerUsername.

4. Click OK to create the dataset.

5. Create a second dataset and name it dsProduct. In the Simple view, choose the connKrystalClearWebASP connection and the tbProducts table. Choose to draw all fields from the table and create a filter where ProductID equals the URL Parameter ProductID.

6. Click OK to create the dataset.

7. With our datasets in place, we can now add content to the page. Place your cursor in the top table inside the main content region and type **Customer Checkout**.

8. Place your cursor in the left cell of the bottom table and type **Please confirm the following product details, shipping information, and credit card information. Update the shipping information and credit card information if necessary. When finished, click the Process button.**

9. Select the two cells in the top row and choose Modify, Table, Merge Cells from the menu bar.

Tip

MERGE CELLS

You can also merge cells by selecting the cells and clicking the Merge Cells button in the Property inspector.

10. Select the two cells in the bottom row and choose Modify, Table, Merge Cells from the menu bar.

11. In the new cell, type **You are ordering 1 productnameplaceholder for the price of productcostplaceholder**.

12. Open the Bindings panel and replace the producttitleplaceholder text with the ProductTitle binding from the dsProducts dataset. Replace the productcostplaceholder text with the ProductCost binding from the dsProducts dataset. With the placeholders in place, your page should now look like Figure 15.7.

13. Press Tab.

14. With your cursor in the new cell, choose Insert, Application Objects, Update Record, Record Update Form Wizard.

15. In the Record Update Form dialog box, choose the connKrystalClearWebASP connection and the tbCustomers table. Choose to select the record from the dsCustomers dataset and set the Unique Key Column to CustomerID.

16. In the On Success, Go To field, type **order_confirmation.aspx**.

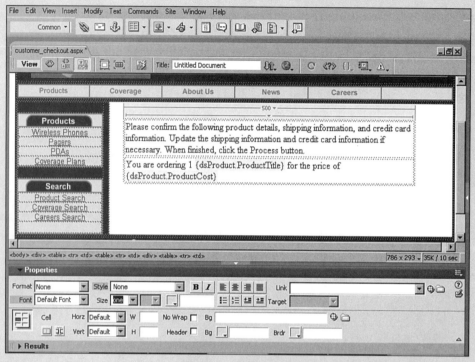

FIGURE 15.7   The page now contains the data placeholders for the product information.

17. In the Form Fields panel, use the minus sign to remove the CustomerID, LastLogin, Password, PasswordQuestion, and PasswordAnswer fields.

18. Change the labels of CustCity, CustState, CustZip, and CustEmail to City, State, Zip, and Email, respectively.

19. Select the CCType field and choose to display the field as a menu. Click the Menu Properties button.

20. In the Menu Properties dialog box, shown in Figure 15.8, add an item with both the Label and Value set to **Visa**. Add a second item with both the Label and Value set to **MasterCard**. Add a third item with the Label and Value set to **Discover**.

21. Click OK to close the Menu Properties dialog box.

22. Click OK again to close the Record Update Form dialog box. As shown in Figure 15.9, the data placeholders for the update page are in place.

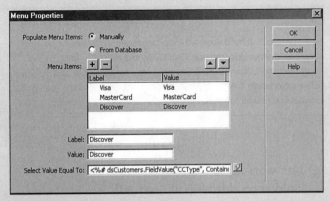

FIGURE 15.8 Add the appropriate items to the menu.

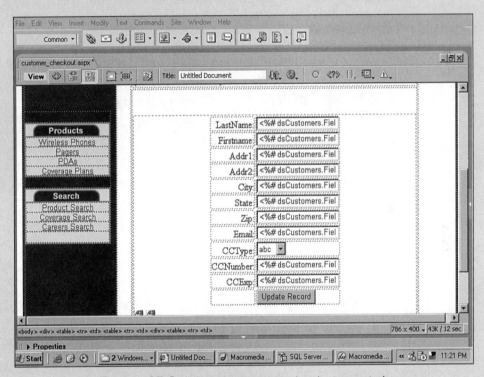

FIGURE 15.9 The checkout page has been created.

23. Save the page.

Exercise 15.3(b)   Building the Page That Confirms the User Information in ColdFusion

1. Open the kcweb_default_template.cfm page and choose File, Save As from the menu bar. Save the file to the orders folder with the name customer_checkout.cfm.

2. Before we can add data to the page, we need to build two datasets—one that contains the customer information and anther that contains the product information.

3. Create a new recordset and name it **rsCustomers**. In the Simple view, choose the connKrystalClearWebCF connection and the tbCustomers table. Choose to draw all fields from the table and create a filter where CustEmail equals the Session Variable MM_UserID.

4. Click OK to create the recordset.

5. Create a second recordset and name it rsProduct. In the Simple view, choose the connKrystalClearWebCF connection and the tbProducts table. Choose to draw all fields from the table and create a filter where ProductID equals the URL Parameter ProductID.

6. Click OK to create the recordset.

7. With our recordsets in place, we can now add content to the page. Place your cursor in the top table inside the main content region and type **Customer Checkout**.

8. Place your cursor in the left cell of the bottom table and type **Please confirm the following product details, shipping information, and credit card information. Update the shipping information and credit card information if necessary. When finished, click the Process button.**

9. Select the two cells in the top row and choose Modify, Table, Merge Cells from the menu bar.

10. Select the two cells in the bottom row and choose Modify, Table, Merge Cells from the menu bar.

11. In the new cell, type **You are ordering 1 producttitleplaceholder for the price of productcostplaceholder.**

12. Open the Bindings panel and replace the producttitleplaceholder text with the ProductTitle binding from the rsProducts recordset. Replace the productcostplaceholder text with the ProductCost binding from the rsProducts recordset. With the placeholders in place, your page should now look like Figure 15.10.

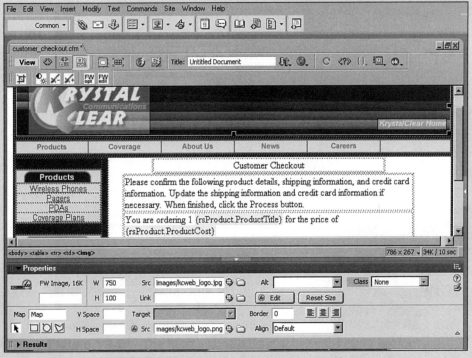

FIGURE 15.10   The page now contains the data placeholders for the product information.

13. Press Tab.

14. With your cursor in the new cell, choose Insert, Application Objects, Update Record, Record Update Form Wizard.

15. In the Record Update Form dialog box, choose the connKrystalClearWebCF connection and the tbCustomers table. Choose to select the record from the rsCustomers recordset and set the Unique Key Column to CustomerID.

16. In the On Success, Go To field, type **order_confirmation.cfm**.

17. In the Form Fields panel, use the minus sign to remove the CustomerID, LastLogin, Password, PasswordQuestion, and PasswordAnswer fields.

18. Change the labels of CustCity, CustState, CustZip, and CustEmail to City, State, Zip, and Email, respectively.

19. Select the CCType field and choose to display the field as a menu. Click the Menu Properties button.

20. In the Menu Properties dialog box, add an item with both the Label and Value set to Visa. Add a second item with both the Label and Value set to MasterCard. Add a third item with the Label and Value set to Discover.

21. Click OK to close the Menu Properties dialog box.

22. Click OK again to close the Record Update Form dialog box. As shown in Figure 15.11, the data placeholders for the update page are in place.

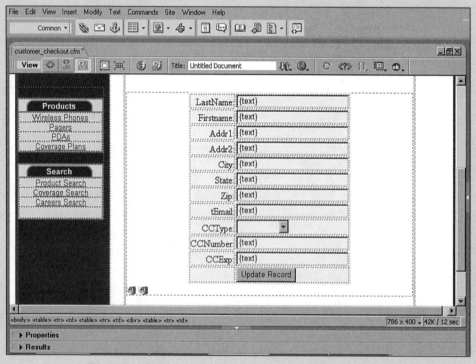

FIGURE 15.11   The checkout page has been created.

23. Save the page.

Processing the Order

Processing the actual order can occur in countless different ways. The order and customer information could be emailed to the processor, the data could be stored in a database record for later review, or the information could be processed immediately by a point-of-purchase system. All of these methods, however, either require technology, financial accounts, or custom software that exceed the scope of this book.

Therefore, to finish the order process, we're simply going to display some basic confirmation details on a page. After you understand the fundamentals of collecting customer and product information, you can then choose what method of processing the information is best for you or your organization.

Exercise 15.4(a)   Displaying the Final Order Details in ASP.NET

1. Open the kcweb_default_template.aspx page and choose File, Save As from the menu bar. Save the file to the orders folder with the name order_confirmation.aspx.

2. In the top table in the main content region, type **Order Confirmation** and center the text on the page.

3. Press Tab.

4. In the second cell, type **Thank you. Your order has been received and processed. Please click any of the navigation links to continue browsing the site.** Center this text as well. Next, remove the remaining empty bottom table. With the text in place and the table removed, the page should look like Figure 15.12.

5. Save the page.

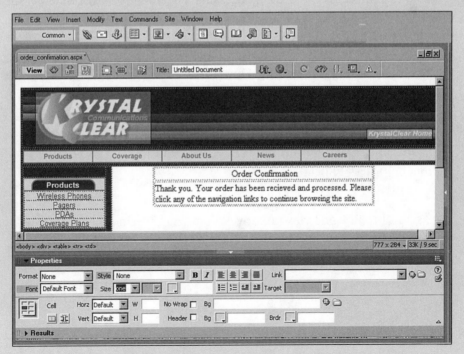

FIGURE 15.12   The order confirmation page has been created.

Exercise 15.4(b)   Displaying the Final Order Details in ColdFusion

1. Open the kcweb_default_template.cfm page and choose File, Save As from the menu bar. Save the file to the orders folder with the name order_confirmation.cfm.

2. In the top table in the main content region, type **Order Confirmation**.

3. Press the Tab.

4. In the second cell, type **Thank you. Your order has been received and processed. Please click any of the navigation links to continue browsing the site.**

5. Save the page.

Making Sure the User Is Logged On

To secure the order processing system, we need to be sure that the user is logged on to his user account. This allows us to collect the appropriate customer data and store it in his individual record and keeps unregistered users from submitting order information that we have no way of tracking.

Because we have already established the ability for visitors to create user accounts, we have half the work done. The only thing left to do is ensure that no one can access the order processing system without first being authenticated.

Exercise 15.5(a)   Locking Down the Pages in the Orders Folder in ASP.NET

We need to lock down the application so that only customers who have logged on can access the pages in the orders folder. Because we previously activated forms authentication in Chapter 12, we can move on to altering the web.config for the orders folder.

1. Create a blank ASP.NET page.

2. In the Code view, remove all code and then add the following code to the page:

```
<configuration>
<system.web>
<authorization>
<allow users="customer" />
<deny users="*" />
```

```
</authorization>
</system.web>
</configuration>
```

With this code in place, your page should look like Figure 15.13 and the forms authentication is activated for the admin folder. Notice that this page allows users who have been authenticated as a member of the customers group, but denies access to any other user.

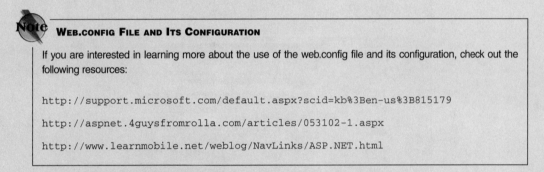

WEB.CONFIG FILE AND ITS CONFIGURATION

If you are interested in learning more about the use of the web.config file and its configuration, check out the following resources:

http://support.microsoft.com/default.aspx?scid=kb%3Ben-us%3B815179

http://aspnet.4guysfromrolla.com/articles/053102-1.aspx

http://www.learnmobile.net/weblog/NavLinks/ASP.NET.html

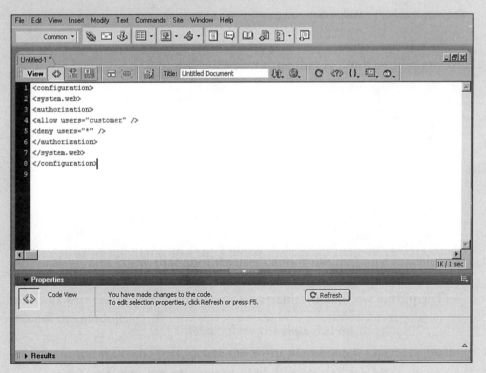

FIGURE 15.13   This code secures the orders folder.

3. Save the page in the orders folder as web.config and close the page.

Exercise 15.5(b)   Locking Down the Pages in the Orders Folder in ColdFusion

1. Open the customer_checkout.cfm page.

2. On the Server Behaviors panel, click the plus sign and choose User Authentication, Restrict Access To Page.

3. In the Restrict Access To Page dialog box, shown in Figure 15.14, choose Username and Password and type **customer_login.cfm** in the If Access Denied, Go To field.

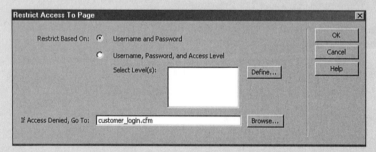

FIGURE 15.14   The Restrict Access To Page server behavior keeps unauthorized visitors out.

4. Click OK to apply the server behavior.

5. Save the page.

6. Repeat this process with the order_confirmation.cfm page.

Summary

With the framework of the eCommerce site in place, we have a relatively functional Web site. Visitors can view the site, click our navigation links, view corporate information, view products, and then purchase those products if they want.

The purpose of this chapter was (obviously) not to show you all the ins and outs of a full-blown eCommerce application. Instead, it was to introduce you to the process involved in the simplest of sales solutions. As elements such as SSL servers, shopping carts, and point-of-service transactions enter the picture, the eCommerce application rapidly becomes more difficult to design and manage.

With the end of this chapter also comes the end of the book. I hope that I have shown you just how easily you can create both intranet and Web applications using Microsoft Access, Microsoft SQL Server, and Macromedia Dreamweaver. In addition, I hope that you have gained insight as to how powerful the combination of these applications can be.

If you have any questions about the book or get stuck, please feel free to email me. My email address is `sean@krystalclearcommunication.com` and I'm always glad to help with problems, hear success stories, and see the sites that you have built with the assistance of this book.

Happy coding!!

Sean

Q-R

U

V

W-Z

inform**IT**

www.informit.com

YOUR GUIDE TO IT REFERENCE

New Riders has partnered with **InformIT.com** to bring technical information to your desktop. Drawing from New Riders authors and reviewers to provide additional information on topics of interest to you, **InformIT.com** provides free, in-depth information you won't find anywhere else.

Articles

Keep your edge with thousands of free articles, in-depth features, interviews, and IT reference recommendations— all written by experts you know and trust.

Online Books

Answers in an instant from **InformIT Online Books'** 600+ fully searchable online books.

POWERED BY

Safari

Catalog

Review online sample chapters, author biographies, and customer rankings and choose exactly the right book from a selection of over 5,000 titles.

New Riders

w.newriders.com

HOW TO CONTACT US

VOICES THAT MATTER

VISIT OUR WEB SITE AT WWW.NEWRIDERS.COM

On our web site, you'll find information about our other books, authors, tables of contents, and book errata. You will also find information about book registration and how to purchase our books, both domestically and internationally.

EMAIL US

Contact us at: **nrfeedback@newriders.com**

- If you have comments or questions about this book
- To report errors that you have found in this book
- If you have a book proposal to submit or are interested in writing for New Riders
- If you are an expert in a computer topic or technology and are interested in being a technical editor who reviews manuscripts for technical accuracy

Contact us at: **nreducation@newriders.com**

- If you are an instructor from an educational institution who wants to preview New Riders books for classroom use. Email should include your name, title, school, department, address, phone number, office days/hours, text in use, and enrollment, along with your request for desk/examination copies and/or additional information.

Contact us at: **nrmedia@newriders.com**

- If you are a member of the media who is interested in reviewing copies of New Riders books. Send your name, mailing address, and email address, along with the name of the publication or Web site you work for.

BULK PURCHASES/CORPORATE SALES

The publisher offers discounts on this book when ordered in quantity for bulk purchases and special sales. For sales within the U.S., please contact: Corporate and Government Sales (800) 382-3419 or **corpsales@pearsontechgroup.com**. Outside of the U.S., please contact: International Sales (317) 428-3341 or **international@pearsontechgroup.com**.

WRITE TO US

New Riders Publishing
800 East 96th Street, 3rd Floor
Indianapolis, IN 46240

CALL/FAX US

Toll-free (800) 571-5840
If outside U.S. (317) 428-3000
Ask for New Riders
FAX: (317) 428-3280

New Riders

WWW.NEWRIDERS.COM

Voices that Matter™

OUR AUTHORS

PRESS ROOM

| web development | design | photoshop | new media | 3-D | server technologies |

EDUCATORS

ABOUT US

CONTACT US

You already know that New Riders brings you the **Voices That Matter**.

But what does that mean? It means that New Riders brings you the

Voices that challenge your assumptions, take your talents to the next

level, or simply help you better understand the complex technical world

we're all navigating.

Visit **www.newriders.com** to find:

- ▸ **10% discount** and **free shipping** on all book purchases
- ▸ Never-before-published chapters
- ▸ Sample chapters and excerpts
- ▸ Author bios and interviews
- ▸ Contests and enter-to-wins
- ▸ Up-to-date industry event information
- ▸ Book reviews
- ▸ Special offers from our friends and partners
- ▸ Info on how to join our User Group program
- ▸ Ways to have your Voice heard

New Riders

WWW.NEWRIDERS.COM